Dynamics of Asian Development

More information about this series at http://www.springer.com/series/13342

Dilip Dutta

Development under Dualism and Digital Divide in Twenty-First Century India

Springer

Dilip Dutta
The University of Sydney
Sydney, NSW
Australia

ISSN 2198-9923 ISSN 2198-9931 (electronic)
Dynamics of Asian Development
ISBN 978-981-10-6342-8 ISBN 978-981-10-6344-2 (eBook)
https://doi.org/10.1007/978-981-10-6344-2

Library of Congress Control Number: 2017949509

Printed on acid-free paper

This Springer imprint is published by Springer Nature
The registered company is Springer Nature Singapore Pte Ltd.
The registered company address is: 152 Beach Road, #21-01/04 Gateway East, Singapore 189721, Singapore

Preface

Structure of the book

Economic development is generally viewed as a continued socio-economic growth associated with a set of interrelated changes in the structure of an economy. These changes involve the composition of domestic demand, production and employment as well as the composition of foreign trade and capital flows. These ongoing structural changes taken together define the societal transformation of the predominately *traditional* socio-economic system to a predominately *modern* one. In a closed auto-centric capitalist economy or a fully planned socialist economy, the highest degree of *articulation* among a society's modes of functioning may exist. However, in reality, a certain degree of 'disarticulation' of any type (sectoral or segmental) exists in the societal formation of almost every society—economically developed or less-developed. But the degree of *disarticulation* is usually more acute in the case of emerging/developing countries that are in the transitional phase—from a predominantly pre-capitalistic or pre-socialistic 'traditional' society towards a 'modern' one. As a result, *structural dualism* has become, in reality, a common feature at the very aggregate level of these disarticulated societies. The co-existence of a *modern* and a *traditional* segment does exist side by side within the same geographical territory of almost all the developed and the emerging/developing societies. Although the degree of co-existence in the form of *structural dualism* varies from society to society, there is, of course, no doubt that this is much more accentuated in the case of the emerging/developing societies.

Chapter 1 focuses on the concepts of societal articulation or disarticulation (segmental/social), economic equilibrium (market/system), nature and laws of dualistic societies, as well as main characteristics of a dual economy. During the transitional phase of the contemporary emerging/developing countries, their political authority or regime has been mostly applying the ideology of either *state capitalism* or *state socialism* in order to guide the future course of socio-economic development. The regime under *state capitalism* borrows socialist ideology—political (one-party state, socialist rhetoric, etc.) and economic (state ownership, planning, etc.)—to accomplish capitalist ends, i.e. the realisation of profit on the basis of exploitation of the wage labour within a class society. The regime under *state socialism*, especially involving a public–private mixed economy, makes effort to incorporate capital into the State by negotiating with the capitalists and without adopting any mechanism of labour repression.

Regarding an appropriate development strategy, every emerging/developing country still needs to follow a judicious combination of both planning/policy and market mechanisms. However, the variation in degree of such a combination depends on the circumstances objectively existing at a given historical moment, particularly under the contemporary globalising forces that began to be felt since the early 1980s. It is often argued that the path of socio-economic development under globalisation is becoming mostly a 'compressed' one in many developing/emerging economies. This compression has been the result of both blurring the stages of development as well as the simultaneous occurrence of industrialisation and de-industrialisation under the globalising forces. Towards the end of Chap. 1, recent decades' economic outcomes of the development strategies followed by China and India have been compared, given that they have been primarily following opposite political ideology, although they are world's two most populous countries and happen to be in Asia. Apparently, from the historical point of view, the path of socio-economic development in China has followed the traditional stages: from agricultural development to industrial development, and then to service sector development, although the industrial sector development has been so fast during the recent decades that it is unparalleled in the world history of industrialisation. In the case of India, the service sector development in the recent decades seems to have leapfrogged the industrial sector development that has been somewhat slow over the decades.

The history of China's economic reforms since 1978 illustrates that China has come a long way since the days when entrepreneurs were banned and central planning dominated economic life. Her continuous experimentation with market-based development—spontaneous marketisation—has certainly been a proven means for her recent economic prosperity. Today entrepreneurship is taught in Chinese universities, markets set most prices and trade is seen as the way to prosperity. The contemporary Chinese State has essentially been a regime based on State capitalism within a *one-party* political system, which has helped in advancing its economic growth very rapidly in the recent decades. On the other hand, the Indian State, although had initially planned to build a 'socialistic pattern of society' after its independence in 1947, but essentially has ended up with a State controlled mixed economy within a democratic *multi-party* political system. Its mixed economic structure jointly with public and private sectors had, however, little success in achieving continuously the targets of planned economic growth until very recently and only during a few of years over the past two decades or so.

The rest of the chapters are focused on growth and development processes exclusively of the Indian society over the past 70 years (1947–2017). The structural forces that the Indian society inherited from its pre-colonial and colonial past had contributed primarily to its *social disarticulation* i.e. essentially a mismatch between the rate of economic growth and the distribution of income from the economy's demand-side point of view. After the independence from the British colonisation over nearly two centuries, the Indian government's initial development strategy was of higher agricultural growth as a preparatory task for industrial development, but soon the plan strategy turned to growth in heavy industry. Despite India being a labour-surplus agrarian economy, its agricultural sector development strategy was nowhere near a comprehensive one. The initial planning process of such a supply-side focused growth strategy within a mixed economic framework contributed to a periodic, shorter-run maladjustment in social allocation of capital, which led to a shorter-run segmental/sectoral disarticulation in the form of disproportionalities at different levels of the Indian society. The disproportionality at the macroeconomic level and particularly because of low effective demand became prominent. From Chap. 2 onwards, the concept of *structural dualism* as a snapshot of the above dynamic process of disarticulation has been used. This approach follows the footsteps of the earlier generations of development economists who were very concerned with the society-wide holistic development of the decolonised less-developed countries with acute *structural dualism* during the post-Second World War period. Because growth rate of employment generation could not keep pace with growth rate of labour force over the past seventy years, there has been hardly any sizable dent on the intensity of *structural dualism* in labour surplus Indian economy. The focus on *structural dualism* is, therefore, expected to serve the book's purpose of analysing Indian society's overall achievement or failure in terms of firstly, the periodic integration of its *unorganised* (or *traditional*) segment into its *organised* (or *modern*) one, and secondly, the application of information and communication technology (ICT) for bridging its *digital divide*. While the former has direct implications for tackling *structural dualism* through socio-economic channels (e.g. direct measures for poverty eradication, resource and income redistribution across states/regions), and the latter has indirect implication for the same through technological channels (e.g. setting up of Community Information Centres, making Government services accessible at affordable costs through National e-Governance Plan, and technology-enabled Direct Benefits Transfer to the social welfare recipients).

Chapter 2 identifies major structural changes and analyses their consequences as a result of India's development plans (long-term) and economic policies (short-term) adopted during 1947–1980. In order to see any clue for the genesis of prolonged *structural dualism* in modern India, the author has looked back to its planned development strategies/policies since her independence in 1947 and until the contemporary globalisation that begins roughly around the very early years of 1980s. This period has been divided into two phases of India's economic strategies/policies:

Phase I: Planned development strategies/policies under the Nehru era (1947–64);
Phase II: Dilution of industrial licensing system and import policy, and more controls (1965–79).

Chapter 2 also examines the widely discussed two major socio-economic consequences of *structural dualism* during the period from 1960 to 1980: (i) industrial deceleration during 1966–79, and (ii) widening development disparity among the Indian provinces or states during 1960–80. The implications of these consequences in terms of the accentuation of India's *structural dualism* have been elaborated in this chapter.

It is often argued that various aspects of *globalisation* are intentional and reflexive, many globalising forces are impersonal and beyond the control and intentions of any individual or group of individuals and even many developing/emerging countries. In response to the contemporary globalisation process, economic liberalisation has been taking place in India–a labour surplus dualistic economy–since the early 1980s. Although India's economic liberalisation during the 1980s was slow, more comprehensive policies of economic liberalisation and social sector development had been adopted by the Indian government under different major political parties or their coalitions since the early 1990s. Chapter 3 records the economic policy changes that have been made by various governments since 1980, which have been divided into three phases:

Phase III: Policy changes *towards* liberalisation (1980–90);
Phase IV: Policy changes *towards* comprehensive liberalisation (1991–2004); and
Phase V: Policy initiatives *under* comprehensive liberalisation (2005–17).

Many argue that the adoption of comprehensive economic reforms in July 1991 was initially, in many ways, erratic, hasty and unplanned. According to the critics, it had eroded the role of the planning process and aggravated the social problems of unemployment and poverty, and had also increased India's external vulnerability especially during the post (comprehensive) liberalisation period of the late 1990s. After highlighting the nature of various changes in the Indian economy, the author has examined the validity or otherwise of the arguments that prevailed then in the 1990s and also the later ones that have emerged afterwards in the twenty-first century. Although the share of the organised segment in India's net domestic product (NDP) (at factor cost) has increased from 30% during 1980–81 to 44.7% during 2012–13, its share in employment has continuously remained very low within a range of only 5 to 9% of total labour force over almost the same period. It continuously declined from 7.89% in 1991 to 5.70% in 2006 before it marginally increased from 5.80% in 2006 to 6.27% in 2012. Consequently, despite the unorganised segment's continuous decline in its share in NDP, it continues to contain over more than 93% of India's labour force (predominantly in the form of self-employment and/or disguised unemployment).

Chapter 3 also closely looks into an often-quoted argument that economic liberalisation in India and its deepening involvement in the process of economic globalisation have created several related adverse trends such as reduced/stagnant employment generation, greater casualisation as well as feminisation (especially in construction and transportation sectors) and deskilling of the work force in general, which have caused erosion of living standards particularly of the impoverished sections of India's unorganised segment. These trends have also given rise to growing income inequality in general and increased regional disparities in particular, because the diversion of industrial benefits going mostly to the industrially advanced states. Despite India's self-sufficiency in food-grain production, about 21.9% of its population was estimated to be below the poverty level in 2011–12.

Towards the end of Chap. 3, there is a short section on demonetisation policy adopted by the government in November 2016 as well as the introduction of Goods and Service Tax (GST) rolled out on 1 July 2017. While the demonetisation is expected to have potential for integration of a part of the unorganised segment into the organised one, similar implication of the introduction of GST seems to be minimal at least in the short run.

As has been noted in Chap. 2, India's prolonged *structural dualism* with the *unorganised* segment's contribution to the net domestic product (NDP) remained virtually constant around 70 percentage even after three decades of the so-called planned economic development and until 1980. This state of socio-economic under-achievement, as reflected on more than 50% of people living below the poverty line during the 1970s, led the Indian planners to search for an alternative development strategy.

Chapter 4 starts with the government's adoption of a strategy of 'Direct Measures for Poverty Eradication' in the Sixth Five Year Plan (1980–85). Since then, starting with special employment programmes in the 1980s, and then subsequently several social sector development programmes have been in operation targeting both the rural and urban poor. During the 1990s, along with the adoption of economy's comprehensive liberalisation policy, the government committed to an expansion of the scope and coverage of direct poverty reduction programmes. Recognising the importance of proper utilisation of human resources, the government launched a number of new schemes related to the fields of education, health and family welfare, housing, water supply, sanitation and employment generation expected to contribute towards the goals of improving the quality of life and ensuring social justice. There had been a substantial increase in the Central Plan Assistance allocations for social sectors and poverty alleviation programmes. Successive governments continued executing several key projects and legislations, including the National Rural Health Mission (2005), National Rural Employment Guarantee Act (2005) and Unique Identification Authority of India (2006). Understanding that social inclusion requires financial inclusion as an essential condition, and disbursement of benefits needs a systematic channel, the Pradhan Mantri Jan Dhan Yojna (PMJDY), the biggest financial inclusion initiative in the world, has been launched by the current government in August 2014. The current government has also adopted a multipronged policy approach to enable skill development.

Although there has been a steady increase in the social sector expenditure in Central Government's total plan expenditure, total public sector expenditure on important social sector heads (such as health and education) remains low compared with international standards and even with many Asian neighbours. During the post-comprehensive liberalisation period, the Indian governments have also been very concerned of India's continued regional inequality alongside with its increasing GDP growth rates. Chapter 4 has a detailed analysis on the distribution of Central Plan Assistance to the provincial states during 1980–2014. The financial resource transfers to the states had followed a set of criteria that had been revised over time; such transfers took place until 2014 through fund disbursal by the Central Government via two channels: (i) grants, loans and advances (plan and non-plan) decided by the erstwhile Planning Commissions; and (ii) a share of central taxes stipulated by the Finance Commissions. These funds constituted a strong redistributive element for dealing with regional inequalities and had played a crucial role in correcting fiscal imbalances between the Centre and the states (general and special categories).

Coming to power in May 2014, the current government has updated/initiated a number of social sector-related development programmes with a vision of attaining an inclusive society via proper delegation of responsibility for managing them in co-operation with different levels of government (centre, state and local) as appropriate (*co-operative federalism*). The idea of *competitive federalism* has been later on added to the initial amalgam of government's policy objectives in order to make the states compete each other not only for the attraction of investments, but also for the better provision of public goods and services. As the current government turns three in May 2017, a number of social welfare schemes have been found successful by reaching out to the poorest of the poor. These include (i) Mahatma Gandhi National Rural Employment Guarantee Scheme (MNREGS)–the inherited one from the previous governments, but recast drastically by the current government; (ii) Assistance to Disabled for Purchase/Fitting of Aids/Appliances (ADIP) scheme has become very effective particularly for the elderly people below poverty line; and (iii) Pradhan Mantri Ujjwalla Yojana (PMUY) launched by the current government with the objective of providing clean cooking fuel to all parts of India.

Chapter 5 utilises an analytical composite framework of actor-network theory (ANT) and national innovation system (NIS) approach to capture the essence of the socio-economic dynamics of the evolution of the ICT industry in India. The basis of ANT is the idea that society and technology are composed of networks linking various actors and actants, while the policy-oriented approach of NIS focuses on national-level analysis for examining the impact of technology on society. The development of the ICT industry in India has been receiving considerable state support since the 1980s. Over the past three decades, the policy-makers have felt an urgency for connectivity of India's vast rural unorganised/informal segment with the counterpart of organised/formal segment initially through telecommunication technology and then through mobile telephones, Internet and other wireless technologies.

Along with a comprehensive coverage of the origin and growth of the Indian ICT industry, this chapter focuses particularly on the growth of India's ICT-enabled service sector that began to evolve in the early 1990s. Software development and information technology-enabled services (ITeS) including business process outsourcing (BPO), business process management (BPM), software engineering R&D services and product development has emerged as one of the most dynamic and vibrant sectors in India's economy. The growth of ICT service industries in general has created employment, higher urban consumption growth and increased demand for technical education, at the both national and regional levels. During the 2000s, there have been various government incentive policies as well as initiatives adopted for bridging the digital divide between the technological haves and have-nots, and also between ICT-intensive and ICT-deficit states.

After recognising the potential of broadband services in the creation of an enabling environment for promoting a knowledge-based society, government had announced a broadband policy in 2004. In order to make sure that the benefits of ICT-related services reach the common people across the country, the government had also announced a programme in 2004 to establish State Wide Area Network (SWAN) up to the block level in 35 states and union territories for providing connectivity for e-Governance, along with setting up of Community Information Centres (CICs) in hilly, far-flung areas of the north-east and Jammu and Kashmir. In 2006, the government approved the National e-Governance Plan (NeGP) for making all government services accessible to the common man in its locality at affordable costs. In 2011, a project of National Optical Fibre Network (NOFN) was approved for providing broadband connectivity to India's approximately 2.5 lakh *gram panchayats* (village governance units). In the same year, another project on the establishment of National Knowledge Network (NKN) as an ultra-high speed backbone for e-Governance was also approved by the government.

In 2012, the Government constituted a high-power National Committee on Direct Cash Transfers in a bid to ensure that benefits flowing out of various governmental welfare programmes go to individuals' bank accounts electronically, curbing pilferage and duplication. Along with the Unique Identification Development Authority of India's (UIDAI) *Aadhaar* programme, the Direct Benefits Transfer (DBT) scheme was rolled in 2013 initially in several identified districts before it was widely applied across the country.

Coming to power in 2014 on the promise of good governance and development for all, the present government continues the previous e-Governance initiatives undertaken by various State Governments and Central Ministries. Recognising the need for further penetration of ICT services domestically, this government envisions 'Digital India' strategy as an ambitious umbrella programme to prepare India for knowledge-based transformation. One of the important components of this programme is the empowerment of the people through availability of entitlements coupled with Aadhaar Authentification Platform. A National Rural Internet and Technology Mission (NRITM) for services in villages and schools, and e-Kranti for government service delivery are the important ones amongst other initiatives. The current government has expanded the previous government's *Aadhaar* program by introducing a potential large-scale, technology-enabled, real-time Direct Benefit Transfer (DBT) system, namely the JAM (Jan Dhan-Aadhaar-Mobile) number Trinity solution. The JAM Trinity is meant to drive the financial inclusion measures as well as make various payments secured through Mobile connectivity, although protection of personal data has been a challenge.

Chapter 6 summarises the recent trends in the Indian society such as overall jobless growth, mass dependence on social sector subsidies, under-funded health and education sectors, relatively higher digital divide, gradual loss of faith on democracy, and above all increasingly high unproductive military expenses. It is concluded that due to these trends, it is unlikely that the intensity of India's *structural dualism* will be substantially reduced in the very near future.

Acknowledgements
I am very thankful to two persons associated with the publisher—*Springer Singapore Private Ltd.* My thanks go to Anthony D'Costa, the Book Series (Dynamics of Asian Development) Editor, for his understanding of why I took more time for the completion of the manuscript, as I genuinely felt the need for including policy updates on Indian economy until 1 July 2017. I'm also thankful to Stephen Jones, Associate Editor, Business and Economics, for his patience on my lapsing of several deadlines for manuscript submission. While I fully appreciate their understanding and patience, I must also express gratitude to my inner self, which constantly inspired me for making the book a chronicle of *structural dualism* during seventy years of independent India (1947–2017).

Finally, I'm grateful to my wife Pompa, sons–Abhi and Ravi, as well as daughter Pritha for enduring my long hours spent at the University of Sydney, roughly from 9 a.m. to 9 p.m. on almost daily basis (including many weekends) over the past three years. Special thanks also go to each of them: Pompa for packing my lunch and afternoon/evening snacks daily without any complaint ever; Abhi, to keep a home computer ready for my night-time typing work; Ravi, for his meticulously correcting the typos in the first draft of manuscript; and Pritha, for her constant online guidance for solving the Microsoft Word-related computing issues. I also appreciate Xin Zheng's help in recreating a number of figures from different issues of Government of India publication–*Economic Survey*–exactly in the way I wanted them to be drawn digitally.

Sydney, Australia Dilip Dutta

Contents

Abbreviations

ACA	Additional Central Assistance
ADIP	Assistance to Disabled for Purchase
AEPS	Aadhaar Enabled Payment System
AIC	Accessible India Campaign
ANT	Actor-Network Theory
BHIM	Bharat Interface for Money
BJP	Bharatiya Janata Party
BPM	Business Process Management
BPL	Below Poverty Line
BPO	Business Process Outsourcing
BSNL	Bharat Sanchar Nigam Limited
BWA	Broadband Wireless Access
CAG	Comptroller and Auditor General of India
CAGR	Compound Annual Growth Rate
CICs	Community Information Systems
CIS	Centre for Internet and Society
CSO	Central Statistics Office
CSS	Centrally Sponsored Schemes
DBT	Direct Benefits Transfer
DEITY	Department of Electronics and Information Technology
DEPwD	Department of Empowerment of Powers with Disabilities
DRDA	District Rural Development Agency
DWCRA	Development of Women and Children in Rural Areas
DWCUA	Development of Women and Children in Urban Areas
EA	External Assistance
EAS	Employment Assurance Scheme
EDS	Electronic Delivery of Services
EPZ	Export Processing Zone
FDI	Foreign Direct Investment
FERA	Foreign Exchange Regulation Act

FFC	Fourteenth Finance Commission
GBS	Gross Budgetary Support
GCS	General Category State
GDCF	Gross Domestic Capital Formation
GDP	Gross Domestic Product
GER	Gross Enrolment Ratio
GFC	Global Financial Crisis
GNI	Gross National Income
GPT	General Purpose Technology
GSDP	Gross State Domestic Product
GST	Goods and Services Tax
GVA	Gross Value Added
HCR	Headcount Ratio
HDI	Human Development Indicators
IATP	Income Adjusted Total Population
IAY	Indira Awas Yojana
ICDS	Integrated Child Development Services
ICT	Information and Communication Technology
ILO	International Labour Organization
IMY	Indira Mahila Yojana
IMR	Infant Mortality Rate
INC	Indian National Congress
IRDP	Integrated Rural Development Programme
ISP	Internet Service Providers
ITeS	Information Technology enabled Services
JAM	Jan Dhan-Aadhaar-Mobile
JGSY	Jawahar Gram Samridhi Yojana
JRY	Jawahar Rozgar Yojana
LDCs	Less Developed Countries
LFPR	Labour Force Participation Rate
MCA	Ministry of Corporate Affairs
MEITY	Ministry of Electronics and Information Technology
MIT	Ministry of Information Technology
MMPs	Mission Mode Projects
MNCs	Multi-National Corporations
MNREGS	Mahatma Gandhi National Rural Employment Guarantee Scheme
MPLADS	Member of Parliament Local Area Development Scheme
MRTP	Monopolies Restrictive Trade Practices
MVAS	Mobile Value Added Services
NAS	National Accounts Statistics
NASSCOM	National Association of Software and Service Companies
NBA	Nirmal Bharat Abhiyan
NCEUS	National Commission for Enterprises in the Unorganised Sector
NDA	National Democratic Alliance
NDC	National Development Council

NDP	Net Domestic Product
NeGP	National e-Governance Plan
NEP	New Economic Policy
NGOs	Non-Governmental Organisations
NIS	National Innovation System
NITI	National Institute for Transforming India
NJAC	National Judicial Appointments Commission
NKN	National Knowledge Network
NNI	Net National Income
NOFN	National Optical Fibre Network
NPCI	National Payments Corporation of India
NREG	National Rural Employment Guarantee
NREP	National Rural Employment Programme
NRHM	National Rural Health Mission
NRITM	National Rural Internet and Technology Mission
NRY	Nehru Rojgar Yojana
NSAP	National Social Assistance Programme
NSDP	Net State Domestic Product
NSS	National Sample Survey
NSSO	National Sample Survey Organisation
OBCs	Other Backward Classes
OFN	Optical Fibre Network
OTR	Own Tax Revenue
PHCs	Primary Health Centres
PMGY	Pradhan Mantri Gramodaya Yojana
PMIUPEP	Prime Minister's Integrated Urban Poverty Eradication Programme
PMJDY	Pradhan Mantri Jan Dhan Yojana
PMUY	Pradhan Mantri Ujjwalla Yojana
PRAGATI	Pro-Active Governance and Timely Implementation
PRI	Panchayati Raj Institution
PSEs	Public Sector Entities
PwDs	Persons with Disabilities
RBI	Reserve Bank of India
RGLIS	Rural Group Life Insurance Scheme
RLEGP	Rural Landless Employment Guarantee Programme
RRT	Redistributive Resource Transfers
RTE	Right to Free and Compulsory Education
RTI	Right to Information
SAGY	Sansad Adarsh Gram Yojna
SC/ST	Scheduled Castes/Scheduled Tribes
SCAoRA	Supreme Court Advocates on Record Association
SCS	Special Category State
SDC	State Data Center
SEEUY	Self-Employment for Educated Unemployed Youth
SEZ	Special Economic Zone

SHASU	Scheme of Housing and Shelter Upgradation
SHGs	Self-Help Groups
SJSRY	Swarna Jayanti Shahari Rozgar Yojana
SMEs	Small and Medium Enterprises
SNA	System of National Accounts
STAR	Standard Training and Assessment Reward
STPI	Software Technology Parks of India
SUME	Scheme of Urban Enterprises
SUWE	Scheme of Urban Wage Employment
SSCs	Sector Skills Councils
SWAN	State Wide Area Network
TCS	Tata Consultancy Services Limited
TRAI	Telecom Regulatory Authority of India
TRYSEM	Training for Rural Youth for Self Employment
UAL	Universal Access Levy
UBI	Universal Basic Income
UBSP	Urban Basic Services for the Poor
UIDAI	Unique Identification Development Authority of India
ULGs	Urban Local Governments
UNESCO	United Nations Educational, Scientific and Cultural Organization
UPA	United Progressive Alliance
UPI	Unified Payments Interface
UPSS	Usual Principal plus Subsidiary Status
USOF	Universal Service Obligation Fund
USTTAD	Upgrading Skill and Training in Traditional Arts/Crafts for Development
UTs	Union Territories
VAS	Value-Added Services
VPT	Village Public Telephone
WTO	World Trade Organization

List of Figures

List of Tables

Chapter 1
Development Dynamics in Two Dualistic Societies of Asia

1.1 Introduction[1]

Any *society* is basically a complex *system*, that is, a set of socio-economic, politico-cultural and technological elements. During a certain period of time, a societal *system* has its own *structure*, defined as a set of relations such that any change in one element or in one relation causes a change in other elements or relations. In social sciences, the word *structure* is one of the most obscure concepts. A structure is not just the set of relations among the elements, it also contains their *transformations*. Again, since transformations involve *laws*, 'the structure is preserved or enriched by the interplay of its transformation laws, which never yield results external to the system nor employ elements that are external to it'.[2] In fact, a structure is 'always the theory of a system … and it is nothing else'.[3] The behaviour of a system is dependent on not only the elements and their structure, but also the structure of the system itself. The *essential* behaviour of a system is, however, determined by the totality of the laws governing it, i.e. by its structure or the set of necessary and essential relations.

---

[1]This section is adapted from Dutta (1991).
[2]Piaget (1970, p. 5).
[3]Boudon (1971, p. 133).

D. Dutta, *Development under Dualism and Digital Divide in Twenty-First Century India*, Dynamics of Asian Development, https://doi.org/10.1007/978-981-10-6344-2_1

The *societal system* is the system of interdependent roles, behaviours, beliefs and values of all social groups and subgroups, classes and categories, and of all institutions—whether socio-economic, politico-legal, technological or religious. In other words, the societal system is a system of systems.[4] Such a *societal system* permits not only *synchronic* description (i.e. 'occurring together in time') of the society, but also its *diachronic* description (i.e. 'successive occurrence in time' and thus with emphasis on history and, therefore, on *path dependence* theory[5]). The *societal structure* is, on the other hand, a *pattern* of interrelated roles, behaviours, beliefs and values of the society. It is, in fact, the reflection of the balance of different socio-economic, political, cultural and other forces of the society. It is to be noted that structure should not be understood solely as a source of constraint on action or strategic activity at the individual or group/class level; rather, it both enables and constrains. In their structuralist theories, social scientists are explicitly concerned with social groups and subgroups or classes. One of the basic facts about such groups/classes is that they, being the centre of transformation, are *dynamic*. Also, since they impose all sorts of constraints and norms (rules), they are *self-regulating*. Differentiation of social status, inequitability in the distribution of economic wealth, concentration of political power among a few groups/classes or sectors/segments must, therefore, be studied dynamically in the process of change as tendencies, not as *static* states of a societal system.

In societal scientific literature, the term *societal transformation* is increasingly used to describe changes of a society's *systemic* characteristics. This incorporates the change of existing parameters of a societal system's social, economic, political, cultural and technological levels. Such changes are wide spread under sporadic globalising forces across both developed and emerging/developing nations. More specifically, a *societal transformation*:

> …firstly influences productive infrastructure which can bring about new technological changes and new patterns of participation in the international division of labour. Historically, this has meant an alteration of the requirements of global information technologies. Secondly, new structures of economic organization are developing. This may imply a change in ownership rights, as well as in investments, production, distribution and

---

[4]Herbert Simon (1962), in his seminal paper: 'The Architecture of Complexity', notes that a 'system of systems', as observed in the social, biological and physical sciences, is like nature which so consistently organises itself into 'hierarchies', although not necessarily in a relational subordination sense, but in the sense of complementarity between different parts of itself. Given the properties of the parts and the laws of their interaction, the larger system as a whole becomes more than the sum of the smaller systems. According to him, 'hierarchy' is a way of limiting complexity of the larger system so that it can evolve with stability. In biological systems, for example, cells, being the building block of human body, organise into tissues, tissues into organs, organs into larger systems. Moving downward from cell, well-defined subsystems such as cell membrane, ribosomes, mitochondria and so on have been identified.

[5]According to the 'path dependence theory', historical events and historically formed institutions have important role to play in determining the future range of possibilities for a nation's growth and development. Once institutions have been established, they tend to lock in a certain evolutionary path for the nation (Cypher and Dietz 2009, p. 79).

> supply. Thirdly, the distribution and use of political power take qualitatively different forms. This involves changes in the structure and performance of state institutions and other bodies of decision-making and control. Finally, a society's value-normative system can change, often in a way that allows the emergence and stabilisation of pluralist institutions.[6]

Many of the less developed countries (LDCs) not only are internally segmented and differentiated by different socio-economic and technological environments, but also have different socio-economic groups/classes. Unlike the neoclassical fiction of well-ordered atomistic-competitive market, markets in the contemporary developing/emerging countries are relatively less organised and narrowly defined. The common structural feature at the highest societal level of most of the LDCs is dualistic in the sense that *traditional* and *modern* segments[7] coexist side by side within their geographical entities. Quite often, the nature of their economic growth and development and the resulting pattern of resource allocation, production, consumption and income distribution are all determined more in the sociopolitical arena than in the market place. To identify this systemic mechanism, it is important to study nature of the *State*[8] and its relationship with (economically/politically) dominant or other socio-economic classes and institutions. Once the society's general socio-economic structure, its laws of transformation and mode of functioning are identified, one can then focus on the economic structure in particular in order to design a plan/policy strategy for its economic growth and development. Economic development is, in fact, viewed as continued economic growth associated with a set of interrelated changes in the economic structure of a developing/emerging country. The structural changes involving the composition of domestic demand, production, employment as well as the composition of foreign trade and capital flows are all very important for analytical purposes in the case of these internally segmented and differentiated economies. Such changes taken together, for an instance, on the economic front of a dualistic economy play a major role in societal transformation from its *traditional* nature to a predominantly *modernised* one. The transformation towards modernisation requires not only the development of society-specific science and technology, but also the application of a growing body of tested knowledge (from developed economies) to various phases and branches of both production and circulation.

---

[6]UNESCO [http://www.unesco.org/new/en/social-and-human-sciences/themes/international-migration/glossary/social-transformation/].

[7]The structural features of the two segments—*traditional* and *modern*—will be elaborated in detail in Sect. 1.3.1.

[8]The modern *State* as a societal entity consists of various elements or institutions such as the government, civil bureaucracy and military/paramilitary forces. From the historical point of view, a *State* may assume a variety of political forms such as military oligarchic, bureaucratic authoritarian, parliamentary or social democratic and one-party republic. It is responsible for rulemaking power within its territory through the institution of *government*. Although the terms 'State' and 'government' are often used interchangeably in general discussion and debate, the term 'government' is specifically meant to play three distinct roles of making the law (legislative role), implementing the law (executive role) and interpreting and applying the law (judiciary role).

In a contemporary society based on the complex division of labour, the interdependence among the elements of competing members/groups/classes is *organic*. The *economy* being the subset of a society is itself a *system* of economic variables and relations as reflected in its various activities and processes such as production, distribution, consumption, accumulation and so on. Generally speaking, at a certain point of history, the structural position of an economy could be, for analytical purpose, identified as an *invariant entity* with respect to its (non-planetary) environment that consists of social, cultural, political, legal and religious aspects of the society. What is, however, important to point out is that not only the economic structures vary across different countries, but also differentiation exists between different segments/sectors[9] of an economy itself and even within these segments/sectors themselves.

1.2 Articulation (Segmental and Societal) versus Equilibrium (Market and System)

In the present-day context of a transitional societal formation, we use the term 'articulation' meaning the interrelationship of a society's one segment represented by a dominant (capitalist or socialist) mode of functioning with one or more of the other segments represented by restrictively defined (pre-capitalistic or pre-socialistic) subordinate mode(s) of functioning through the law of motion and mechanism of the former's own reproduction.[10] It should be noted that the concept of 'articulation' between a dominant capitalist segment and one or more pre-capitalistic segments follows from the literature on *functional socialism*[11] or State socialism of a transitional socialistic society, especially involving mixed-economic framework where some

[9]While 'segment' refers to the compartmentalisation of the economy on the basis of specific modes of functioning (e.g. pre-capitalistic *traditional* and capitalistic *modern*), 'sector' refers to the compartmentalisation of any segment on the basis of specific goods/services under production. In the literature, the modern segment is more often assumed to have two productive sectors producing capital/services and consumer goods/services.

[10]Wolpe (1980, p. 41).

[11]As Tinbergen (1985, p. 179) points out, the concept of *functional socialism* is 'an alternative between communism and capitalism'. Unlike in the case of *natural socialism* with complete public ownership of all the means of production, a common element in the societal formation under other varieties of socialism, i.e. under *functional socialism,* is the 'limited relevance of ownership'. The functional approach also has elements in common with the distinction made between aims and means. Means usually constitute processes, a concept related to functions. Ownership as a means is too partial an answer to the question of how to attain the aims. Whether the aims are attained depends on a good deal on the way ownership is used, i.e. on management, which is itself a *function* (Tinbergen 1985, p. 180). Although public ownership is limited under *functional socialism*, several functions of the production and distribution processes (related to, e.g. child labour, minimum wage, unhealthy work, old-age pensions, statutory working hours, worker's participation in management, etc.) are generally 'regulated by law, and brought under public control'.

private ownership is still allowed. In fact, there could be a great difference in the degree of articulation in the societies with or without State ownership of capital (partly or fully). In the literature, it is often referred to as an extreme case of abstract auto-centric, closed capitalist economy with two productive sectors producing capital goods/services for derived demand and consumer goods/services for final demand. In the following analysis, we'll, however, mainly emphasise the case of a *dual* economy where two segments—*modern* (capitalistic and/or socialistic) and *traditional* (pre-capitalistic and/or pre-socialistic)—coexist side by side. The modern segment may produce both capital and consumer goods/services and hence may have two productive sectors. The traditional segment is, on the other hand, generally assumed to produce raw materials and wage goods/services as well as to provide information and communication technology (ICT)-related various low- and semi-skilled services. In the literature on petty commodity production within the traditional segment, numerous and diverse-dependent linkages (direct or indirect) between 'small-scale enterprises' and the 'capitalist segment' as well as between different levels of petty commodity production within the capitalist mode of functioning have been provided. Examples of such linkages include direct incorporation through subcontracting and employing outworkers as well as more complicated procedures such as the utilisation of agents in retail distribution and ICT-related subsidiary service providers who put up their own deposits for relieving the mother company of many of the risks involved.

Keeping the above possible reference of linkages in mind, one can distinguish two types of articulation based on an economy's supply and demand sides point of view. Both supply and demand will be referred to the economy's either *segments* or *sectors*. From the supply-side point of view, the economy is said to be *segmentally/sectorally articulated* between the two modal segments or productive sectors if linkages[12] exist between the segments/sectors such that investment accelerators are generated, i.e. an increase in the production of wage goods/services creates an increase in the derived demand for capital goods/services. This segmental/sectoral articulation is, in fact, the objective determinant of the social allocation (or division) of labour between the modal segments or between the productive sectors. In the process of growth, the periodic, shorter-run maladjustment in this social allocation of labour leads to shorter-run *segmental/sectoral disarticulation* (in the form of disproportionality), which, in turn, leads to business cycles with market *disequilibria*. Shorter-run business cycles[13] phenomena are self-correcting, but they generate endogenously the conditions necessary for a subsequent adjustment.

From the demand-side point of view, the economy is said to be *socially articulated* across the segments or sectors if the necessary relation between the generation of production and consumption capacities (i.e. between *derived demand* for

[12]Under sectoral articulation, for example, both forward *linkage* in the production of raw materials and *backward linkage* in industrial production do exist. According to backward linkage effects (i.e. output utilisation), every activity that does not by its nature cater exclusively to final demands will induce attempts to utilise its output as inputs in some new activities.

[13]Shorter-run business cycle phenomenon is here distinguished from short-run trade cycle.

capital goods and *final demand* for wage goods/services) exists. Production capacity is determined by the *return to capital* (i.e. profit), while consumption capacity is determined by the *return to labour* (i.e. wage). It is thus implied that under *social articulation*, there exists an objective relationship between profit and wages and, therefore, between the rate of growth and the distribution of income. When the necessary relation between production and consumption capacities does not imply a relationship between return to capital and return to labour, the economy is said to be *socially disarticulated*.[14] 'The key difference between social articulation and disarticulation thus originates in the sphere of circulation—in the geographical and social location of the market for the modern sector. Under social articulation, market expansion originates principally in rising national wages; under social disarticulation, it originates either abroad or in profits and rents'.[15]

In the process of growth, the periodic maladjustments in the above necessary relation lead to shorter-run social disproportionality in the distribution of income, which, in turn, leads to business cycles and structural crises. It is noteworthy that, unlike shorter-run phenomena of business cycles, structural crises are not self-correcting and, therefore, require structural changes for their elimination. Structural changes are generally meant to be changes in the structure of an economy involving changes in the composition of demand, production, employment and distribution as well as in the legal, political, institutional and social frameworks in which economic activities take place. In order to be *structural*, a change must, therefore, be permanent (i.e. long term) and not temporary, real and not monetary, fundamental and not policy related, drastic and not small, or a change of conditions ordinarily assumed unchanged.[16] The analyses of segmental/sectoral articulation and social articulation are primarily *structural* in nature; here, not only the technological relations among the modal segments/productive sectors or the functional relations among the social groups and classes are emphasised, but also their transformations are identified.

In today's globalising world, forces of sectoral/social articulation and disarticulation are all being tossed and tackled *simultaneously* by the States and at a faster rate particularly in those societies that have been closely involved in both production and circulation processes either domestically and/or globally. Focusing on East Asia and taking a broad perspective that spans the economic and social dimensions of development, Whittaker et al. (2010) have argued that the path of socio-economic development is now better conceived as one of 'compressed

[14]The term 'disarticulation' has been applied over the past decades by a number of political economists and sociologists to describe different types of socio-economic and political distortion in the context of both domestic and global economy (e.g. Therborn 198; de Janvry 1981; de Janvry and Sadoulet 1983; Stokes and Anderson 1990; Huang 1995, Breedlove and Armer 1996; Cypher 2001 and Kostzer 2004).

[15]de Janvry (1981, p. 34).

[16]Machlup (1963 [1958], p. 927).

development'.[17] The result of compression is not just blurring the stages of development, but also simultaneous industrialisation and de-industrialisation. Similarly, focusing on India and China, D'Costa (2014) contends that capitalism is 'compressed' in these societies meaning that the phases of capitalism do not follow one another in sequential order. Instead, primitive accumulation of petty commodity producing sectors may be delayed or be experienced simultaneously with an advanced accumulation of the corporate sector under mature capitalism.

Let's now make reference to the working of the markets in terms of transactional activities of individual participants irrespective of their any functional group identity or class differences (i.e. homogeneous individuals). If we assume that markets are well organised and widely monetised, and if aggregate income (on the supply side of the markets) equals aggregate expenditure (on the demand side of the market), then the economy is said to be in *market equilibrium*. In the framework of an abstract, closed and autocentric capitalist economy, when both markets (capital and consumer goods) are in equilibrium, wages are then spent on consumption, profits are spent on investments and government expenditures are compensated by taxes. For an instance, if in a mature capitalist economy, aggregate expenditures lag behind aggregate incomes, i.e. if there are more money holdings (or, increased liquidity preference) in the hands of the public (say, due to some future uncertainty), investment will lag behind saving. This will, in turn, lead to less production, less employment and then less consumption. In order to achieve full employment again or moving towards full employment, Keynesian policies of government borrowing or taxing away excess savings could create an effective demand (backed by income generation) without increasing the productive capacity of the system, but such policies, however, are only effective as a counter-cyclical measure for slowdowns originating in underconsumption.

If one could separate out structural or permanent (i.e. long-term) government *expenditure* and *revenue*[18] and if they are structurally interrelated, then the fiscal or budgetary process is said to be in *Keynesian articulation*. When they match, the state of the budgetary process is said to be in *fiscal equilibrium*.[19] It should,

[17]To my knowledge, the word 'compressed' had been used by Therborn (1980, p. 115) in the context of processes of change involving masses of people and aiming at a transformation of the social and political regime.

[18]According to Tanzi (1982), permanent government expenditures or revenues are those items that are *sustainable* or *maintainable* over some period of time or more appropriately over the long run. These are *structural* in nature—often linked with either the performance in foreign trade (e.g. export boom, worsening terms of trade) or public enterprise performance, also sometimes influenced by tax structure, administrative control mechanism and in the degree of political stability.

[19]Tanzi (*Ibid.*) also adds that this *fiscal equilibrium* may exist despite temporary imbalance between total revenue and total expenditure. He gives a list of causes of decrease in total government revenue and increase in total government expenditures. The facts contributing to the fall in public revenues are: (a) decline in export prices; (b) unrealistic customs valuations for determining import duties; (c) widespread use of specific (*ad valorem*) rates for both exercise taxes and customs duties; (d) increasing use of (quantitative) import restrictions; (e) administrative difficulties in collecting revenues; (f) substantial collection lags; and (g) increasing exemptions granted

however, be noted that *fiscal equilibrium* may be accompanied with *monetary disequilibrium*, especially when government deficit is financed by borrowing from the central bank of the country. In the process of growth, there might be short-run, periodic Keynesian or fiscal disproportionality causing either aggregate expenditures to lag behind the aggregate incomes or permanent government expenditure to lag behind permanent government revenue. It may happen due to, for example, individual enterprises' informational deficiency regarding future certainty, government's wrong price or tax policy during the fiscal year and so forth. In any case, contrary to the concepts of *market equilibrium* (with zero net excess demand in a single market or with zero net excess aggregate demand in the economy as a whole) or (Walrasian) *general equilibrium* (with zero net excess demands in all markets) or *fiscal equilibrium* (with zero net excess permanent government expenditure), there is another concept of equilibrium—called *system equilibrium*—which is also very often used in economic analysis. One could note that the latter kind of equilibrium is based on the *functional* theory of equilibrium, whereas former kinds of equilibrium are based on the *mechanistic* theory of equilibrium. The basic difference between the two types of theories is based on the different kinds of logical procedure applied.

> Functionalist theory focuses on the unity and directedness of a total system, while mechanistic theory tends to concentrate on the precise determination of the relationships between parts of a system. Functionalist theory assumes a system to have a basic organizing principle of goals and self-regulating mechanisms. Mechanistic theory takes a system to be derived from the relationships between the parts. Both types of theory, organizing their explanations in different ways, develop equilibrating systems. .... Economics, more than any other social science, has tried to organize the relationships with which it deals in the form of mechanistic equilibrium theories.[20]

A *system equilibrium* is defined, in Machlup's (1958, p. 9) terminology, as 'a constellation of selected inter-related variables so adjusted to one another that no inherent tendency to change prevails in the model which they constitute'. As Krupp (1965, p. 73) further points out, the *stability* of an equilibrating system is established by the system's tendency to react in a constant way to a change introduced into the system. Special *self-regulating mechanisms* are generally present in systems exhibiting stability. They can also be introduced into the systems to help create stability. These mechanisms operate by creating compensatory adjustments in some variables when disturbing changes occur in other parts of the system. Unlike other social sciences, many of the *self-regulating mechanisms* are more

(Footnote 19 continued)

to investors and importers. Similarly, the factors attributed to the rise in public expenditures are: (a) subsidies to consumers via supply of consumer goods at low prices (controlled); (b) subsidies to enterprises via supply of raw materials at low prices; (c) wage increases and creation of new entitlements; (d) administrative difficulties in controlling expenditures; and (e) spending on capital projects and repayment of past domestic and foreign debts.

[20]Krupp (1965, p. 68).

clearly formulated in mainstream economics. The stabilisers such as unemployment insurance, progressive tax or escalator clauses in wage contracts are constantly being debated with regard to their effectiveness as stabilising mechanisms. It is very likely that the economic system may be in equilibrium even if there is no market equilibrium or fiscal equilibrium in some parts of the system.

The general concept of equilibrium (in the tradition of mainstream economics) is *static* in nature. The equilibrium system as such, in fact, represents 'a system without time'.[21] But the concept of articulation (of any variety) is primarily a *dynamic* concept of the societal formation. In other words, the concept of equilibrium is associated with a state of (an economic) system or some of its subsystems in a point of time, while the concept of articulation is associated with a (socio-economic) process of a system or a sub-system repeated or reproduced over some period of time. Equilibrium does not necessarily mean articulation except in the extreme cases like closed autocentric capitalist economy or fully planned socialist economy. In the extreme case of a capitalist economy, for example, the Keynesian articulation corresponds to market equilibrium, which, in turn, corresponds to the (Walrasian) general equilibrium. This is so because all markets separately and together are in equilibrium. In fact, articulation of any variety in the context of this extreme case with these two restrictive assumptions is said to be perfect (or pure, in the terminology of de Janvry and Sadoulet (1983, p. 279)). Thus, if there is perfect segmental/sectorial and social articulation, then there must be not only a system equilibrium, but also a general equilibrium, and hence, equilibrium in all markets.

All the above analysis suggests that equilibrium, being a concept of *rest*, is a snapshot in the dynamic process of articulation of a society and, therefore, is a very restricted concept.[22] Articulation, on the other hand, being a very broad concept, is to be understood in different degrees and in different stages of social formation. Highest degree of articulation corresponds to the perfect articulation in the context of a closed, autocentric capitalist economy or in the context of a fully planned socialist economy, although its realisation is a distant possibility.

Before we discuss the actual state of disarticulation and disequilibrium (more so under globalising forces) in a subsequent section: *Market and structural disequilibrium under disarticulation*, let's first briefly describe nature and laws of dualistic societies.

---

[21]Even the concept of *temporary* equilibrium is a snapshot of a dynamic economy evolving through time. As Nagatani (1981, p. 34) points out, a *temporary equilibrium* is different from a *static* equilibrium for two reasons: (a) each *period* is not self-contained, and it is constrained by past history and by the state of expectations about the future; (b) it is generally not a position of *rest* but is subject to certain dynamic forces, i.e. the motion of the economy in a given position.

[22]As in Marx who stressed the capitalist process of production as a 'process-in-circuit' of capital through all its various stages, the real issue 'is not that of equilibria in a sub-markets (money-market, labour-market, commodity market for the means of production or consumption), or equilibrium in the "production process" or the "circulation process". … [Instead] … equilibrium has to be seen and understood as an equilibrium within the overall framework of all these stages' (Grossmann 1977, p. 82).

1.3 Nature and Laws of Dualistic Societies

In the preceding section, we have defined various types of articulation—segmental/sectoral, social, Keynesian, etc—that may be present in the process of societal formation of a country. We have also noted that the perfect (or pure) form of articulation is only a theoretical possibility. In reality, a certain degree of 'disarticulation' of any type exists in the societal formation of almost every society—economically developed or developing—and more so in the case of developing/emerging countries that are in the transitional phase towards a higher level of development and under centralised/decentralised socio-economic and political institutional framework. As a matter of fact, no society is absolutely monomorphic and homogeneous[23] having only one single mode of functioning of either capitalism or socialism. The 'modern'[24] segment (with the capitalistic or socialistic mode of functioning) does exist side by side with the 'traditional' segment (with the pre-capitalistic or pre-socialistic mode of functioning) in almost all contemporary developed and developing societies.[25] Although the degree of coexistence varies from society to society, there is, of course, no doubt that this is much more accentuated in the case of the developing/emerging societies. As Higgins (1977, p. 120) rightly declares, '… nearly all developing countries are dualistic'.

We have already mentioned that in the modern capitalist society, the traditional pre-capitalistic segment not only simply exists, but also often performs *functions* that are critical to the capitalistic segment in different ways. It is rather very rare (except for some tribal communities in some countries) that the traditional segment is in complete isolation from the modern segment of the contemporary societies. Thus, a fully disarticulated society is also an abstract concept as is the fully or perfectly articulated one. Many empirical studies identify complex linkages and dependent relationships between production and distribution systems not only within the traditional segment, but also in relation to the modern segment. We have also noted that the framework of complex petty commodity production is rather more realistic in understanding the traditional segment of developing countries. This approach, in fact, focuses on the 'relationship between the different elements of the ensemble' (in the terminology of structuralism) rather than on defining the

[23]Using the concepts of *market rationality* and *modernisation*, and basing on the premise that social and economic structures are generated by continuous variables (like production, income, consumption, security, status or prestige), the mainstream economists tend to integrate all social groupings and economic activities into a so-called homogeneous society. 'The market [does] not seem to allocate persons and resources nor [does] the spread of communication work to diffuse belief, motive, and social structures in the sort of continuous array' (Berger and Piore 1980, p. 2).

[24]Although the term 'modern' has many characteristics of its own as will be discussed below, the modern segment includes a manufacturing production process based on 'assembly line' method of production in a factory system.

[25]In the literature, the terms—'formal', 'regular' and 'organised'—are often interchangeably used for the term 'modern', while the opposites—'informal', 'irregular' and 'unorganised'—are similarly used for the term 'traditional'.

organised-unorganised, formal-informal, capitalistic-pre-capitalistic types of distinction of the economy.

It is true that there is a variety (though not a continuum) of productive activities within both segments of a society, and more so in the traditional or informal one. It is also true that the two segments are qualitatively very much different, especially in terms of distinct mode of functioning. In the terminology of Berger and Piore (1980, p. 2), societies seem to be *lumpier*. Whatever may be the number of *lumps* or social segments, these are *coherent wholes*; these are united from the consistency of their internal rules and organisation and the stability of their relationships to each other in a particular interval of time. If one sticks to the general term of 'mode of functioning' as the criterion to identify different lumps or segments of say, a non-socialist developing society, then, broadly speaking, the distinct segments—*capitalist* and *pre-capitalist*[26]—are to be found to exist in many of such societies. This pattern of socio-economic segmentation is generally known as *dualism* in economics literature. This significance of *dualism* does not mean that 'a society is divided into two autonomous and discontinuous segments'; it simply means that 'a society is divided segmentally and not continuously'.[27] 'Equally, social segmentation does not', as they (*Ibid*., p. 142) further add, 'rule out some mobility between sectors [segments], so long as the volume and character of this mobility still permit the maintenance within each segment of different values, rules and institutions'.

1.3.1 Main Characteristics of a Dual Economy

The two segments—*capitalistic/socialistic* and *pre-capitalistic/pre-socialistic*—are generally called *modern* and *traditional,* respectively. These are two different socio-economic and technological environments that coexist within the same geographical territory of a country.

[26]Under the name of pre-capitalist segment, we very often lump together a number of restricted/extended modes of functioning like 'feudal', 'semi-feudal', 'servile' (though not 'slavery'), 'lineage', which may exist in different small pockets of the contemporary societies—transitional or not.

[27]The social and economic structures are not generated by continuous variables, and hence, number of segments cannot be multiplied indefinitely. In fact, the continuous array of variation could only be possible in a unitary, unsegmented, monomorphic model of society. The very existence of finite number of segments follows from the fact that there exist qualitative differences in both behavioural characteristics of the principal actors (e.g. workers and managers) and the nature of human experiences. As Berger and Piore (1980, pp. 16–17) argue in the context of labour market dualism, '[s]uch basic economic processes as wage determination or education and training are fundamentally different in different market segments and cannot be captured by a single model of human behaviour. Because the nature of experience is different, well-being of workers in one stratum is fundamentally incommensurate with that of workers in another and cannot be expressed by a single monetary scale'.

As to the *social* and *organisational* distinction, jobs in the traditional segment are usually regarded as inferior and with demeaning social status. Working conditions are poor; highly personal; social relationship often prevails between workers and supervisors; wages tend to be determined directly or indirectly by statute; jobs usually utilise basic human skills and capabilities, or require little skill if any; they provide little security or career advancement. 'The labour force in these hobs is composed of distinct groups who derive their principal identity from social roles outside the work place; women, adolescents, peasant workers, or temporary migrants. Such workers are typically unstable, with a high rate of voluntary turnover, and frequent movement in and out of the labour force'.[28] Jobs in the modern segment are, on the other hand, attractive, relatively skilled, and better paying and generally with greater social status and more stable work environment. They usually provide substantial job security and offer more extensive opportunities for career advancement with high geographical and institutional mobility. Professional and managerial employment involves formal education prior to employment, while workers mostly acquire their skills on the job in the process of production. Wages are usually set through either collective bargaining via formal union organisations or informal procedures mediated by informal groups. 'Work and authority are, as a result, governed by custom and formal rules and procedures, and the exercise of authority is frequently subject to a review process'.[29]

As to the *economic* distinction, the traditional segment is, by and large, peasant owned, though there are varieties of petty production including those by artisans and traders. The mode of functioning is pre-capitalistic in the sense that it uses relatively little wage labour or rented land, and retains most if its product for consumption. The functional distribution of income among the various inputs to the production process and the demarcation between subsistence and surplus are all blurred in such a segment. Here, per capita income is very low, and (open) unemployment and (disguised) under-employment are its persistence features. All these make the traditional segment economically stagnant. The modern segment, on the other hand, has a capitalistic mode of functioning in the sense that wage labour mostly works with capital (i.e. plants and equipment), whether privately or socially owned,[30] and most of the product is sold in the market with main consideration for profit or surplus. Functional distribution of income between labour and capital, as well as division between surplus and subsistence, is satisfactorily defined in terms of the distinction between profits and wages. Here, the degree of industrialisation is high, factors of growth are in operations, productivity and wages tend to increase, and per capita income is fairly high.

---

[28]Berger and Piore (1980, p. 18).

[29]*Ibid.* (pp. 18–19).

[30]In fact, the overlapping of *mixed* economy (with private and public sectors) and *dual* economy (with modern and traditional segments) is very common in many of the developing/emerging countries.

As to the *technological* distinction, the two environments have different methods of production. Depending on the natural resource endowment of the economy, it may act as a constraint and hence can severely limit output in traditional segment, especially in agriculture. For an instance, land may be a scare factor of production in traditional segment, while it is less important in the production of modern segment's output. Both segments use capital of different types, and once this is installed in either segment, it is not easily shiftable to the other one. The traditional segment generally uses primitive methods of production with high labour-to-capital and labour-to-land ratios, and the labour productivity as such is very low. The modern segment, on the other hand, does use mechanised methods of production with high labour productivity. There may be some exceptions, for one can easily find some modern farms and plantations and also some close substitutes for manufactures (like woven cloth) that are produced in factory's assembly lines, although using traditional handicraft methods. Similarly, some petty commodity producers might all along introduce new technological inventions. As Moser (1978, p. 1058) gives an example, some crafts such as watch-mending owe their very existence to European inventions.

As to the distinction from the point of view of the technological fact of *specialisation*, the traditional segment produces mainly primary products including food, which, apart from some requirements for seed, can only be used for consumption in both segments. Petty producers of goods and services generally satisfy a part of the local demands. The modern segment, on the other hand, produces mainly manufacturing goods which can be used as either consumer goods or investment goods in both the segments. Since the *division of labour* is very much effective in manufacturing industries of the modern segment, the operation of increasing returns to scale is quite operative. The fundamental reason is that, for any industrial activity which involves processing or transformation of say, basic materials, increasing returns to scale dominate due to the nature of technological progress and not necessarily to any particular technology.[31] In the case of primary products of traditional segment, the increasing returns are not usually operative at least at the level of individual producer. Diminishing returns generally operate in agriculture of the traditional segment due to the large seasonal variations in the flow of free solar energy causing the utilisation rate of land to fluctuate over the annual agricultural cycle in temperate zones.[32]

As to the distinction of the two environments from the point of view of *location* and *community organisation*, the traditional segment is predominantly *rural* with relatively close ties among the people, while the modern segment is predominantly *urban* with loose ties or even sometimes with no such ties whatsoever.

As to the *market institutions*, the markets for manufacturing products of the modern segment where increasing returns play a dominant role, are, by and large, imperfectly competitive. This is mainly because the manufacturers themselves

[31]Kaldor (1972, p. 1242).

[32]Felix (1977, p. 192).

maintain their own inventory stocks and adjust production rates in tune with sales demand. The markets for most of the primary products of the traditional segment do, on the other hand, consist of many small producers generally facing diminishing returns and, hence, are very competitive. Due to various types of uncertainties that the traditional segment has to go through, merchants or dealers play the important role of shock absorption and, thereby, make the market stable so that individual producers can sell, and individual consumers can buy at given prices. The activities, the organisations and the institutions of each of the two segments thus reflect particular differing modes of socio-economic behaviours, values and relationships. They also express differing levels of technological sophistication and specialisation. The two environments thus, simply, reflect two stages of development. Characterisation of a dual economy can be made in terms of the following distinctions:

Environmental, social and organisational distinctions:

Traditional	Modern
• Rural, poor working conditions; • Close ties, low-paying jobs, inferior social status; • Wages flexible (more towards downward) or may be statutorily regulated, unstable labour force with high turnover, low skill and little job security	• Urban, better work environment; • Loose ties, better-paying jobs, superior social status; • Wages usually set through formal procedures, relatively stable labour force, high skill and high job security

Economic distinctions:

Traditional	Modern
• Peasant owned or with petty producers, i.e. pre-capitalistic with little wage labour or rented land; • Greater role of use value of production; functional distribution of income (between rent, interest and profit) unsatisfactory; • Stagnant economy, low employment and low utilisation of resources; • Low per capita income	• Capitalistic with market wage labour or socialistic with social wage fund; • Capital owned privately or socially; • Greater role of exchange value of production; • Functional distribution of income satisfactory; • High degree of industrialisation with high employment and high utilisation of resources; • High per capita income

Technological distinctions and production specialisation:

Traditional	Modern
• Primitive or non-mechanised methods of production based on parallel arrangement of small-scale production units;	• Mechanised methods of production based on assembly line large-scale production units; • Low labour–capital ratio;

(continued)

(continued)

Traditional	Modern
• High labour–capital and labour–land ratios; • Low labour productivity; • Specialisation in primary production; • No increasing returns to scale (at least at the level of individual producers)	• High labour productivity; • Specialisation in secondary and tertiary products; • Increasing returns to scale highly operative

Market institutional distinctions:

Traditional	Modern
• Markets narrowly defined due to the existence of various non-market transactions; • Large number of small producers; • Markets are competitive	• Markets fully developed; • A few big producers; • Markets are usually oligopolistic

1.3.2 Economic Dualism versus Functional Dualism

The concept of *dualism* that is generally referred to by the liberal economists with full faith on market forces and modernisation process is known as *economic dualism*; this is in the sense that as if some sort of market exchange (though with unequal terms) between the two segments takes place on voluntary basis (with or without State intervention). Markets in both the segments are implicitly assumed to be more or less organised as it is the case in neoclassical calculus. Unlike the neoclassical two-sector growth models,[33] the models based on economic dualism try to incorporate some social mechanism (and, hence, appropriate social institutions) operating along with market economic forces. However, there is no reference of the political economy[34] as such to the mechanism of labour transfer in a dual economy. Sometimes, the State authority deliberately keeps the subsistence segment in existence as a reservoir of surplus labour so that labour could be transferred at some low wage rate to the capitalist agriculture or industry whenever needed.

[33]In neoclassical calculus, institutions (other than market) are, as Taylor (1983, p. 3) notes, conspicuously lacking as is the recognition that men, women and children are political and social as well as economic animals. In fact, two-sector growth models in the neoclassical tradition are purely economic models of two productive sectors interacting via the market mechanism.

[34]*Political economy* is the branch of social science that deals with (i) the interaction between politics and economics on the surface of a society as in the *above-class* (orthodox) economic approach and (ii) *social relations of production* analysed as a unity with the *technical productive forces* as in the *class-based* (Marxian) approaches, in which social relations are determined by the organisational arrangements (e.g. capitalistic) and economic relations of men and women (as wage earners and profit earners) in order to make the labour-generation and capital-accumulation processes effective.

In the context of the dependency literature on centre–periphery relationship, the agricultural sector of Latin America itself is characterised by a *functional dualism*[35] in the sense that the pre-capitalist peasant segment is (involuntarily) functional to capitalist class—national and international, or peripheral and central. Functional dualism emerges between the (modern) capitalist segment which produces commodities on the basis of hired skilled as well as semi-proletarian labour, and the (traditional) peasant/self-employed artisan segment which produces petty commodities and use values (for home consumption) on the basis of mainly self-employed/family labour. The traditional segment delivers cheap wage labour to the capitalist segment. The wage is sustained at a level below the cost of maintenance and reproduction of the labour force. Here, under functional dualism, wage is only a complement between the subsistence needs (of the worker and his/her family) and net production in the traditional segment. Since part of the labour's subsistence needs is derived from production for home consumption, functional dualism thus provides the structural possibility of meeting the necessity of cheap labour for capitalist development.[36]

Two modes of functioning under functional dualism are articulated in the general sense of Wolpe (1980), though not necessarily in the strong sense of two-way perfect (or pure) interrelation of social and segmental articulation. As we have seen, functional dualism is characterised as a source of primitive accumulation (through cheap semi-proletarian labour and cheap food); it could be shown as a contradictory process that leads to the destruction of the subsistence segment of peasantry.[37] The principal manifestations are the demographic explosion, increasingly landlessness under competition (for land in the development of capitalist agriculture), forced commercialisation, more and more peasant's involvement in land tenancy contract, urban migration and overall ecological collapse. Since industrialisation under capitalism tends to occur on the basis of capital-intensive technology, a very limited proportion of the surplus labour from the traditional agriculture is absorbed in the modern industry. As a result, a considerable size of the urban labour surplus gets reproduced out of the fundamental dualism and it constitutes the marginal mass redundant and excluded from any function in the accumulation process. Thus, the lack of proper articulation of the traditional segment or the society in relation to the modern one is the basic condition of the huge 'marginal mass'. This also leads to autonomous attempt (via self-employment in petty commodity production including artisan production and trading) at what Portes and Walton (1981, p. 78) call 'survival through a myriad of interstitial economic activities'. The fact that 'marginal mass' is excessive even relative to the requirements of the reserve army helps depress the wage of the labourers in the capitalist segment further below the level that could prevail if such an extra surplus was not present. Thus, due to the presence

[35]*Functional dualism* is considered in literature to be only a transitional phase of the development of capitalism, which lacks its own stable *laws of reproduction*.

[36]de Janvry (1981, p. 37).

[37]de Janvry (1981, p. 85) discusses in detail.

of 'marginal mass', the functions exercised by the 'reserve army' in capital accumulation are more than fulfilled. Although disjointed overlap of a smaller segment excluded from any participation in modern production or consumption is not fully disarticulated, the articulation is biased to the modern segment. We will call this a situation of weak articulation or simply, disarticulation as opposed to strong articulation with two-way segmental/sectoral and social posed to strong articulation with two-way segmental/sectoral and social interrelationship between modes of production/productive sectors.

1.4 Market and Structural Disequilibrium under Disarticulation

The discussion that we will now intend to enter into is the enumeration of either different types of market disproportionalities or incompatibilities of a set of selected interrelated variables—*periodic* and *structural*. State of market disproportionality or non-market clearing situation is generally known as the state of *disequilibrium*, when prices do not clear markets *currently*, and individuals perceive quantity constraints. The 'state of disequilibrium' is, precisely speaking, a state of 'temporary equilibrium with rationing' (Drazen 1980, p. 285) or a 'quantity constrained equilibrium' (Drazen 1982, p. 1039).

The concept of 'disequilibrium' itself is, therefore, a static one too. Unlike the static concept of equilibrium or rest, the concept of disequilibrium is, however, based on the view that the typical market remains out of equilibrium for some time interval. Thus, any analysis of such a disequilibrium state requires a proper dynamic theory for the same reason as the physicists adopt to identify which state of the system is in equilibrium and which is in disequilibrium. But the economists, in distinguishing two such state, tend to be less precise and very often do not even explicitly use an underlying dynamic theory of behaviour or mechanism. For an instance, in the situation of non-market clearing disequilibrium state, 'the economics usually has', as Hey (1981, pp. 3–4) points out, 'at the back of mind, an informally derived, and ad hocly appended, dynamic theory'. Accordingly, it is taken for granted that there will be an inherent tendency to change (e.g. in prices) when market does not clear. In using such intuitive acceptable procedure, one really 'violates the assumptions under which the supply and demand curves were constructed in the first place'. It is to be noted that the proper identification of the nature of the weak articulation or simply disarticulation will definitely give the basic dynamic (equilibrating or disequilibrating) force operating behind the markets, in the surface of which we observe the interaction of demand for and supply of various economic activities.

Depending on the nature and causes of the economic state for being out of equilibrium, the disequilibrium states could be divided into two categories—*transient* disequilibrium (generally known as *market* disequilibriun) and *persistent* disequilibrium (generally know as *structural* disequilibrium). As opposed to the former, the degree of disproportionality is, in the latter case, much higher and the adjustment lag is much larger. It is noteworthy that market disequilibrium is predominantly a phenomenon of the developed capitalist countries. Here, markets are broadly defined institutions in the sense that they are sufficiently organised, monetised and impersonalised; economic principle of voluntary exchange among the atomised economic units is already the dominant transactional mode on the basis of which all the resource allocation, work organisation, product disposition, etc, take place. Structural disequilibrium is, on the other hand, a phenomenon found more often in the less developed countries (LDCs) and manifests its existence recurrently for some period of time. Here, markets are narrowly defined in the sense that they are inadequately monetised, highly fragmented, transactional modes of both market and non-market economies exist in some limited degree.

Following a whole generation of social anthropologists and empirical economists, Bardhan (1980, p. 58) mentions that in the narrowly defined markets, traditional system of obligatory payments, custom-determined rewards, communal sharing and insurance, etc., are being eroded by the steady penetration of market forces. Due to the existence of a certain degree of sensitivity to market stimuli, tractions of this kind cannot be described as mere expression of social, traditional or cultural factors. Also, behind the operation of supply and demand, a network of personalised dealings is still present in these markets. Relationship between attached labour and the employers and relationship between small-scale enterprises and the capitalist sector through subcontracting are some such examples that are found in the narrowly defined markets.[38]

Also, if we focus on the governmental budgetary aspects of the developing countries, we could very frequently see that government revenue and, perhaps, government expenditure often do not have a permanent character. This situation of Tanzi's (1982) fiscal disequilibrium is predominantly structural in nature. This is so, especially because public sector in most of the LDCs, instead of being a monolithic entity with one decision-making centre, is composed of different parts such as the central government, the local government, nationalised enterprises and many governmental institutions. As we'll see later on, the governmental decisions in the economic sphere are mostly the direct results of the political, social and institutional structures of the country. Similarly, unemployment is also basically an example of structural disequilibrium in labour market of the LDCs, especially with large numbers of surplus labour. Because of underdeveloped and unplanned modern

[38]Bardhan (1980) also mentions the distinguishing characteristics of purely *non-market* transactions. According to him, the transactional mode of non-market economics is primarily one of the obligatory payments based on non-market relation of *extra-economic* (social and legal) coercion and some commitment to sharing based on non-market principle of reciprocity and redistribution. Master–serf relation under feudalism, constant gist and counter gist giving in tribal community, patron–client relationship of Indian *Jajmani* system are some examples of non-market relations. In the case of imperfect markets, market exchange is, on the other hand, already the dominant transactional mode, but there exists *asymmetry* of information, assets and economic power.

industrial sector in many of such LDCs, vast unemployed and underemployed populations give rise to persistently open or disguised involuntary unemployment. The problem of unemployment, however, differs from that in the developed capitalist economies. While the inadequacy of effective demand is the main cause of unemployment in the developed capitalist economies, shortage of capital equipment and limited opportunities for technical substitution as well as restrictive economic mobility of factors of production are its basic causes in the LDCs. This is of course not to deny that in an underdeveloped economy there may not be any deficiency of effective demand. There are, in fact, many instances of countries whose capital equipment, meagre though they are, will nevertheless be under-utilised. However, even if such equipment is fully utilised in the LDCs, they are, in contrast to developed economies, still not capable of absorbing all available labour. Therefore, unemployment is primarily a structural problem in the LDCs, though it might be the result of the deficiency of effective demand in some segmented region or in some specific sector for some types of labour.

Structural disequilibrium could be found either at the factors level or at the goods level. In its manifestation at factors level, a single factor is found to receive different returns in different uses or the relationships among the factors' prices are seen to be out of line with factors' availabilities. The disequilibrium (or imbalance) at the factor level thus involves questions, of both resource allocation and use (i.e. sectoral and/or segmental articulation) on the one hand, and product circulation and income distribution (i.e. social articulation across the sectors/segments) on the other. Similarly, structural disequilibrium at the goods level means the goods' relative prices do not reflect the allocation of factors among various production units appropriate to existing factor prices. This may be due to imperfect competition in the market; also, this may arise either because of excessive factor response (as found in Cobweb Theorem) or because of factor rigidity which permits no response. The existence of such structural disequilibria is very common in dual economies. Here, factor prices (especially, wage and capital interest) are very much out of line with factor proportions if we focus our attention on both the segments—modern and traditional.

Structural disequilibrium may also arise due to external reason of say, either chronic balance-of-payments deficit or extroverted and disarticulated process of capital accumulation (as under *peripheral* or *semi-peripheral* capitalism). Having access to foreign capital, the modern export sector of the developing countries is able to employ factors combinations yielding relatively higher marginal productivities compared to the rest of the economy. As a result, factors of production in combination with foreign capital could receive higher return in modern export sector than in the traditional subsistence segment with scarce domestic capital. Unequal prices for the same factor in alternative uses will, in turn, generate structural disequilibrium, and hence, it may directly cause significant income differentials across an economy's different socio-economic segments, productive sectors and groups of factor owners. The degree or extent of the inequality very much depends on the level of economic growth and development, as well as on the intensity of the existing structural disequilibrium of various forms. Due to cumulative causation, this inherently disequilibrating market forces in a downward direction do certainly worsen economic inequalities and also have a high likelihood for stifling economic growth. It is also, however, to be noted that the nature of economic growth and development of the LDCs and the resulting pattern of income distribution are all determined more in the political arena than in the market place. To understand this mechanism, it is therefore absolutely necessary to study the social class structure,[39] the nature of the State and its relationship with the (economically and politically) dominant or other socio-economic classes.

In his taxonomy of a society's class structure, Weisskopf (1983, p. 471) distinguishes ten separate classes categorised into three broad groups—*top-most stratum* of elite (or bourgeoisie) classes, *middle stratum* of independent classes and *lowest stratum* of proletarian classes. The *top-most stratum* consisting of five classes of elites (traditional feudalistic, agricultural, business, foreign and educated) is small in number but strong in economic and political power; it generally owns and controls large units of production, and it also hires and directs substantial number of employees in the productive activities. The *middle stratum* consisting of two classes (peasantry and petty-bourgeoisie) owns or controls small units of production, and hence can afford to be self-employed and self-directed in production; it also hires and directs generally a few within the immediate family or kinsman circle. The *lowest stratum* consisting of three classes (urban, rural and lumpen proletariats) does not have any significant claim to any means of production and is, therefore, either employed or directed by others or chronically lacking in work opportunities. In most of the developing/emerging countries of today, the class structure, more or less of the above type, does exist very much distinctly.

In understanding the dynamics of the societal formation in such countries, one must need to answer the following questions:

- Who (i.e. which socio-economic class, group or alliance of classes) controls the State or strives for the power of the State?
- How strong is the power of the State, or alternatively speaking, whether the State has *relative autonomy* from any dominant class or any faction under a dominant class?
- What are the roles of the State especially in the transitional period (either to *state capitalism* or to *state socialism* or a mixed one) of the developing/emerging countries?

In the next section, we'll answer these questions in greater detail.

---

[39]Wright (1982, pp. 332–333) summarises the basic distinction in the Marxist and non-Marxist concepts of socio-economic class. Non-Marxist concepts of class typically take one of the two forms: either they are structured around distributional categories (in terms of occupation or market capacity) without reference to domination, or they are structured around categories of domination (in terms of power or authority relations of *command classes* and *obey classes*) without reference to any economic institutions of distribution. The Marxist account of class, on the other hand, subsumes both of these images of class relations through the concept of exploitation. Class relations are stressed to be the unity of appropriation relations (the Marxist way of theorising categories of distribution) and political domination. Thus, in the Marxist tradition, political dimension is part and parcel in analysing class structures even at the highest level of abstraction.

1.5 Nature and Role of State Institution

1.5.1 *Nature of State under State Capitalism and State Socialism*

The modern State, resulting from the socio-economic and historical forces, is a societal entity recognised as a 'compulsory form of human association'. Of various institutions (socio-economic, political and legal) comprising the State system, important ones are the government (as its executive organ, apart from its legislative and judicial ones), civil bureaucracy and military. The government (central and sub-central) consisting of individuals or groups directly controls the State apparatus. Civil bureaucracy (administration) includes ministries, public corporations, central banks, etc. The State may assume a variety of forms—absolutely monarchy, a narrow oligarchy, military oligarchy, military dictatorship, bureaucratic authoritarian, parliamentary democracy, social democracy, people's democracy, etc. The substance of a State, however, does not vary much across the societies, as it always allows a distinction between government (by which the State will is carried into effect) and subjects. The question of form must, of course, affect the question of substance, but its real reference is, in fact, to the prevailing type of government. That is, in part, also a question of the basis upon which responsibility is to rest.[40] Such a definition of the modern State excludes the equation of the State with society unlike under feudalism where both are combined. The exclusion is possible due to the fact that there are many social relationships that are not expressed through the State. Institutions such as religious organisation, trade union and family, which obviously act upon their respective members as social determinants are not, however, merely part of the State, even though the State may affect them.

The general way of thinking about the State is, in fact, common to both liberal and Marxist varieties of social theory. The crucial difference of opinion between these two broad traditions is over the type of means the political arena distinctly embodies: fundamentally, consensually based legitimate authority or fundamentally coercive domination. On the basis of this difference, two polar extreme forms of societies (and, hence, of States) can be distinguished as *pure socialist* (i.e. classless and, hence, *apolitical* by definition) and *pure capitalist* (with surplus appropriating and property owning) dominant class or classes.[41] In reality, no society is, in fact, purely socialist or purely capitalist in the strict sense of their definitions.

While the State participation in the process of socio-economic development is in the form of *commanding authority* at least in the non-socialist developing/emerging countries, it is, in fact, in the form of mere *intervention*. Intervention is, again, of two types—*support* type and *control* type. Apart from the maintenance of a certain societal structure, the support type of intervention takes a number of forms: the

[40]Laski (1968, p. 16).

[41]Skocpol (1979, p. 25).

provision of physical infrastructure such as roads, ports, irrigation and railways; the supply of cheap industrial inputs such as power, steel and minerals. Under support type of State intervention, one could hardly expect State's independent and comprehensive planning towards a restructuring of the economic system as a whole. Under the control type of State intervention (through investment licenses by adopting proper project evaluation technique, through selective credit facilities, wage and price control as well as appropriate fiscal and monetary policies), role of the State is, on the other hand, independent (of the private sector) to some extent. Surplus mobilisation could largely be centred on the State; the object of investment becomes the development of the public sector, and, therefore, not the private profit alone.

Because of inadequately developed private capital and insurance markets in many of the developing/emerging countries, it is the State that can often provide the required capital and underwrite the risks involved in huge initial investment ventures in the early stage of industrialisation. Because of the greater involvement of giant multinational corporations in the contemporary globalised world, urgency of more expanded role on part of the State has been felt in many developing/emerging countries. As a result, State capitalism has emerged in some of the developing countries as the force of economic development. 'State capitalism' is different from both 'State monopoly capitalism' of the advanced capitalist countries and 'State intervention' of most of the developing countries (including the peripheral ones with externally induced expansions). While highly concentrated industry and highly centralised capital (private monopoly and State capital) constitute the economic base of the State monopoly capitalism, in the case of State capitalism, it is the State that is the sole owner of productive and profitable firms as a substitute for the private sector. The regime under 'State capitalism' 'borrows "socialist forms"—political (one-party state, socialist rhetoric, etc.) and economic (State ownership, planning, etc.)—to accomplish capitalist ends'[42]—the realisation of profit on the basis of exploitation of the wage labour within a class society. Similarly, under 'State intervention' (with simply selective support type or control type of measures), the State acts to support accumulation in the private sector and, thereby, to encourage the domestic enterprises (often in alliance with the foreign counterparts), but the regime under 'State capitalism' tends to move against foreign capital in order to facilitate national capitalist accumulation. What is clear from the above discussion is that under each type of State participation with or without State ownership, patterns of capital accumulation and the consequent class structures are different.

[42]Petras (1976, p. 433).

1.5.2 The Notion of Relative Autonomy of State

Political theorists, in studying concrete societal formations of different societies, have drawn considerable attention regarding the relationship between the socio-economic classes and the nation state specifically in the context of the advanced capitalist States. The notion of *relative autonomy* of the State from the dominant class, in particular, constitutes one of the most important debates. It is argued that the capitalist (or bourgeois) class is internally divided into several fractions: commercial, industrial and financial capitals. The economic interests of these fractions do not always match, and hence, the capital as a class is not always capable of achieving a hegemonic level of unified political power over the other subordinated classes. As a result, the capitalist can, under these conditions, only grant the hegemony to the internally divided ruling capitalist (bourgeois) class 'through the functioning of a relatively autonomous political structure' which is not under the direct control of any fraction of this class. Thus, due to its relative autonomy (or independence from the capitalist class), the state can intervene to make necessary compromises between the competing interests of various fractions of the economically dominant capitalist class. This autonomy also allows the State to present itself and legitimise itself as the embodiment of the political unity of the nation's entire population through the arrangements of universal suffrage and parliamentary representation or like, through the provision of social goods and services, through reformism and concessions like civil rights to its individuated citizens. As the unit of overall cohesion of the political forces of dominant capitalist classes and the organiser of bourgeois hegemony, the State tends to insure the survival and reproduction of both.[43]

The above general concept of *relative autonomy* of the advanced capitalist states cannot, however, be applied in analysing the societal formation of the developing/emerging countries in which the productive forces are to a greater extent at a lower or pre-capitalist stage of development. These countries are either on the transition to capitalism or in the struggle for socialism, and hence, the States are not the direct instrument of a *single* capitalist class. Regarding the difficulty of the application of this concept in the post-colonial developing countries, Alavi (1972, p. 62) argues that the problem arises not with reference to 'diverse fractions' of a single class (as is the case for an advanced capitalist society), but rather with reference to three different propertied socio-economic classes, namely the metropolitan bourgeoisies, the indigenous bourgeoisie and the landed classes. Since these three classes have different material bases and mutually competing (but, reconcilable) class interests, they do not constitute a whole in the form of a dominant class. Under this multi-class relationship of the State, the government (parliamentary democratic or military oligarchic) mediates between competing interests of the three propertied classes, while at the same time, being active on behalf of them all, it preserves the societal order in which their interests are embedded,

[43]Bamat (1977, p. 57).

namely the institution of private property and the capitalist mode of functioning as the dominant one. In this sense, the State is said to be relatively autonomous in the post-colonial societies. As to the autonomy in the economic sphere as such, they directly appropriate a very large part of the economic surplus on the basis of exploitation of wage labour and deploy it in bureaucratically directed economic activity in the name of achieving national economic aspirations of growth and development.

Similarly, one can easily notice that there is absence of a dominant class hegemony in the social formation of the neocolonial (with externally induced expansion) societies with *peripheral* or *semi-peripheral* (fully or partly dependent) capitalism as well. Being dependent largely upon economic interests and State power in the more advanced metropolitan formations, the capitalist mode of functioning in such a dependent societal formation is not *self-centred* (or *articulated*). Because of the transfer of the generated surplus value to a large extent to the metropoles, there remains a little left for the local capital accumulation, more so in the case of directly dependent *peripheral capitalism*. Consequently, pre-capitalist elements and classes continue to persist under peripheral capitalism. Although historically, capitalist production had been concentrated in the export sector mainly of mineral and agriculture production, in recent decades, industrialisation has also been taking place in many of the dependent countries. The effects of past and present positions under the centre–periphery relationship have been profound in structuring the local dominant classes and in determining the functions of the peripheral state in the dependent social formations. In spite of dominating the most profitable productive sector(s) of the economy, the local dominant classes have been unable to establish political and ideological hegemony. Because of their dependent and diversified economic base, and therefore, inadequate share of surplus value, the landowners and various capitalists (industrial, commercial and financial) frequently have been unable to present their own interests as representative of the general interest of the people or nation. The dependent States have had difficulties in legitimatising the system through social services or redistributive schemes. Representative 'democratic' forms of State have mostly been ineffective, politically, ideologically and economically in their 'developmental' role, and therefore, the peripheral/semi-peripheral State has often assumed more authoritarian and repressive forms in its effort to impose the interest of the dominant classes.

1.5.3 Role of State under State Capitalism

From the above analysis of the nature of relationship between the State and the heterogeneous dominant proprietary classes in the developing countries, it is evident that these classes may often be directly dependent upon the State inputs, or alternatively speaking, the position of the State in relation to such classes may be strengthened. Consequently, the State may have a very vital role to play in shaping the societal formation that emerges in the context of the developing/emerging countries. In the absence of the means of production, however, power passes on to some extent from the State to the economically dominant group(s) and class(es). Though the constraints posed by the imperatives of the dominant proprietary class are sometimes binding to the State action, one cannot 'ignore the large range of choices in goal formulation, agenda setting and policy execution that the state leadership usually has and the powerful impulses shaping policies and actions that are generated within the state'.[44]

It is now appropriate to make an attempt for answering the earlier question as was debated in the early 1980s: Who then controls and manipulates the State?

In both post-colonial and neocolonial developing countries, the State is generally dominated and controlled by the bureaucratic leaders, drawn from a narrow stratum of the State bureaucracy or the public functionaries (civilian and military). Because of the economically weak position of the national bourgeoisie, the State may gradually acquire the ownership of the major means of production and distribution and, thereby, in its own right, becomes an agent of capital accumulation. As a result, the top bureaucratic leaders can be seen as a State bourgeoisie. The resulting new class, also known as bureaucratic class, is most directly a case of the economic (class) structure's dependence on political.[45]

In addition to the above active role in the development of the productive forces in the processes of transition to capitalism, the State could attempt to create an organic and interrelated (i.e. articulated) national economy by eliminating the remnants of pre-capitalist relations of production. If the State is strong enough compared to the power of feudal landlords, it could, through agrarian reform measures, expropriate their large tracts of land and then transfer to the middle- and small-holding peasantry, along with agricultural implements, credits, etc. The peasantry can, thereby, be incorporated into the cooperative arrangement in the rural area. Parallel to this, the State could nationalise the major means of production for the development and implementation of more broad-based industrialisation programme along with appropriate State control and regulation of commerce.

Following the ILO Country Missions and City Studies, and a few other studies, Moser (1978), in the past, had put together a variety of policy recommendations for the growth and development processes[46] of both the formal and the informal parts of a developing dual economy. Some of these are relevant from the specific 'nation' as a whole or its part ('region' or 'city') points of view, and others are relevant from the specific approach ('functional dualist' or 'pretty commodity production') point

---

[44]Bardhan (1983, p. 2).

[45]A few examples of such cases are given in Bardhan (1983, p. 4): 'Deliberate political announcements from the state can make or break fortunes in stock markets; political decision on public investment … may turn a petty real estate owner … into a rich capitalist; politically administered price and distribution policies causing artificial scarcities can catapult a petty trader into a more elevated class; by overpricing or rationing a publicly provided input … the state can drive a business to bankruptcy'.

[46]These two processes of growth and development will be discussed quite elaborately in the following section.

of view. Apart from major structural institutional changes of 'land reform', 'fiscal reform', 'nationalisation of important means of production', and, thereby, restructuring of the entire 'industrial mix' of the country, other changes and reforms, to mention a few, may include the following: 'development of labour-intensive urban industrial employment in such areas as construction and handicrafts'; 'comprehensive rural works programmes to create irrigation facilities' and, 'thereby, raising cropping intensity'; 'wages policy to reduce differentials and limit consumption growth to a minimum'; 'a wage freeze in the protected labour market until wages outside it have increased to the same level'; 'reorganization if the educational system to cope with structural imbalances'; 'short-term strategy to reduce unemployment among the young educated through a compulsory youth service with nominal wage rates'; expansion of migrant centres 'to include the provision of information in available jobs, and schools and other training facilities'; 'income and fiscal policies … to release [investible] resources from the rich through taxation and *voluntary wage constraints*'; 'developing vocational and managerial skills' and 'intensifying technical research and development work on products suitable for production or use' in the informal segment; redirecting 'final demand [specifically for consumer durables and non-durables, small-scale tools, etc.] towards the informal [segment]' to generate a more equal distribution of income via its employment promoting impact; encouraging 'investment in informal [segment] enterprises by experiments with lending procedures based on expected production instead of existing collateral'; increasing 'the government's contribution to public sector investment' in medical and community centres, and also on other facilities such as sewerage, drainage, drinking water, transportation and communication systems, etc., to improve quality of both rural and urban life.

It is often found that the effectiveness of many of the above policies, when adopted, has been very limited, especially if the state-capitalist regime is weak both economically and politically. Some degree of proletarianisation of petty producers could ensue as the growing enterprises attract labour commensurate with increased capacity, but the majority of such producers find their markets severely cut, and their access to raw materials even more difficult as economies of scale become more noticeable and real accumulation process begins in the enterprises of the few. In fact, during the process of growth of the productive forces during the transition to state capitalism, various contradictions and conflicts do arise between the State and the heterogeneous proprietary classes.

> The very basis of the [State-capitalist] regime; … social ownership based on capitalist social relations is inherently an unstable and conflictive circumstance. Short-term trends towards public ownership conflict with the long-term conversion toward new forms of integration into the world capitalist system… (N)ew forms of social differentiation within state-capitalist society are in part products of differential political power rather than 'overt' ownership of property (Petras 1976, pp. 442–443).

Conflicts may develop even between the State and individual capitalists (but not necessarily the capitalist class as a whole). This arises when individual capitalist enterprises hinder the long-term development of national capitalism and capitalist industrialisation.

> The centralisation of property-ownership in the state, the narrow social basis and exploitive social relations result in the emergence of the 'coercive' state: the state performs its essential duty of disciplining the labour force hence appearing to the labour force as an alien power… Class struggle under state capitalism becomes considerably and directly 'political' in the double sense that the masses directly confront the state as the employer and the state confronts the workers as the source of capital expansion. As the class struggle deepens, there is a possibility of further differentiation between nationalist and 'socialist' sectors within the regime, leading directly to the struggle for socialism and state power (Petras, *Ibid*).

The class balance and heterogeneity of the proprietary classes do not necessarily always help the State to play the role of capitalist in capital accumulation, as in the developing countries with mere State intervention and not State ownership. Because of the heterogeneous nature of the contending classes, though they cannot pull themselves together under a strong coalition with a common direction,[47] they, however, exert strong pressures on the State for their respective major shares in the national cake through varieties of demands. To pacify all such diverse elements of the dominant coalition of proprietary classes, the State grants a substantial number of subsidies and concessions[48] with the consequent reduction in available surplus for capital formation. In his concrete example of India's societal formation in earlier decades, Bardhan (1983, p. 10) indicated one kind of predictable outcome in this circumstance, that is, the State's role more as a successful grantor of subsidies and dispenser of various permits and licenses than as a successful capital accumulator. By keeping all the diverse elements of the coalition of the interest groups happy, surplus for reinvestment in public capital formation may be drastically reduced leaving the State in an *abortive* form.

The burden of consequent slower economic growth falls (in the form of inflation and unemployment) mostly on the large section of the traditional segment's population which are excluded for the benefits of the so-called *disarticulated* economic growth. As a result, the *clientelist democratic* system might face difficulty in maintaining its political *status quo*. The continuous pressure from the bottom may lead the State towards *absolutism* in the name of securing political order and stability for capitalist production. The legitimacy of the State can also be reinforced by its success in institutionalising class conflicts and in its reform efforts.

---

[47]In Bardhan's (1983, p. 11) judgment, this inability to form a strong coalition of the heterogeneous proprietary classes has largely to do with the difficulty or taking collective action amidst large and diverse heterogeneities as Olson (1982) and others have emphasised in another context.

[48]A list of such subsidies and concessions is given in Bardhan (1983, p. 10). Those are, for example, provision of public sector-produced inputs and utilities at subsidised prices, high support prices for farm products, concessional credit from public lending institutions, automatic protection of domestic markets for import-substituting industries and export bounties. In the Footnote 12, these have been mentioned in the list of causes of decrease in government revenue or increase in its expenditure.

Institutionalising class conflicts in the context of the capitalist development may take the form of new labour legislation, arbitration of labour disputes and the direct or indirect incorporation of working class parties and organisations within the existing political framework, etc. The major reform efforts are generally confined in the area of land distribution and fiscal policy/management. The intensity of class conflict may also be reduced through 'various forms for socialisation (to establish the legitimacy of the existing system) and social control (when legitimacy breaks down) ranging from the elaboration of ideology and its propagation through the educational system, media, etc., to coercion—e.g., strike breaking, police repression, etc.'[49]

The above discussion suggests that in the context of capitalist development, the State is not merely just a set of institutions; rather, it is a structure in itself. It basically includes 'the network of relationships of "political" domination activated and supported by such institutions in a territorially defined society, which supports and contributes to the reproduction of society's class organisation'.[50] Alternatively speaking, in the process of transition to capitalism, the State, being the embodiment of all socio-economic classes, is nothing but an expression of the class struggle itself.

1.5.4 Role of State under State Socialism

As we have noted above, the State, during the transitional period to capitalism, rules over the society as an alien power, and thereby, the *political* sphere seems to be separate from the *economic* sphere. In this sense, the State is primarily separate from the society during the transition to capitalism. On the other hand, some sort of unity in separation is found to exist (at least in the secondary sense), especially when the State itself reflects and perpetuates the conflicts and contradictions among the socio-economic classes, and, thereby, forces the economic (class) structure to be dependent (at least indirectly) on the political one. As to its historical purpose, socialism, on the other hand, tries to resolve the conflicts and contradictions of capitalism. By the *socialisation* (or more appropriately by the *statisation*) of all the major means of production, capitalist alienation (the capital and wage labour relation) is abolished, and the economic spheres become directly dependent on the political decisions. Though, primarily, there is unity between the State and the society, it will be shown below that some kind of separation within this unity could also exist.

Under the transition to socialism, the regime draws its (political) support mainly from the non-elitist classes (agricultural labourer and the peasantry, wage and salary earners, petty commodity producers, etc.). Historically, prior to the achievement of the socialist regime, established regimes in many of the developing countries were

[49]Hamilton (1975, p. 84).

[50]O'Donnell (1978, p. 24).

politically and economically oppressive towards these classes. After the achievement of political power by the socialist regime, its foremost task is to establish economic democracy to guarantee equality of socio-economic conditions to all segments of the economy. Worker-peasant management along with appropriate political institutions (including the *vanguard* party) and a certain minimum level of economic development are the indispensable ingredients of socialism to start with.

Generally, agriculture being by far the largest producing sector in many of the developing countries, the first step the State should adopt is that of a drastic land-reform measure. After the parasitic landlords are eliminated, lands are to be distributed among the cultivators themselves. If large-scale collectivisation or State farming is not feasible at the very beginning of the transition, some sort of local level cooperatives must be formed. Along with the long-term emphasis in constructing appropriate heavy infrastructure (in terms of irrigation, flood control facilities, roads, railways, cold storage, etc.), the State could at least introduce agricultural extension services, the price-support arrangements, the provision of marketing and credit facilities, etc. This will, on the other hand, help the peasant households to become viable producers and, on the other hand, eliminate all the exploitative middlemen.

Over the period of prolonged transition to socialism, especially involving a public–private mixed economy, the crucial question that a socialist regime faces is: how to incorporate capital into the State by negotiating with the capitalists and without adopting any mechanism of labour repression. During the initial period of transition, the strategic areas of production (manufacturing, mining, energy, etc.), distribution, transport, financial and foreign trade (of both domestic and foreign ownership) may selectively be nationalised with the establishment of worker-State management councils. If political, administrative and economic factors do not permit, other major enterprises may remain private with some form of worker's control (codetermination or wage earners funds, etc.). Certain numbers of producer, consumer and credit cooperatives could be established in both rural and urban areas. Individual and family enterprises—peasants, artisans and small tradesmen of the traditional segment—could also be organised to bring them under these cooperatives not only to reduce their risk, but also to check excess profiteering. The coexistence of the different ownership sectors[51] makes the socio-economic equilibrium obviously very unstable as it is under State capitalism. The aim of economic policy under the transition to socialism is, of course, not to preserve the equilibrium of this coexistence, but rather to control the dynamics of change in such a way that the different sectors are 'oriented to converge institutionally, towards one single labour managed economy'.[52]

In the course of the transition, some economic threats could come from both capital and labour. If the capitalist class does not cooperate with the regime either

---

[51]As Marglin (1981b, p. 3) warns, one must not lump capitalists and small proprietors together as the mainstream economists have the tendency to do so under the rubric of market economy.

[52]Hovert (1981, p. 957).

by withdrawing economic and financial resources from the economy or by refusing to follow new norms, it can seriously undermine economic development. In this circumstance, it is important for the regime to take necessary measures and actions to ensure the credibility of its authority (i.e. power plus legitimacy) and policy. As Petras (1983, p. 18) writes:

> Resolute actions should be firmly taken in a visible fashion, directed at those firms that fail to co-operate…. To sacrifice authority for economic expediency (under the guise that management expertise is lacking) is to completely misunderstand the dynamics of political struggle. Without political authority, the regime cannot retain the support of its members and it can no longer discipline its adversaries. On the other hand, a decline in economic operation that may result from premature assumption of economic management can be corrected over time (training programs, hiring foreign consultants, etc.)

Similarly, threat from labour—the political base of the regime—could undermine political stability, especially when severe austerity measures (restraints on wages, social welfare spending, etc.) are imposed without compensatory measures in the direction of socialisation or greater worker participation. 'The equalisation of socio-economic conditions facilitates', as Petras (*Ibid*., p. 21) further adds, 'political acceptance by the working class, farmers, and other popular classes. In sum, there must be a trade-off between equity and economic sacrifice'. In other words, under socialism, it is the articulation (both social and sectoral) of the whole economy that invariably takes place along with the capital accumulation and, hence, economic growth. This is so unlike under capitalism where the capital accumulation necessarily goes along with social (though not necessarily sectoral) disarticulation.

With the progress of socialism, as the socialist democratic system develops, the role the State planning/policy and administration in the direct management of the economy is increasingly transferred to various local self-governing bodies. Though the decentralised setting is eventually appropriate for the effective participation of the individuals or the local organisations, the initial phase of socialism, it is argued, requires strict centralisation. This is primarily because of the fact that at the beginning, only a few trained people are available in the government to initiate the process of economic, educational and cultural development. Centralisation in planning may, therefore, be used as a temporary expedient and not as a permanent tool. In the course of the socialist transformation, the administrative experts or the managers of the society are expected to exercise State's bureaucratic authority on those who depend on the direction of the bureaucracy, namely the *clientele*. Whatever may be the duration of centralised planning, just like under State capitalism, it is, in fact, very likely that a new class division between the State bureaucracy and its clientele may emerge from within socialism. *Socialisation* of the means of production and thereafter its management does not necessarily mean that this new class has to emerge. Though there will always be a tendency in the State bureaucratic elements (with brain power as their property) to become a class, but for its realisation, they must be aware of their class interests in order to promote those interests. 'Thus a dialectical relationship develops', as DuRand (1984, p. 25) emphasises, 'between the bureaucracy and the clientele in which the power of the former emerges as the alienated power of the latter'. Consequently, there may arise some cases as above when the State becomes separated from the society, even though primarily the State needs to be united with the society under socialism. This contradiction, though not unique to a socialist society, is, of course, against its classless nature. 'The state no longer just reflects and preserves', as DuRand (*Ibid.*, p. 24) further notes, 'existing [social] relations of production, it becomes a part of the new relations of production. Indeed, the very relation between state and society itself becomes a relation of production'. Unless, right at the beginning of the transition, careful safeguards are adopted by the social planners (e.g. the party leaders), the new relation of production will very likely continue to accentuate in the form of a main contradiction throughout the long transition.

Instead of relying mainly on the State officials (at the centre) in formulating, organising and implementing developmental projects and programs, the regime could have several safeguards by establishing proper institutions or by making appropriate changes in the existing institutional frameworks so that the central bureaucracy could be prevented from being a class of its own. The first safeguard could be to transfer the *delegation of authority* from the centre to the local governments as much as possible. The centralised decision in few important spheres is 'fully consistent with the local autonomy in day-to-day businesses'. Besides, local self-government, once established, 'has its own vested interests which will act as a countervailing force'.[53] Another safeguard could be to enforce *codetermination* from the very beginning of the transition. This, with the support of trade unions, will help the social plans to move towards self-management. To prevent the new class to emerge, the regime could also follow *affirmative action* in the admission procedures to universities as it was adopted in China during the cultural revolution. The purpose is to check the *class closure* that passes class position on from generation to generation through higher education. As a result, the bureaucracy will consist of heterogeneity in terms of class background. Despite the fact that State socialism is premised on non-market principle, but, for the sake of safeguarding the new bureaucratic class, *market socialism* could be adopted. If it is implemented in the face of opposition from the dominant bureaucracy, it will significantly alter the relation between the State and the society. Consequently, there will be a drastic shift of managerial authority over the means of production from the State to civil society or its segment so that the latter's role becomes firmly rooted in production.

Most of the above safeguards against the State bureaucrats could, however, very likely promote the interests of the *petty bureaucrats* (at the level of enterprise managers) and the *technocrats* (who also get benefits from greater autonomy at the production point). As a matter of fact, an interclass conflict may arise if the State bureaucrats with support from petty bureaucrats strive for dominance over the technocrats allied with the workers. It is, no doubt, ironic that the safeguards against the State bureaucrats help generate class consciousness among themselves and, thereby, completing the class formation of the State bureaucrats as such if at all it so happens.

---

[53]Hovart (1981, p. 959).

1.6 Economic Development: Major Views and Strategies under Globalisation

Economic development is generally viewed as a process of continued *economic growth* along with a set of interrelated changes in the socio-economic structures of the society within a given political structure under either *state capitalism* or *state socialism* or a mixed one. The interrelated changes involve the composition of domestic demand, production, distribution and employment as well as the composition of foreign trade and capital flows. These structural changes on the socio-economic level taken together define the *societal transformation* of the predominately *traditional* socio-economic system towards a predominantly *modern*[54] one. This societal transformation must help not only to expand the *entitlements* of the masses, but also to strengthen their *capabilities* these *entitlements* generate.[55] Alternatively speaking, the structural changes on the socio-economic level, if strategically designed and carefully executed, must help to move a developing/emerging society with segmental/sectoral and societal disarticulation towards the establishment of one with higher level of articulation.

The common major goals of economic development to be carried out by a State or the government are: (i) to increase per capita net national income for the maintenance of sustained rate of economic growth, (ii) to increase employment opportunities for full utilisation of human resources, (iii) to establish equitable income distribution and to maintain some minimal standard of living by providing the society with the very basic nutritional, medical, housing and educational needs, along with the required infrastructural facilities of transportation and communication to the majority of the people, (iv) to maintain international balance of payments at least in the long run in order to achieve economic independence and self-reliance, and finally, (v) to increase environmental protection by reducing/reversing environmental degradation resulting from economic growth. Because of the availability of more efficient technology, necessary importable goods and services, and other influences from the developed countries, today's transition in many developing

[54]As Nash (1977, pp. 20–27) explains, the historically based view of modernisation stresses social transformation (not the mere bit-by-bit incorporation of *disjecta membra*) … At the centre of the transformation towards modernisation is the application of growing body of tested knowledge of all phases and branches of production. The application of tested knowledge to the process of production requires a special sort of value system and social structure, and it requires the presence of the modernising society. Horvat (1981, p. 961) mentions the personality of *associative* character that achieves full integration with the community … Modernisation is thus the process of transformation towards the establishment and institutionalisation of the framework of modernity.

[55]As Sen (1983, pp. 754–755) defines, *entitlements* refer to the set of alternative commodity bundles that a person can command in a society using the totality of rights and opportunities that he/she faces. On the basis of 'entitlements', a person can acquire some *capabilities*, i.e. the ability to do this or that (e.g. can live long, escape avoidable morbidity, be well nourished, be able to read and write and communicate, take part in literary and scientific pursuits and so forth), although he/she may fail to acquire some other capabilities.

countries is much more rapid compared to that in the case of industrialising economies of the nineteenth/early twentieth century.

Economic development, being a multidimensional concept, is actually a process involving more than simply growth in per capita income. Economic development is a *positive function* of increasing per capita income, increasing economic equity, increasing employment opportunities, increasing economic independence and increasing environmental protection. Depending on the existing socio-economic and technological structure of a country and her stage of development, appropriate weight for each of the above major objectives (*growth* and *non-growth*) needs to be fixed. Apart from socio-economic judgments, some sort of explicit ethical judgments are also implied in the choice of such weights. Questions of stressing higher employment level, reducing economic inequality, promoting economic independence/self-reliance from the foreign dominance, reducing/reversing environmental degradation, etc., arise very much from both socio-economic and ethical points of view. Economic development, accompanied with economic growth, needs to assure all people of a decent material standard of living. In fact, 'a person's sense of dignity, self-worth and efficiency' are hampered if an able-bodied person cannot participate in the productive activities of the society. Similarly, the right of all people to participate effectively and democratically in social and political decisions could be denied if some are in much better economic position than others within the society, or if members or institutions from other society 'exert some degree of control over indigenous attitudes, motivations, policies, and decisions'.[56]

The crucial question that now arises is whether the management of the rapid socio-economic structural changes requires *balanced* or *unbalanced* development strategies. Economic development is *balanced* if some positive gains are recorded with respect to each non-growth objective and *unbalanced* if zero or negative gains are recorded with respect to one or more non-growth objectives.[57] Kornai's concept of *harmonic growth*[58] can very well complement the above concept of *balanced development*.

Let's now focus our attention to the concepts of *balanced* and *unbalanced* growth from a purely technological point of view. There is plenty of theoretical literature on the notion of both balanced and unbalanced growth. Even if we leave aside von Neumann's *uniformity* notion[59] of balanced growth, which is applicable

---

[56]Weisskopf (1983).

[57]Weisskopf (1983, p. 455).

[58]According to Kornai (1972, Chap. 2), there are four factors shaping the requirements of *harmony* in economic growth: (i) rules or proportionality among human needs on a level corresponding to their environment (biological and social), their material and cultural circumstances; (ii) technological relationships between inputs and outputs (e.g. phenomenon of complementarity); (iii) efficient and economic use of resources by the rational effort of economic leaders and engineers; and (iv) political and ethical considerations.

[59]According to von Neumann's *uniformity* notion of balanced growth, the economy changes only in scale and not in composition. In other words, the mutual proportions in which commodities are produced are maintained at a constant level. This type of model of long-run equilibrium is based

mainly for the developed economies, and focus on the version put forward as a remedy for LDCs' *saving* and population traps (also known as *poverty trap* or *low-level equilibrium traps*), one could find different versions balanced stressing different aspects by different national and international agencies and by different authors, most of which belong to the structuralism school of development economics. Broadly speaking, whenever several non-infinitesimal investment decisions (or economic decisions in general) depend for their success upon each other, the notion of balanced growth requires simultaneous investment (action) in a series of industries in conformity with the pattern of consumer demand and their demand for each other's products. The case for *balanced growth* thus rests upon the relation of *complementarity* between wants, between factors and between factors and products at various stages of production. The non-infinitesimal nature of investment emphasises the fact that the overall size of the investment programme must be large enough to overcome technical indivisibilities and the smallness in the size of domestic markets caused by the LDCs' low level of purchasing power. In fact, the importance given by many LDC policy-makers to the lack of aggregate (effective) demand is the basis of adopting the strategy of *Big Push*. Besides, the use of imported technology and sometimes the import of a complete industrial complex allow the LDCs to skip virtually the whole epochs of technological development process. This *discontinuous shift* to international technology not only acts as a major hindrance to technological creativity in the modern segment of the developing countries, but also causes some *discontinuities* in different socio-economic variables.

There is no doubt that balanced growth is meaningful as long as it satisfies the complementary nature of investment. Alternatively speaking, investment in steel mills must require investment in coal mining; otherwise, production without market is meaningless. It is, however, also true that economic growth is a lengthy process during which interaction takes place not only between industries, but also up and down and across the whole of an economy's input–output matrix, and for many decades. Besides, because of non-infinitesimal nature of investment, it may not be feasible in terms of available investible resources to adopt a balanced programme of economic growth across the country, especially in the early stage of economic development. The indivisibilities, discontinuities and *externalities*[60] are so prominent in LDCs that the comprehensive reallocation of investible resources along with appropriate structural adjustments for redistribution of income is absolutely

(Footnote 59 continued)

on highly restrictive assumptions such as known technical possibilities, constant return to scale, perfect competition, zero saving propensity of workers, unit saving propensity of the propertied class and neutral money, which are likely to change only in the long run.

[60]The *externalities*, or more specifically, the *external economies,* are essentially caused by production *complementarities*. *Horizontal* or extensive external economies provide the inducement to invest. *Vertical* or intensive external economies operating through cost reduction, on the other hand, fail to maintain the inducement to invest.

essential. All initial development programmes are thus programmes for unbalanced growth in this sense.

It is not always right to claim that unbalance necessarily delays or halts growth. In the early stage of development and under certain conditions, unbalance may stimulate rather than impair progress and too greater an emphasis on balance may cause, rather than prevent, stagnation. It is to be often argued by the earlier development economists like Paul Streeten, for the feasibility of unbalance first for consumption and then for production with both *static* arguments (concerning the indivisibilities in the fact of given wants and technology) and *dynamic* arguments (dealing with the stimulus to new wants, new activities and technical innovations). In his advocacy of unbalanced growth, Albert Hirschman once postulated that development policy must concern itself with the judicious setting-up of the kind of sequences and repercussions rather than with any attempt to suppress them. If the economy is to be kept moving ahead, the task of development policy is to maintain tensions, disproportions and disequilibria.

Whatever strategy of growth—balanced or unbalanced—is adopted, there remains the important question of development objective to be specified and procedures (market or planning) to be followed. As far as the specification of the development objective is concerned, there is, therefore, much ambiguity in the cases of both balanced and unbalanced growth doctrines. It is not very clear whether Ragnar Nurkse's doctrine of balanced growth maximises 're-investible surplus (capital accumulation), inducement to invest, external economies, complementary industries, structural changes or the growth rate of total output'. In the case of the doctrine of unbalanced growth, while Hirschman seeks to develop decision makers, external economies (of vertical type) and the growth rate, Streeten emphasises anabolism of wants, technological progress and the growth rate.

Because of the existence of structural disequilibria in the economic sphere of the LDCs as the reflection of the sociopolitical contradictions as well as technical indivisibilities and complementarities, the doctrine of balanced growth should somehow be formulated in such a way that certain degrees of sectoral imbalance among some sectors are incorporated. And, therefore, planning is supposed to be more successful procedures to adopt at least in the early stage of development. After the achievement of certain level of economic development, especially, after the pre-capitalistic remnants are mostly eliminated, market mechanism can be combined with planning method (as in both China and India). All countries use the market as source of information and a guide to decision-making, and, in varying degrees, as a mechanism for allocating resources and distributing goods and services. It is to be noted that every country always follows a combination of both central planning and market mechanism; however, their degrees vary, although the variation in degree depends on the circumstances objectively existing at a given historical moment.

On the basis of growing evidence over the past two decades or so, the development economists and international community have been convinced that information and communication technology[61] (ICT) can be used as a powerful tool in accelerating development progress. It is argued that ICT can not only play an important role by providing new and more efficient methods of production, but also could bring previously unattainable markets within the reach of poor, improve the delivery of government services and facilitate management and transfer of knowledge.

Use of ICT in some of the developing countries has been found to have considerable impact in their *modern* segment. However, many developing countries are highly *dualistic* in the sense that the *modern* segment coexists with a huge *traditional* segment. In these types of developing countries, generally with surplus labour force (both skilled and unskilled), ICT needs to be applied in the specific areas of agricultural and rural development, poverty alleviation, human resource development, etc., so that acute *digital divide* within these dualistic countries can also be avoided.

What is essential for the dualistic developing countries is to incorporate an ICT strategy into their economic development plan. These countries must adopt policies that could improve the existing social capital (i.e. social and political organisations and national infrastructure) in order to become more receptive of the global technological changes. Appropriately designed technology strategy is expected to improve a country's competitive position by identifying the current and potential use of ICT and managing diversifications required in response to both local and global market demand. Informatics has therefore now become a catalyst which not only supports a country's production base and helps utilise its surplus (skilled) labour force, but also maximises the use of technology in a society as a whole.

As noted above, structures of either advanced socialist or (closed) matured capitalist economies are more or less segmentally and socially articulated. What is also clear from the above discussion is that the reality under *state socialism* or *state capitalism* in developing/emerging countries is dominated by various conflicts of interest, tendencies towards structural economic disequilibria and recurring breaks in the continuity of overall development process. Under *state capitalism* in less developed countries (LDCs), the socio-economic contradictions and conflicts are likely to be increased due to their inherent nature of *structural disarticulation* (socially and segmentally/sectorally), and thereby, their *structural disequilibria* on the economic sphere will very likely be accentuated over time. Under *state socialism*, on the other hand, contradictions and conflicts could emerge, but they, instead of being completely eliminated (at least from the pragmatic point of view of political reality), could be reduced to a minimum level if sufficient and timely safeguards are adopted by introducing various institutional mechanisms. Here comes the role of institutionalist thoughts on socio-economic analysis of the contemporary developing/emerging countries.

---

[61]Information and communication technology (ICT) usually consists of hardware, software, networks and media for collection, storage, processing, transmission and presentation of information (voice, data, text, images, etc.).

1.6.1 *Convergence of Structuralist and Institutionalist Views on Development*

In the 1980s, there was a resurgence of neoclassical free-market decentralised approach towards economic management, which led to the emergence of the *Washington Consensus*.[62] For much of the 1980s and into 1990s, this so-called consensus on development policy that reflected the free-market approach to development, with total disregard for underdeveloped countries' structural, institutional and historical legacies of their past, had great influence, especially through 'pressures from the international financial agencies in favour of implementing the consensus'.[63]

As an alternative to the orthodoxy, neoconservative adjustment and restructuring programs of the 1980s, a theoretical framework of *neostructuralism* emerged.[64] Neostructuralists share the basic structuralist view that the sources of underdevelopment are not primarily due to policy-induced distortions in relative prices, but are rooted in endogenous *structural rigidities* of individual countries/regions. Ramos and Sunkel (1993, p. 7) provide a tangible proof of the neostructuralist view with three crucial aspects of Latin America's economy in the late 1980s:

(1) an international specialisation in products lacking dynamic potential;
(2) the prevalence of an uncoordinated, vulnerable and highly heterogeneous production pattern that tends to concentrate technical progress and is incapable of fully and productively absorbing new entrants into the labour force; and
(3) the persistence of a growth pattern that excludes the vast majority from the fruits of progress, evidencing the system's inability to lower poverty significantly.

During 1980s and 1990s, various strands of 'institutionalisms' have also flourished within the social sciences in general and the discipline of economics in particular. They under the banner of *new institutionalism* have stimulated 'significant discussion not only of formal rules and governance structures, but also of informal norms and social networks, and of the relationships between them'.

---

[62]The *Washington Consensus* is often summarised in ten policy reforms: (i) fiscal discipline; (ii) redirection of public expenditure priorities towards fields offering both high economic returns and the potential to improve income distribution, such as primary health care, primary education and infrastructure; (iii) tax reform (to lower marginal rates and broaden the tax base); (iv) financial (e.g. interest rate) liberalisation; (v) unified and competitive exchange rates; (vi) trade liberalisation; (vii) liberalisation of (i.e. elimination of barriers to) direct foreign investment (FDI) inflows; (viii) privatisation; (ix) deregulation (in the sense of abolishing barriers to entry and exit); and (x) secure property rights.

[63]Ficker (2005, p. 153).

[64]Mostly, Latin American and North American economists who are behind this framework include: Alejandro Foxley (1983), Albert Fishlow (1985, 1990), Lance Taylor (1983, 1991), Patricio Meller (1991), Osvaldo Sunkel (1993), among others (Ramirez 1993, p. 1026).

As Rutherford (2001, p. 190) summarises:

> 'Institutional analysis has been used both to explain the failings of unfettered markets and the need for a greater degree of government intervention, and the failings of government interventions and the need for a greater degree of market freedom. But a common theme is that institutions matter a great deal, and that economists need to think hard about the ways in which institutions shape economic behavior and outcomes, and are themselves shaped by economic, political, and ideological factors.

As successful development policy must entail 'an understanding of the dynamics of economic change if the policies pursued are to have desired consequences', Douglas North (1995, p. 22), a Nobel Laureate *new institutional* economist, had cautioned that

(a) political institutions will be stable only if they are supported by organisations with an interest in their perpetuation. Therefore, an essential part of political/economic reform is the creation of such organisations;
(b) it is essential to change both the institutions and the belief systems for successful reform since it is the mental models of the actors that will shape choices;
(c) evolving norms of behaviour that will support and legitimise new rules is a lengthy process, and in the absence of such reinforcing norms, policies will tend to be unstable;
(d) while economic growth can occur in the short run with autocratic regimes, long-run economic growth entails the development of the rule of law and the protection of civil and political freedoms; and
(e) informal constraints—norms of behaviour, conventions and codes of conduct—are a necessary (but not sufficient) condition for good economic performance, and therefore, societies with norms favourable to economic growth can sometimes prosper even with unstable or adverse political rules.

In their *holistic* approach towards a general understanding of socio-economic evolutionary processes, both the structuralist and the institutionalist views emerge as critiques on limitations of *orthodox* economic doctrine or policies designed from that doctrine. According to these views in *heterodox* tradition, any analysis of growth and development processes of the contemporary developing/emerging economies needs a very close look at their diverse and differentiated socio-economic structures. Specific cultural, political and economic frameworks of such countries have some inherent structural and institutional biases as the reflection of the *unequal* distribution of resources, power, entitlements and action capabilities among their individuals and groups/classes or *uneven* growth and development across their different parts, regions and segments/sectors.[65] It is often argued that the emergence of institutionalist development theory has essentially supplemented the 'structuralist views' over the past three decades or so.

[65]Dutta (2014, p. 12).

1.6.2 Development Strategies under Globalisation in China and India

1.6.2.1 China

China's structural transformation from an agriculture-based economy to one dominated by industry and service sectors has been possible mainly by a number of factors such as (i) economic reform policies, (ii) fiscal and administrative decentralisation, (iii) increased investment in social services and rural development and (iv) integration into global economy through trade and foreign direct investment (FDI). *Firstly*, China's highly distorted and inefficient centrally planned economy has been gradually replaced by 'an economic system that depends, to a great extent, on market forces to allocate resources, enforces private property rights, and operates within a set of relatively developed regulatory institutions'. The reform process that started in the early 1980s in the agricultural sector through the introduction of household responsibility system and development of Town and Village Enterprises replaced the inefficient rural collective system. The *second* factor is the fiscal and administrative decentralisation from the central government to local tiers of institutions. This decentralisation created competition among local governments and improved efficiency through better decision-making based on local conditions and better information flows. Both the above reforms 'unleashed enormous creativity and incentives of individuals, firms and local governments that strived to maximise economic returns, by seeking out opportunities, both domestically and globally'. *Thirdly*, 'China's long-term commitment to public investment in infrastructure, education and health, and basic services…resulted in China's impressive human development outcomes despite its low per capita income'. *Fourthly*, China's economic growth was further strengthened by its integration into the rest of the world, particularly through its admission to the World Trade Organisation (WTO) in 2001. Now, the 'global economy offers China a nearly unlimited market for its export of goods and services', and also 'provides China with the opportunity to import technology and ideas, know-how and modern management skills that are embodied in FDI and joint ventures'. Another important channel of knowledge transfer is through various exchange programs. The Chinese government has been inviting a stream of foreign experts to help its policy-makers learn about the functioning and features of a market economic system, while at the same time sending many waves of Chinese students and government officials for their training in the US and European universities.[66]

China has been experiencing a rapid economic growth since it opened up its economy in 1979 after the 'open door' policy was politically approved in December 1978.[67] By 2010, the Chinese gross domestic product (GDP) increased with an

---

[66]Wang (2014).

[67]It was under the guidance of Deng Xiaoping, China adopted the 'open door' policy. As Dorn (2016) argues, the socio-economic devastation during the Great Leap Forward (1958–60), the

Table 1.1 China's growth in GDP at factor cost in 1996 prices (%)

	2004–05	2005–06	2006–07	2007–08	2008–09	2009–10	2010–2011	2011–12
GDP (value added)	**11.3**	**12.7**	**14.2**	**9.6**	**9.2**	**10.4**	**9.3**	**7.7**
Agriculture, forestry, animal husbandry and fishery	0.8	3.3	10.6	9.2	5.2	7.9	8.7	8.1
Mining	30.2	12.8	3.5	35.3	14.3	17.4	20.6	−2.5
Manufacturing	11.8	14.1	14.1	8.8	8.0	11.0	7.2	5.0
Production and supply of electricity, gas and water	12.1	13.6	11.4	−21.9	4.4	5.7	4.4	3.7
Construction	14.7	15.3	14.5	13.7	20.2	11.6	11.1	8.9
Services[a]	11.7	13.9	16.8	9.5	13.4	10.0	9.7	10.8

Sources: Various issues of *Statistical Yearbook of China* over the period of 2005–2014. The author is thankful to Dr. Yibai Yang for computing data used in Table 1.1
Notes: [a]Services include Transport, Storage and Post, Information Transmission, Computer Services and Software, Wholesale and Retail Trades, Hotels and Catering Services, Financial Intermediation, Real Estate, Leasing and Business Services, Scientific Research and Technical Services, Management of Environment and Public Facilities, Services to Households and Other Services, Education, Health, Social Security and Social Welfare, Culture, Sports and Entertainment, and Public Management and Social Organizations

average growth rate of 10.58% annually.[68] This has enabled China to drastically reduce its people living below the poverty line (i.e. US $1.25 a day) to 12.6% of total population in 2008. On the basis of a new poverty line of US $1.90, the World Bank estimate shows that China's 2008 poverty headcount ratio would be 14.7%, which has further reduced to 11.2% in 2010.[69]

China's continuing high growth rates of gross domestic product (GDP) in recent years have been the result of high growth rates in mining, manufacturing, utilities (electricity, gas and water), construction and services (Table 1.1). However, the regional disparities in economic and income growth between the coastal and the two inland regions were evident. For example, during 1996–2010, growth rate in the Eastern region was 14.45% on average, while it was 13.95% and 13.78% in the Western and the Central regions,[70] respectively (Dutta and Yang 2014, p. 79).

(Footnote 67 continued)

Great Famine (1959–61) and the Cultural Revolution (1966–76) led Deng to elevate economic development to the primary goal of socialism. His vision of 'market socialism with Chinese characteristics' and his mantra—'Seek truth from facts'—paved the way for the emergence of the non-state sector and the return of private entrepreneurs.

[68]In 1979, the GDP of China was US $263,190 million, and it grew to US $5,951,462 million in 2010. See United Nation National Accounts Main Aggregates Database 2012 for the sources.

[69]http://povertydata.worldbank.org/poverty/country/CHN.

[70]For this chapter, the *Eastern* region includes the provinces of Guangdong, Fujian, Jiangsu, Zhejiang, Shanghai, Shandong, Hebei, Beijing, Tianjin, Liaoning and Hainan; the *Western* region includes the provinces of Shaanxi, Chongqing, Sichuan, Gansu, Qinghai, Xinjiang, Ningxia,

Although the Chinese government has made efforts for balancing the economic growth across the three regions by reducing income disparity, which lead to some growth convergence between these regions, in 2010, the income per capita in the Eastern region was still 1.96 and 1.65 times as much as in the Western and Central regions, respectively. There are many factors that are responsible for these regional per capita income disparities in China, but the major factors include favourable economic policies towards the Eastern provinces, a coast-oriented policy to adopt technology and thereby an attraction of foreign investment to the Eastern/coastal region.

There are different strands of literature that analyse different aspects of China's regional disparity. One group of authors (e.g. Fujita and Hu 2001 and Lee et al. 2012) examines the influence of globalisation and economic liberalisation on regional economic/financial disparity, while another strand of literature (e.g. Sun 2002; Zhang et al. 2002; Özyurt and Mitze 2012) focuses on the impact of foreign direct investment (FDI) and trade on China's regional economic development. In addition, Sun and Dutta (1997) had studied the regional disparities of development and income mainly between Eastern (coastal) and Western (far inland) regions in China during 1984–1993 (the earlier post-reform era).[71] They found that the dualistic growth patterns of the two regions stemmed from the structural characteristics of their own. Three characteristics identified by them are economic structure, openness of the economy and investment structure.

1.6.2.2 India

After the adoption of a comprehensive economic liberalisation policy in July 1991, the Indian economy underwent a substantial change.[72] As can be evident from Table 1.2, India has become one of the world's best performers, with average annual GDP growth of more than 8% during the period of 2005–2011 except in 2008–09 due to the *Global Financial Crisis* (GFC), although there had been some signal of future growth deceleration as can be seen from the first revised estimate of 2012–13 and provisional estimate of 2013–14 GDP growths. In 2011, India became the third largest economy in the world (in PPP terms). Although poverty has declined in India on an average by 1.5% points per year between 2004–05 and 2009–10, still 29.8% of people are below the poverty line (US $1.25 a day). An earlier World Bank estimate computed on the basis of a new poverty line of US

(Footnote 70 continued)

Guizhou, Yuannan and Tibet, while the *Central* region includes the provinces of Shanxi, Inner Mongolia, Jilin, Heilongjiang, Anhui, Jiangxi, Henan, Hubei, Hunan and Guangxi.

[71]Sun and Dutta (1997, Table 4, p. 850) had, however, provided a regional distribution of foreign direct investment between three regions of Coastal (East), Central inland and Western inland.

[72]The author has a detailed analysis in Dutta (2011).

Table 1.2 India's growth over previous year in GDP at factor cost in 2004–05 prices (%)

	2005–06	2006–07	2007–08	2008–09	2009–10	2010–11	2011–12 (2R)	2012–13 (1R)	2013–14 (PE)
GDP	**9.5**	**9.6**	**9.3**	**6.7**	**8.6**	**8.9**	**6.7**	**4.5**	**4.7**
Agriculture, forestry and fishing	5.1	4.2	5.8	0.1	0.8	8.6	5.0	1.4	4.7
Mining and quarrying	1.3	7.5	3.7	2.1	5.9	6.5	0.1	−2.2	−1.4
Manufacturing	10.1	14.3	10.3	4.3	11.3	8.9	7.4	1.1	−0.7
Electricity, gas and water supply	7.1	9.3	8.3	4.6	6.2	5.3	8.4	2.3	5.9
Construction	12.8	10.3	10.8	5.3	6.7	5.7	10.8	1.1	1.6
Trade, hotels, restaurants, transport and communication	12.0	11.6	10.9	7.5	10.4	12.2	4.3	5.1	3.0
Financing, insurance, real estate and business services	12.6	14.0	12.0	12.0	9.7	10.0	11.3	10.9	12.9
Community, social and personal services	7.1	2.8	6.9	12.5	11.7	4.2	4.9	5.3	5.6

Source: *Economic Survey 2012–13* (Table 1.1, p. 3) and *Economic Survey 2013–14* (Table 1.1, p. 4)
Notes: *2R* Second revised, *1R* First revised, *PE* Provisional estimate

$1.90 shows that India's poverty headcount ratio had fallen sharply from 31.4% in 2009 to 21.3% in 2011.[73]

According to the new GDP series[74] with base year of 2011–12 (Table 1.3), the real GDP growth in 2012–13 was 5.1%.

There are, however, two trends in India which are noteworthy: *firstly*, India's rapidly growing middle class, which is currently about 250 million of people, and *secondly*, its demographic dividend, that is, half of India's population being under 25; India is projected to add 12–15 million workers to its labour force every year over the coming decades.[75] The Indian Government has set a target of providing skills training to 500 million workers across 30 sectors by 2022.

The *Economic Survey 2015–16* notes that in spite of Indian economy's better growth performance since 2002, this is still below the potential. Using institution

[73]http://povertydata.worldbank.org/poverty/country/IND.

[74]According to *Economic Survey 2014–15* (Vol. I, Box 1.3, p. 6), the improvement in data and methods applied in the new GDP series puts India on par with international standard of GDP estimation.

[75]The year 2016 was a turning point in global demographic trends in the sense that it was the first time since 1950 that the combined working-age (WA) population (15–59) of the advanced countries declined. Over the next three decades, the United Nations (UN) projects that China and Russia will each see their WA populations fall by over 20%. India, however, seems to be in a demographic sweet spot with its working-age population projected to grow by a third over the same period (Economic Survey 2016–17, p. 30).

Table 1.3 India's growth over previous year in GDP and major sectors in 2011–12 prices (%)

Sector	2012–13	2013–14 (2R)	2014–15 (1R)	2015–16 (PE)
GDP at constant market prices	**5.1**	**6.6**	**7.2**	**7.6**
Agriculture, forestry and fishing	**1.2**	**4.2**	**−0.2**	**1.1**
Industry	**2.3**	**5.0**	**5.9**	**7.3**
Mining and quarrying	−0.2	3.0	10.8	6.9
Manufacturing	6.2	5.6	5.5	9.5
Electricity, gas, water supply, etc.	4.0	4.7	8.0	5.9
Construction	−4.3	4.6	4.4	3.7
Services	**8.0**	**7.8**	**10.3**	**9.2**
Trade, hotels, transport and communication	9.6	7.8	9.8	9.5
Financing, real estate, professional services, etc.	8.8	10.1	10.6	10.3
Public administration, defence and other services	–	4.5	10.7	6.9

Source: *Economic Survey 2014–15* (Volume II, Table 1.2, p. 4) and Economic *Survey 2015–16* (Table 1.2, p. 7)
Notes: *2R* Second revised, *1R* First revised, *PE* Provisional estimate

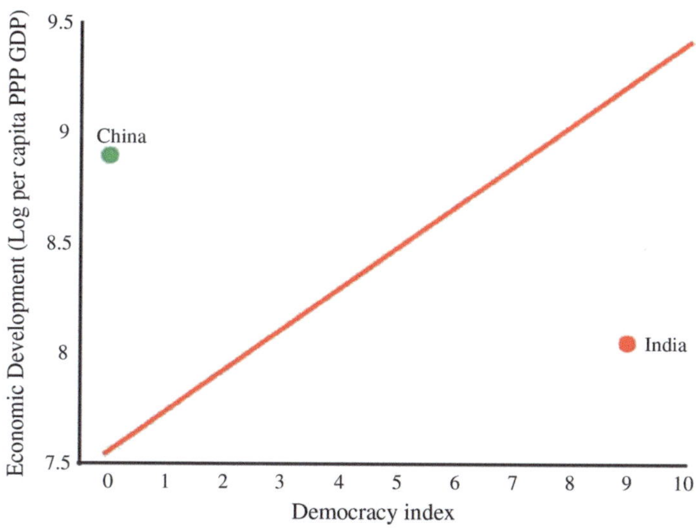

Fig. 1.1 Institutions matter—India and China *Source* Adapted from *Economic Survey 2015–16*, Government of India, Figure 1, Vol. 1, Box 1.1, p. 5

buildings as the key determinant of long-run growth, the empirical research has found that the upward-sloping line in Fig. 1.1 reflects a strong relationship (on average) between political institutions and economic development validating the

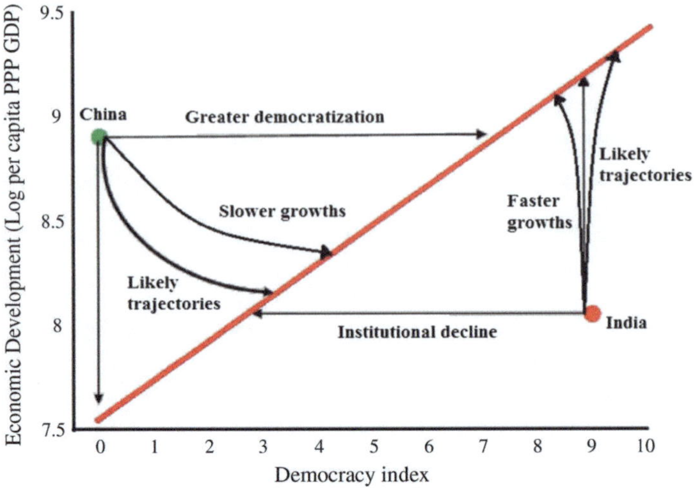

Fig. 1.2 Hypothetical growth convergence—India and China *Source* Adapted from *Economic Survey 2015–16*, Government of India, Figure 2, Vol. 1, Box 1.1, p. 6

central argument of the 'institutions matter' hypothesis. Having been far away from the line of best fit, China and India are the two outliers in the sense that each of these two countries is an exception. China which is above the line and at the north-west position shows its very high per capita GDP, but with low democracy index (i.e. weak democratic institutions). India, on the other hand, is way below the line and at the south-east position indicating its low per capita GDP, but with high democracy index (i.e. strong democratic institutions).

Assuming that mean reversion can happen in different ways for both the countries, typically it is expected that for China which experiencing growth slowdown in the recent years may adopt a path towards political democratisation, while India has the option to move towards higher growth potential with either the same level of democracy index or even better[76] (Fig. 1.2).

[76]Although India is, in general, a democratic success by contemporary standards, still there is, as Drèze and Sen (2014 [2013], p 252) assert, plenty of scope for improvement, especially in electoral politics involving 'women's political representation, the funding of elections, inner party democracy, judicial accountability', etc. The same applies when there are 'violations of democratic practice in specific contexts, on alleged grounds of national security and other concerns' (*Ibid.*, p. 248).

Chapter 2
Development in Modern India under Structural Dualism (1947–1980)

2.1 Introduction

When India got independence in 1947, the first Prime Minister, Jawaharlal Nehru, put it, 'the soul of a nation, long suppressed, finds utterance'. Although the 'suppression' dates back prior to the Mogul era that begins in the early sixteenth century, there is no doubt that Nehru made this reference of 'suppression' specifically to the period of almost two hundred years of British colonisation (1757–1947).[1] It is not surprising that during this colonial period, economic development in general and industrial development in particular, regardless of whatever little took place, was not only extremely uneven, but also very slow leading. This structural force within the Indian society led to the formation of its socio-economic dualism. Foreign capital occupied a dominant position in Indian industry and absorbed a large portion of her newly created wealth in India's so-called nascent 'modern' segment. Native capital of India's 'traditional' segment, on the other hand, mostly engaged in money lending, invested in land or commerce, rather than in the new type of manufactures. Apart from these, banking facilities were inadequate, technical education was virtually lacking, natural resources such as coal were unevenly distributed, and, most importantly, the colonial government had an apathy[2] to genuine economic transformation of Indian society. With this background of weak transition, from traditional Indian society to modern, the Nehru government, after the independence, made attempts to give it meaningful expression using the 'utterance' that the 'soul' of the Indian nation found at 'the midnight hour' of

[1]It was Lord Clive's victory at Plassey in 1757 that inaugurated official British rule in India by the East India Company. As a result of the Mutiny of 1857, the Government of India was subsequently transferred from the hands of the Company to the Crown in the same year.

[2]As to the colonial government's apathy towards India's genuine industrial development, one could easily verify the fact that even towards the end of the colonial period (e.g. 1938–1939), about three-fourths of India's imports consisted of manufactured articles, while raw materials and (agricultural) foodstuffs together showed about the same proportion to her total exports.

D. Dutta, *Development under Dualism and Digital Divide in Twenty-First Century India*, Dynamics of Asian Development, https://doi.org/10.1007/978-981-10-6344-2_2

August 14, 1947. The very manifestation of this 'utterance' could be found in the declaration, by the Nehru government, of a Sovereign Democratic Republic India. The adoption of a new Constitution with the 'Directive Principles of State Policy, designing of Industrial Policy, setting up of the Planning Commission, launching of Five-Year Plans for India's economic development, etc, are some of the other crucial steps that were taken during the early stage of the Nehru administration. The idea was to tackle the state of socio-economic dualism inherited from the colonial administration. But, as we will see below, India's inherited socio-economic dualism in absolute term continued as a prolonged *structural dualism* in relative term due to social and economic underperformance, particularly during the 1960s and 1970s.

2.2 Organised versus Unorganised Segments

In order to test the validity or otherwise of the above assertion, let us first explain what a *structural dualism* at the very aggregate level of the Indian society means. This means that India has two different socio-economic-technological environments —the *organised* (or modern) segment (predominantly *capitalistic*) and the *unorganised* (or traditional) segment (predominantly *pre-capitalistic*).

The *organised* (or modern) segment is divided into two sectors: public government sector and private corporate sector employing 10 or more persons, while the *unorganised* (or traditional) segment is essentially the household sector, which 'includes conceptually not only farm households engaged in agricultural production, but also unincorporated enterprises[3] engaged in industry, trade, transport and finance, private 'charitable' trusts, as also households that are not directly involved at all in production of any kind (except very marginally perhaps through ownership of residential houses)'.[4] The *organised* segment thus includes all establishments in the public sector irrespective of their size and non-agricultural establishments in the private sector employing 10 or more persons. The *unorganised* (or traditional) segment is usually defined to be the segment that is not recorded under any factory legislation. This segment is mostly comprised of self-employed households and

[3]Recently, 'quasi-corporations'—defined in the UN's *System of National Accounts* (SNA 2008) as 'an unincorporated enterprise that has sufficient information to compile a complete set of accounts as if it were a separate corporation and whose de facto relationship to its owner is that of a corporation to its shareholders'—has been reclassified in the new series as part of private corporate sector. Some selected trusts and non-profit organisations are designated as quasi-corporations in India.

[4]RBI (1982, p. 1).

casual labourers with no steady employment and, therefore, no secure or sustainable incomes, and above all with no access to the benefits of social security.[5]

The *Report of the National Commission on Labour* (1969, p. 417) provides a list of major unorganised sectors employing large numbers of workers, most of whom are under- and unemployed. These categories include contract labour such as construction workers; labour employed in small-scale industry; hand-loom/power-loom workers; bidi and cigar workers; employees in shops and commercial establishments; sweepers and scavengers; workers in tanneries; tribal labour; casual and other unprotected labour; etc. This segment is usually characterised by low capital-labour ratios, low levels of formal schooling, low-paying jobs, poor working conditions, little job security, inferior social status, and, above all, lack of governmental support. India's poverty syndrome is directly associated with the very state and nature of its vast *unorganised* segment, although it is functionally related to its *organised* segment.

Although it has been more than four decades since the publication of this *Report*, the characteristics of the *unorganised* segment remain virtually the same. At the beginning of the new millennium, the Government of India set up the National Commission for Enterprises in the Unorganised Sector (NCEUS) on 20 September 2004 to review the status of India's unorganised/informal segment including the nature of its enterprises, their size, spread and scope, and magnitude of employment. In NCEUS's first report on 'Conditions of Work and Promotion of Livelihoods in Unorganised Sector', it is recorded that despite the Indian economy being on a sustained path of economic growth since the early 1990s when economic reforms were introduced, 'the picture that emerges for an overwhelming majority of Indians is one of extremely slow improvement or even deterioration in the quality of work'.[6]

The *unorganised* segment's contribution to the Indian economy's net domestic product (NDP) was virtually constant around 70% until 1980. Sundrum (1987, Table 6.18, p. 169) reports that the *unorganised* segment's *average* contributions to India's NDP were 72.8 and 69.0% for the periods 1960/61–1969/70 and 1970/71–1981/82, respectively. It has, however, been steadily declining since then, although with marginal up and down fluctuations within a range between 54.4 and 56.1% during the recent period from 2007–2008 to 2012–2013 (see Table 3.9).

[5]Concept of *social security* in the context of developing countries (especially, with huge *unorganised* segment) needs to be broader than the one applied to the developed countries. Many rightly argue that economic security and social security are intimately connected in developing societies. There is, however, 'a general recognition that social security must be expanded to include not only new elements such as food provision, housing and sanitation; but also income and employment' (Jhabvala 1998, p. L8).

[6]NCEUS (2009, p. 17).

2.3 Genesis of Prolonged Dualism under Modern India[7]

The Indian experiences of economic development can be divided into four major phases:

Phase I: Planned development strategies/policies under the Nehru era (1947–1964);
Phase II: Dilution of industrial licensing system and import policy, and more controls
(1965–1979);
Phase III: Policy changes towards liberalisation (1980–1990); and
Phase IV: Comprehensive liberalisation and its impacts (since 1991).

2.3.1 Phase I: Planned Development Strategies/Policies under the Nehru Era (1947–1964)

The new *Constitution*, adopted on 26 November 1949, contains the 'Directive Principles of State Policy'. The State is, accordingly, directed 'to promote the welfare of the people by securing and protecting as effectively as it may a social order in which justice, social, economic and political, shall inform all the institutions of the national life'.[8] Meanwhile, the Government issued its *Industrial Policy* on 6 April 1948 with the main thrust being the assurance that the existing industrial structure would remain undisturbed at least for ten years. Yet, as the Congress Party gained some confidence in the Government, more control gained momentum. The Government secured passage of *the Industries Bill* of 1949 ensuring more control over industry.[9] Because Nehru had a dream of planned economic development of the entire country, he, notwithstanding of some opposition even from his own Cabinet, took special interest in setting up the Planning Commission on 28 February 1950, with himself as its Chairman. It was July 1951 when the Planning Commission presented the draft outline of the First Five-Year Plan (1951–1956). In this Plan, greater emphasis had been given to agriculture, food and matters pertaining to agriculture, as a preparatory task for industrial development in the near future. The First Plan was, in fact, merely a set of internally coordinated specific investment projects including public irrigation, and, therefore, it cannot really be called a comprehensive one. However, the Plan was successful in the sense that its very modest (12%) targeted increase in national income was surpassed over the

[7]Discussion under the first three phases has been adapted from Dutta (1992).
[8]Article 38 under 'Directive Principles of State Policy' in Part IV of *The Constitution of India.*
[9]The present author has a summary of details on the nature of control in Dutta (1990, p. 90).

plan period. This was possible mainly because the production of food grains (cereals and pulses) increased from around 52 million tonnes to 66 million tonnes.[10]

As the political stability of his government grew, Nehru strengthened the planning process and as a result, the Second Five-Year Plan (1956–1961) was made highly comprehensive. The basic development strategy of this Plan was 'Growth in Heavy Industry'. The basic objective was to be eventually less reliant on imports of producer goods from abroad. The Plan recommendation was that the new producer goods industries would be installed mainly in the State-owned public sector.[11] This was in conformity with the government's declaration for the establishment of a 'socialistic pattern of society'. For successful implementation of the development objectives, various regulatory control mechanisms were designed, one after another.[12] These controls used, were to be 'exercised primarily through the executive branch of the State and especially through the bureaucracy'.[13] The rate of growth of industrial production was satisfactory with an increase in the general index of industrial production from 139 in 1955–1956 to 194 in 1960–1961 (with 1950–1951 = 100),[14] although the overall growth rate achieved during the Second Plan period was 3.9% per annum as against the target of 4.5%.

The general strategy of development in the Third Five-Year Plan (1961–1966) was very similar to that in the Second Plan i.e. the continuation of the strategy of sizeable investments in heavy industry, although traditional agriculture received some attention in this Plan. By the time the *Third Plan* was designed, a widening gap between targets and achievements became visible. The planners took notice of it. As a result, the *Third Plan* had laid emphasis 'on implementation, on speed and thoroughness in seeking practical results and creating conditions for maximum production and employment and the development of human resources'.[15]

The Nehruvian approaches to the role of State through planning mechanism and its implication for inclusiveness in Indian Society.[16]

Because Nehru wanted both a 'Welfare State' and a 'socialistic pattern of economy' in a multi-class society like India, he had to go through necessary and inevitable compromises with the vested interest groups. His approach towards socialism was, in fact, tempered by democratic and humanitarian ideals as will be evident from our analysis below. As we have already mentioned, he did not want to accept either of the two major ideologies—capitalism and socialism—in their strict,

---

[10]Following *Third Five Year Plan* (1961, p. 39), Chakravarty (1987, p. 19) quotes these figures.

[11]The public sector is widely defined to include the administrative machinery of the government as well as public enterprises.

[12]A list of major regulatory control mechanisms are given in Dutta (1992, pp. 83–84).

[13]Sen (1982, p. 131).

[14]Quoting from the Government of India's *Third Five Year Plan* (1961) document, Chakravarty (*op. cit.*, pp. 19–20). also notes that in spite of the spectacular increase in the machinery index during the *Second Plan* period, growth in iron, steel and chemicals was less spectacular and that of cotton textiles was virtually unchanged.

[15]*Third Five Year Plan* (*op. cit.*, p. xiv).

[16]This section has been adapted from Dutta (1990).

rigid or 'doctrinaire' sense. The exploitative capitalist system of the colonial State at home and abroad had always made him very repulsive towards the ideology of capitalism. To him, the 'acquisitive society' based on capitalism was no longer suited to the present age. Although he was an advocate for the ideology of socialism, he tried to avoid its extreme kind—State socialism in which the State is all-powerful entity governing practically all political and economic activities. Since Nehru believed that the State was relatively autonomous, that is, politically independent and very powerful, there was perhaps no need for the State to be fully involved in economic spheres as well. The argument in his own language runs as follows:

> If you are going to make it [the State] very powerful economically also it would become a mere conglomeration of authority. I should, therefore, like decentralisation of economic power.[17]

Socialism to Nehru was more than an 'economic doctrine'—it was a 'philosophy of life'. According to him, socialism could be viewed from two approaches[18]—scientific and non-scientific. The first approach is basically economic and is less open to argument, while the second one 'is a certain human approach, of humanity growing and developing'. Although Nehru did not deny the class contradictions that exist in the Indian society, he wanted 'to deal with the problem in a peaceful and cooperative way by lessening rather than increasing these conflicts and trying to win over people instead of threatening to fight them or to destroy them'.[19] In other words, to deal with class contradictions, he chose the Gandhian solution of 'class synthesis' rather than the Marxian solution of 'class struggle'. Although he repeatedly emphasised that political democracy without social democracy could not bring any real benefit for the masses, he followed easier methods of persuasion and reformism from the top rather than any painstaking path of mobilisation from the bottom. Consequently, India's hierarchical social structure with its corresponding uneven power relations (economic as well as political) remains almost unchanged.[20] National planning as a technical instrument for economic development has, in fact, served the political need of the vested interests. In his interview with Karanjia, Nehru explicitly agreed with this view and tried to legitimise in the name of scientific socialism:

> Our approach, being Socialist, is primarily an economic approach which has made politics revolve around economic policies….We have adopted also the planned and scientific approach to economic development in preference to individual enterprise of the old laissez faire school. We are, therefore, proceeding scientifically and methodically without leaving things to chance or fate.[21]

---

[17]Nehru expressed this thought on socialism in the spring of 1958 (Brecher, p. 532).

[18]Karanjia (1960, pp. 51–52).

[19]*Ibid.*, pp. 76–77.

[20]The far reaching implication of these uneven power relations that exist in India has been elaborated in Dutta (1989).

[21]Karanjia (*op. cit.*, pp. 39 and 49).

Nehru's Scientific approach to socialism—State control from the 'commanding heights' of the economy, and 'decentralization of economic power' between the bureaucrat and elite groups-dominated public sector on the one hand, and big and petty bourgeoisie-owned private sector on the other hand, did very little to bring the vast majority of people into the process of planned economic development. Nehru believed that he was trying to move towards a socialistic pattern of society; but, on the contrary, the society actually moved towards the State-led capitalism.

In the midst of the Second Five-Year Plan, Nehru realised that the planned economic development had lagged far behind his expectation. He himself described the situation in a frustrating tone:

> India today presents a very mixed picture of hope and anguish, of remarkable advances and at the same time of inertia, of a new spirit and also the dead hand of the past and of privilege, of an overall and growing unity and many disruptive tendencies.[22]

One could specifically mention such disruptive tendencies reflected in various newly established institutions. For example, basic institutions under Panchayati Raj (village councils) became 'merely a means through which rural oligarchies consolidated their power'.[23] Similarly, the administrative bureaucracy at the top 'have their power unabated, occupied heights of decisive importance in all new institutions, undertakings and enterprises'.[24] In spite of the fact that Nehru was aware of these ominous tendencies, and he was concerned morally and emotionally, he, however, could not do much. Later on, he seemed to lean more towards the non-scientific approach to socialism. By this approach, he basically meant Gandhian approach to rural development that lays emphasis on traditional agriculture with cooperative farming. Although the general pattern of development in the Third Five-Year Plan was essentially similar to that in the previous one, traditional agriculture was prioritised. He had a very high expectation of success in the Third Plan:

> We are determined to succeed in this great adventure. We have faith in it because we have faith in our people, and it is the hard work and co-operative spirit of our people that will bring success and the advancement of our people to greater prosperity and equality of opportunity. The Third plan will, we hope, take us out of the rut of poverty that has brought so much unhappiness and degradation to our millions.[25]

Nehru's simply tremendous faith in planning and people in a society based on social hierarchy and economic unevenness did help in no way to realise his hope or even to move nearer to his ideal. Towards the very end of his life, we, therefore, find him bitterly disappointed and uttering:

---

[22]Nehru (1960, p. 43).

[23]Chand (1966, pp. 38–39).

[24]*Ibid.*, p. 43.

[25]'An Appeal on 5 July 1961' in Gopal (1983, p. 332).

Table 2.1 NSS estimates of incidence of poverty in rural India: 1960–1961 to 1970–1971

Year	Consumer price index	Rural per capita monthly consumption (in 1960–1961 prices)	Poverty line (Rs. per capita for 30 days)	Incidence of poverty (Percentage poor)
1960–1961	100	21.47	15.0	38.9
1963–1964	118	21.51	17.7	44.5
1964–1965	142	18.62	19.8	46.8
1967–1968	206	16.21	30.9	56.5
1970–1971	192	18.39	28.8	47.5

Source: Nair (1979, p. 135)

> One thing that distresses me very much greatly is that….there is a good number of people in India who have not profited by planning, and whose poverty is abysmal and most painful.[26]

The following Table 2.1 gives a dire picture of increasing the incidence of rural poverty with decreasing per capita consumption and increasing consumer prices during 1960s.

One could ask the question: Was Nehru himself responsible for this failure? The answer is both 'no' and 'yes'. The answer is 'no', because of his commitment to the liberal democracy and, therefore, the consequent constant compromises with the vested interest groups that had forced him to shun any drastic measure to break the power relation nexus of the Indian society. The answer is 'yes', when one finds that the Nehruvian State had managed to achieve a considerable degree of autonomy and Nehru himself had a great deal of room to manoeuver the country's uneven pattern of power relations. In spite of this, Nehru chose not to disturb the power structure—both economic and political. 'On the most decisive question of all, his policy was', as Moore (1965, p. 407) puts it, 'one of rhetoric and drift'.

2.3.2 *Phase II: Dilution of Industrial Licensing System and Import Policy, and More Controls (1965–79)*

The delay in tying up foreign loans at the beginning of the Third Plan, sharp increase in defence spending after the Indo-Chinese conflict[27] in 1962 and suspension of credits by the USA towards the end of this Plan period worsened the foreign exchange shortage. Meanwhile, Nehru, the architect of Indian Planning,[28]

[26]'A Speech in the Lok Sabha on 11 December 1963' in Gopal (1983, p. 317).

[27]The Indo-Chinese conflict lasted from 20 October to 21 November in 1962.

[28]That Nehru was the architect of Indian Planning has been documented in detail by the present author (Dutta 1990).

died on 27 May 1964. The new Prime Minister, Lal Bahadur Shastri,[29] faced further deterioration in the foreign exchange situation especially when the Indo-Pakistan conflict,[30] in 1965, and the monsoon failure during 1965–1966, necessitated large-scale imports of food grains. Caught into the continued increase in defence spending on the one hand, and additional need for food import on the other hand, the government had to cut back public investment very sharply. This dampened economic growth, which led to 'the emergence of significant excess capacity in the heavy and capital goods sector'.[31]

Due to the sudden death of the Prime Minister Shastri on 11 January 1966, the Indian economy started experiencing renewed instability. When Mrs. Indira Gandhi became the Prime Minister on 24 January 1966, she inherited an unstable economy that seemed to have drifted from its planned trajectory of economic growth and development. The government also temporarily abandoned the method of five year planning and instead adopted annual plans. The International Monetary Fund and the World Bank imposed special conditions, such as rupee devaluation and liberalisation of licensing mechanisms, in exchange for the resumption of the flow of aid/assistance. Consequently, the government allowed for a progressive dilution of the industrial licensing system along with the devaluation of the rupee by approximately 37% (in terms of exchange rate with the US dollar) in June 1966. As a panacea to the ailing economy, both large business houses and foreign capital were allowed into the 'core' sector industries,[32] given permission to increase the production limit by 25% of their licensed capacity, and also unauthorised capacity was legalised in a wide range of industries.

Towards the end of the three Annual Plans (1966–67, 1967–68 and 1968–69), which were nothing more than simple budgetary exercises, Mrs. Gandhi's government managed to gain some degree of political stability and launched the Fourth Five-Year Plan (1969–1974). The main thrust of this Plan was to overcome the continued 'agricultural stagnation', and, therefore, 'Modern Agricultural Growth' became the development strategy of this Plan. The use of *seed-fertilizer*-based agricultural technology resulted in increased output to such an extent that this phenomenon became what is known as the Green Revolution in India. Although the Green Revolution certainly broke the agricultural stagnation, 'it conferred more than proportionate benefits to the better-off farmers in the infra-structurally better endowed regions'.[33]

[29]After Nehru's Death, Gulzarilal Nanda was the Interim Prime Minister from 27 May to 8 June in 1964, and then Lal Bahadur Shastri became the new Prime Minister on 9 June 1964.

[30]The Indo-Pakistan conflict took place from 5 August to 23 September in 1965.

[31]Chakravarty (*op. cit.*, p. 22).

[32]The 'core' sector consisted of industries which were important because of their links to other industries such as synthetic rubber and certain chemicals.

[33]Chakravarty (*op. cit.*, p. 27).

Export promotional measures that had found some support during the second half of the sixties, gained momentum in official circles only at the beginning of the 1970s. A Cabinet Committee Export Policy resolution was passed in 1970. From 1971 onwards, a new dimension to the export promotion effort was added in the form of creation of a number of organisations aimed at providing export services to the exporting community.[34] Unfortunately, multiplicity of different organisations later on found to be inefficient for 'providing export services such as advice on product development, product adaptation, adoption of technologies, information on marketing policies and procedure in other countries, etc.'[35]

From the points of view of both accelerating industrial development and improving the administrative efficiency, the Fourth Plan (1969–1974) document had shown greater willingness to modify the existing system of controls. In fact, the State sought for more controls,[36] especially following the Reports of the Committees[37] that revealed there had been impressive gains by the large industrial houses based on middle-class consumer goods industries catering to the urban population. Although the licensing system continued in much the same way as before, the *New Industrial Licensing Policy* announced by the Government of India in February 1970 had tried to reconcile the conflicting objectives of promoting economic growth and restricting concentration of economic power in the hands of larger private industrial groups. It has tried to encourage the growth of new and smaller entrepreneurs (i) without any need for obtaining a licence for projects requiring investment up to Rs. 1 crore, and (ii) promising liberal licensing for middle-level investments up to Rs. 5 crores and protecting them from the competition from the larger industrial units by not allowing the latter into these areas. Another new concept of the public-private 'joint sector' ventures in the core and heavy industries had been floated in the *New Industrial Licensing Policy*, but the private sector viewed it as utopian.[38] The existing *Foreign Exchange Regulation Act* (FERA) was also revised in 1973 specifically to kerb excessive remittance of

---

[34]Panchmukhi (1985, p. 296). Among the significant developments during the early seventies, included are the creation of *Export Promotion Councils*, *Commodity Boards*, *Trade Development Authority* and *Indian Institute of Foreign Trade*.

[35]*Ibid.*, pp. 297–298.

[36]Some examples of more controls include the passing of the *Monopolies Restrictive Trade Practices* (MRTP) Act in 1969, the nationalisation of fourteen commercial banks in July 1969, the introduction of new Industrial Policy in 1970, the revision of the *Foreign Exchange Regulation Act* (FERA), etc.

[37]Reports of two Committees are noteworthy: R.K. Hazari Report (1966) to the Planning Commission on "Industrial Planning and Licencing Policy" and the "Industrial Licensing Policy Inquiry Committee Report" (July 1969) known as Dutt Committee Report to the Government of India.

[38]Larger private industrialists' views have been summarised in Wadhva (1977, pp. 298–301).

profits abroad. Among other measures, the Act sought for giving the *Reserve Bank of India* greater control over foreign investors and reducing the equity positions of foreign companies in their Indian subsidiaries.

With an excessive price rise during 1973–1975 being accompanied by the oil crisis, the Draft Fifth Plan (1974–1979) required thorough revision. The above sentiment for more control measures, prevalent since the late sixties, acted as the basic background for the Draft Fifth Five-Year Plan's development strategy of 'Growth with Distribution'. The Draft Plan emphasised the objectives of employment generation and poverty eradication and favoured public ownership of financial institutions as an instrument for exercising an effective form of 'social control'. The whole process of long-term planning was, however, temporarily halted. Three Annual Plans were, instead, announced for 1974–1975, 1975–1976 and 1976–1977, in order to provide some breathing space before price stability was achieved and the revised Fifth Plan was ready. As a matter of fact, on 1 July 1975, Mrs. Gandhi announced the 20-point New Economic Programme[39]—a short-term crash programme to fill in the gaps of long-term planning. The Programme's objective was to uplift the poorer and weaker sections of the society, particularly in the rural areas. The above Programme was, however, discontinued when the Janata Government[40] came into power in March 1977 with more focus on promoting economic self-reliance and indigenous industries, requiring multinational corporations (MNCs) to have partnership with Indian companies and to adhere to a particular provision of what was then the Foreign Exchange Regulation Act (FERA).[41]

After terminating the Fifth Plan on 31 March 1978, the reconstituted Planning Commission, under the Janata Government, decided to experiment with a Decentralised Planning Model. This Model was supposedly trying to link the Central Planning Authority with the grass-root units, consisting mostly of Party Cadets, and the intermediate bodies comprising expert representatives of agriculture, industry, trade and commerce. However, the experiment did not get any chance for its implementation because of the Janata Government's collapse towards the end of 1979.

---

[39]The 20-point programme included measures to bring down prices of essential commodities, promote austerity in government spending, crack down on bonded labour, impose ceilings on ownership and possession of vacant land, acquire excess land and distribute among rural poor, liquidate rural indebtedness and make laws for a moratorium on recovery of debt from landless labourers, small farmers and artisans.

[40]The declaration of a State of Emergency by Mrs. Gandhi on 26 June 1975 and later on its lifting for elections in March 1977 are believed to have paved the way for the Janata government—the first non-Congress government at the Centre. Morarji Desai was its Prime Minister until he resigned on 15 July 1979. Afterwards, Janata(S), formed by Raj Narain in early July 1979 and claimed to be a secular party, formed the government with Charan Singh as its Prime Minister sworn in on 28 July 1979.

[41]This policy under the Morarji Desai government with George Fernandes as its industry minister led to the exit of high-profile MNCs like Coca-Cola and IBM from India in 1977.

2.4 Major Structural Changes of the Indian Economy (1951–1980)

One of the major structural changes during 1951–1980 was in the composition of output (see Table 2.2). Although *agriculture* continued to be the major production sector, its share in gross domestic product (GDP) declined from an average of 59.0% during 1951–1956 to 38.8% in 1979–1980. The share of *industry* (manufacturing, mining and construction) increased from an average of 14.7–22.4% during the same period, while that of infrastructure (electricity, gas, water supply, transport, storage and communication) rose from an average of 4.0–8.4%. The remaining components (trade, hotels and restaurants, financing, insurance, real estate, business and other services) of GDP increased from an average of 22.3–30.4% over the same period.

There had also been major changes in *industrial structure* and *industrial organization*. As to the former one, there had been a shift in production from traditional agro-based industries to chemicals and engineering industries. During the period from 1956 to 1980, the production weight of food decreased from 15.7 to 8.9%, while that of textiles decreased drastically from 47.0 to 19.7%. During the

Table 2.2 Composition of India's gross domestic product (1951–1980) (at 1970–1971 prices) (per cent)

Plan period	Agriculture and allied sectors	Manufacturing and construction, mining and quarrying	Electricity, gas, water supply, transport, storage and communication	Others	Total
First Plan (1951–1956)	59.0	14.7	4.0	22.3	100.0
Second Plan (1956–1961)	55.5	16.8	4.6	23.1	100.0
Third Plan (1961–1966)	49.5	20.1	5.5	24.9	100.0
Annual Plans (1966–1969)	46.0	21.4	6.3	26.3	100.0
Fourth Plan (1969–1974)	45.9	21.1	6.5	26.5	100.0
Fifth Plan (1974–1979)	43.3	21.4	7.5	27.8	100.0
1979–1980	38.8	22.4	8.4	30.4	100.0

Source: Averages for Plan periods are computed from annual data published in *National Accounts Statistics* (*Central Statistical Organisation*, Government of India). Adapted from RBI (1985, Table 2)

Table 2.3 Composition of India's industrial structure (1956–1980) (Sectoral weights (%))

Manufacturing sector	1956	1960	1970	1980
Food	15.7	14.2	9.5	8.9
Textiles	47.0	31.9	21.5	19.7
Rubber, chemicals and petroleum	11.7	12.9	18.2	21.4
Non-metalic minerals	2.8	4.5	4.1	3.9
Basic metals and alloy industries	10.4	8.7	10.9	15.7
Engineering (manufacture of machine tools, parts and appliances)	8.3	19.7	25.9	23.9
Others	4.1	8.1	9.9	6.6
Total manufacturing[a]	100.0	100.0	100.0	100.0

[a]Total Manufacturing does not include miming, quarrying and electricity sectors of the Index of Industrial Production

Source: This table has been partly adapted from RBI (1985, Table 3). Figures for 1980 have been computed by the author from *Statistical Abstract India 1997*, CSO, Government of India (Vol. 1, Table 9.7, p. 166)

same period, the production weight of engineering industries increased rapidly from 8.3 to 23.9%, while that of rubber, chemicals and petroleum industries together increased from 11.7 to 21.4% (see Table 2.3).

There had also been a major transformation in the *industrial organization* with the growth and development of the *public sector*. The public sector had played a vital role in India's growth and development. The following statement in the document of the *Second Five-Year Plan: Summary* (1956, pp. 10–11) clearly outlines the role of the public sector in India's planned economic development and its implications for the role of private sector:

> For creating the "socialistic pattern of society" the State has to take on heavy responsibilities. The public sector has to expand rapidly. It has to play a dominant role in shaping the entire pattern of investments– both private and public– in the economy and has to initiate developments which the private sector is unwilling or unable to undertake. The responsibility for new developments in certain major lines of activity which require the use of modern technology, large-scale production and a unified control and allocation of resources must be undertaken in the main by the State. Public ownership, partial or complete, and public control or participation in management are specially required in those fields in which technological considerations tend towards a concentration of economic power and of wealth. Private enterprise has to play its part within the framework of the overall plan. In a growing economy there is scope both for public and private sectors to expand simultaneously, but if development is to proceed at the pace envisaged and is to contribute effectively to the larger social ends in view, it is inevitable that the public sector must grow not only absolutely but also relatively to the private sector.

The public sector did, indeed, grow rapidly, and reached commanding heights in the economy in 1980 by contributing nearly one-fourth of gross domestic product (GDP) and nearly one-half of gross domestic capital formation (GDCF). This is evident from Table 2.4 that average share of the public sector in GDP increased from

Table 2.4 Share of public sector in GDP and GDCF (1951–1980)

Plan period	% Average share of public sector in	
	Gross domestic product (GDP) (at factor cost)	Gross domestic capital formation (GDCF)
First Plan (1951–1956)	8.5	14.3
Second Plan (1956–1961)	9.3	21.9
Third Plan (1961–1966)	11.5	32.3
Annual Plans (1966–1969)	13.9	35.3
Fourth Plan (1969–1974)	16.0	39.4
Fifth Plan (1974–1979)	18.9	46.3
1979–1980	22.6	47.7

Source: RBI (1985, Table 7) has computed the figures from annual data published in various issues of *National Accounts Statistics* (Central Statistical Organisation, Government of India)

8.5% during the First Five-Year Plan (1951–1956) to 22.6% in 1979–1980,[42] while its corresponding share in the economy's GDCF increased from 14.3 to 47.7%. Even though the *public sector* had grown steadily, it by no means dominated the total economy. By 1980, the economy was predominantly a mixed one with the *household sector* or the *unorganised segment* contributing as high as about 70% of GDP; out of 30% share of the *organised segment*, the *public sector* contributing about 22.6% and the corporate (domestic and foreign) *private sector* contributing the residual of roughly 7.4% of domestic income.[43]

The corporate private sector, particularly its private industrial sector, had expanded in absolute terms under the government's protection from both *internal* competition (through industrial licensing policies) and *external* competition (through rigorous import trade control). The private-sector industrial units, particularly the major ones, had also benefitted from the government's liberal policy of financing their capital expenditures in both local currency and foreign exchange requirements at a very low interest rates through government's various term-lending institutions, such as the Industrial Development Bank of India (IDBI), Industrial Finance Corporation (IFC) and Industrial Credit and Investment Corporation (ICIC). Instead of investing into planning-authority-declared socially high-priority areas, namely the

[42]In fact, the percentage share of the Public Sector in GDP increased up to a maximum of 27.3 in 1992–93 (*National Account Statistics of India: 1950–51 to 1995–96,* EPW Research Foundation, 1997, p. 45) and then gradually declined to 19.9 in 2007–08; subsequently, it remained within a range between 20 and 21% during 2008–2014 (*National Account Statistics 2014*, p. 67 and *National Account Statistics 2015*, p. xxxviii).

[43]The variation of domestic income measured in terms of GDP and NDP has been ignored for the sake of approximation.

Table 2.5 Performance under the Five-Year Plans during 1951–1990 (Per cent growth)

Plan period	National Income		Per capita income		Agricultural production		Industrial production	
	T	A	T	A	T	A	T	A
First Plan (1951–1956)	2.1	3.6	0.9	1.7	–	2.9	7.0	5.9
Second Plan (1956–1961)	4.5	3.9	3.3	1.9	–	3.2	10.2	6.4
Third Plan (1961–1966)	5.6	2.3	3.2	0.1	6.0	−0.5	10.7	6.8
Annual Plans (1966–1969)	5.0	3.7	N.A.	1.4	N.A.	6.2	N.A.	2.6
Fourth Plan (1969–1974)	5.7	3.3	–	0.9	5.0	2.6	7.1	3.7
Fifth Plan (1974–1979)	4.4	4.9	–	2.6	4.0	3.4	9.0	6.3
Sixth Plan (1980–1985)	5.2	5.4	3.5	3.2	3.8	5.5	6.9	6.2
Seventh Plan (1985–1990)	5.0	5.8	3.2	3.6	4.0	3.4	8.3	6.5

T Target, *A* Achievement

Source: Agrawal and Varma (1996, Table 19.1 based on various *Plan Documents* and *Economic Survey, 1993–94*)

core-sector and export-oriented industries, many private-sector industrial units, including some foreign-based ones units, had diversified investment into low-priority areas.[44] When both public and private sector results are pooled together, the overall performance of Indian Planning operation, particularly during the Second, Third and Fourth Plans and including three Annual Plans (1966–1969), had been poor. As can be seen from Table 2.5, although the shortfalls had been less pronounced in the achievements of the economy's specific targets in the Second Plan, these had further been deteriorated during the Third and Fourth Plans[45] before their improvement started marginally in the Fifth, Sixth and Seventh Plans until 1990.

---

[44]Several diversifications of investment into low-priority areas have been cited in Wadhva (1977, p. 146). For example, the Sarabhai Group (an Indian group—family based), which had traditionally been operating in the textiles field had diversified into radio business. Delhi Cloth Mills (DCM) (an Indian company—family based) had diversified into the production of electronic desk calculators and PVC plastics. Among the foreign-based multinational companies operating in India who had diversified into low low-priority fields of business were Hindustan Levers, ITC Limited (Principals: Imperial Tobacco Company) and Union Carbide. Hindustan Levers which had traditionally been operating in soap, clear butter (ghee) (prepared from edible vegetable oil) and baby foods business had planned to diversify into Sodium Tripolyphosphate and related raw materials required for the production of detergents. ITC (formerly, the Indian Tobacco Company) had diversified into hotel industry. Union Carbide which had been operating in the dry cells industry had diversified into deep-sea fishing. It is interesting to note that India's Central Bureau of Investigation (CBI) and Enforcement Directorate (ED) have been currently looking into whether Vijay Mallya, a beleaguered liquor baron, had used a part of the IDBI Bank loan given to his now-grounded Kingfisher Airlines for buying a racehorse that cost Rs. 9 crore (*The Economic Times*, 27 April 2016).

[45]India's slow rates of national income growth (around an average of 3.5%) in the earlier three decades since 1950 were coined as 'Hindu rate of growth' by the Indian economist Raj Krishna while referring to the results of the Congress Party's socialistic economic policies in India. In fact, Raj Krishna was the Deputy Chairman of the Planning Commission under the first non-Congress government at the Centre.

2.4.1 Implications for the Unorganised Segment

The public sector absorbed a high proportion of labour in tertiary activities, namely transport, storage and communication, as well as community, social and personal services, while the private sector did the same in manufacturing activities (Table 2.6). Employment in public sector's tertiary activities increased from 5.45 million in 1961 to 9.88 million in 1981, while that in private sector's manufacturing activities increased from 3.02 million to 4.42 million during the same period. But, the total employment level in the organised segment not only remained very small (as percentage of total labour force), but also increased at a snail's pace compared to the total labour force during 1961–80. As can be seen from Table 2.7, employment

Table 2.6 Employment in the organised segment (public and private sectors): 1961–1980 (Figures in lakh)

Industry division brief description	Employment in public sector (as at the end of March)				Employment in private sector[a] (as at the end of March)			
	1961	1971	1979	1980	1961	1971	1979	1980
Agriculture, hunting, etc.	1.80	2.76	4.08	4.31	6.70	7.98	8.41	8.60
Mining and quarrying	1.29	1.82	7.71[b]	7.97	5.50	4.04	1.24[c]	1.25
Manufacturing	3.69	8.06	14.16	14.46	30.20	39.55	44.33	44.17
Electricity, gas, water, etc.	2.24	4.35	6.34	6.61	0.40	0.46	0.34	0.34
Construction	6.03	8.80	10.32	10.68	2.40	1.39	0.83	0.73
Wholesale and retail trade etc.	0.94	3.28	0.99	1.10	1.60	3.04	2.81	2.74
Transport, storage and communication	17.24	22.17	25.97	26.51	0.80	0.96	0.71	0.71
Financing, insurance, real estate, etc.	–	–	6.47	6.91	–	–	2.01	2.06
Community, social and personal services	37.27	56.07	70.71	72.24	2.80	10.00	11.40	11.67
Total	**70.50**	**107.31**	**150.45**	**150.78**	**50.40**	**67.42**	**72.08**	**72.27**

[a]For March 1961, the data relate to non-agricultural establishments in *organised* private sector employing 25 or more persons. Since March 1966, the coverage has been extended so as to include establishments employing 10 or more persons

[b, c]The rise (fall) in employment in the public (private) sector from March 1972 onwards was mainly due to nationalisation of coking coal mines by the government and the consequent shift of employment from the private to the public sector

Source: Employment figures for 1961 and 1971 are from *Economic Survey 1981–82* (Tables 3.1 and 3.2, pp. 108–109); the same figures for 1979 and 1980 are from *Economic Survey 1982–83* (Tables 3.1 and 3.2, pp. 114–115)

Table 2.7 Selected decadal key indicators (1950–1951 to 1990–1991)

Item	Unit	1950–51	1960–61	1970–71	1980–81	1990–91
Population	Million	361	439	548	685[a]	846
Population growth rate	Per cent	1.26	1.93	2.24	2.28	2.14
Labour force	Million	140.79	188.77	186.32	253.45	321.48
Labour force as a proportion of population	Per cent	39	43	34	37	38
Employment in the organised segment (Public + Private)[b]	Million	N.A.	12.09	17.47	22.31	26.35
Employment in the organised segment (as a proportion of total labour force)	Per cent	N.A.	6.40	9.38	8.80	8.20
National Income (at 1980–1981 prices)	Rs. Crores[c]	40,454	58,602	82,211	1,10,685	1,84,460
Per capita income (at 1980–1981 prices)	Rupees	1,127	1,350	1,520	1,630	2,197
Per capita private consumption expenditure (at 1980–1981 prices)	Rupees	1,006	1,193	1,322	1,462	1,860
Gross domestic saving as per cent GDP		10	13	16	21	24
Rate of investment[d]	Per cent	10	16	17	23	27
Share of public sector in GDP (at 1980–1981 prices)	Per cent	N.A.	9.4	12.7	19.7	26.2
Share of agriculture in GDP (at 1980–1981 prices)	Per cent	56.5	52.1	45.8	39.6	33.1
Index number of agricultural productivity (1967–1970 = 100)		77.1	94.2	107.9	122.7	174.7
Index number of agricultural production (1967–1970 = 100)		58.5	86.7	111.5	135.3	192.2
Index number of industrial production (1980–1981 = 100)		18.3	36.2	65.3	100.0	212.6
Index number of wholesale prices (1981–1982 = 100)		17	20	35	91	183

[a]Includes projected figure of Assam
[b]These employment figures (except for 1990–1991) have been taken from Table 2.6 and converted into million
(1 million = 10 lakhs). The employment figure for 1990–1991 has been taken from Dutta (2004, Table 11.2)
[c]Rs. 1 Crore = Rs. 10 million
[d]Gross domestic capital formation (GDCF) as percentage of GDP at current prices
Source: Agrawal and Varma (1996, pp. 15 and 75)

in the organised segment had been only 6.40%, 9.38% and 8.80% of the total labour force in 1960–1961, 1970–1971 and 1980–1981, respectively. This implies that the unorganised segment had to carry the liability of employing more than 90% of the total labour force mostly as self-employed households and casual labours.

The very slow trends in the organised segment's growth and employment shown above clearly indicate why *structural dualism*[46] persisted even after three decades of so-called planned economic development. The entire framework of government controls and regulations gradually reflected 'the inadequacies of the licensing authorities and other administrative authorities concerned with implementation of controls. … The same [was] the case with the working of promotional agencies such as the term-lending institutions'.[47]

2.5 Two Major Socio-Economic Consequences of Structural Dualism (1960–80)

Two major socio-economic consequences of structural dualism often highlighted by the economists and other social scientists are (i) industrial deceleration and (ii) widening development disparity among the Indian States during 1960s and 1970s.

2.5.1 Industrial Deceleration (1966–79)

Due to various external and domestic economic and political factors,[48] experienced during 1966–1979 of the Phase II (1965–1979), industrial growth, in general, had been slow as compared to the last 6 years of the previous Phase I. Ahluwalia (1983) had noted two major trends as shown in Table 2.8: (i) industrial sector as a whole experienced a decline in the growth rate per annum of both *value-added* (from 8.0 to 5.7%) and *value-of-output* (from 8.8 to 6.5% per annum) figures; (ii) most of this deceleration was concentrated in non-consumer goods and particularly on basic goods and capital goods (if *use-based classification* is followed), and specifically, the metal-based industries (if *input-based classification* is followed). Various explanations are put forward for the underlying reasons for the above industrial deceleration:

> These explanations, some mutually reinforcing, others mutually conflicting, have highlighted the following set of factors: poor agricultural performance despite the Green Revolution, relative price movements resulting in a shift in terms of trade against industry, unequal income distribution and resulting lack of demand, slowdown in import substitution, declining levels of public investment and increasing inefficiencies in the industrial structure resulting from governmental controls and policies.[49]

---

[46]The phrase 'structural dualism' is here used as a short form of 'structural-functional dualism'.

[47]Wadhva (*Ibid.*, p. 147).

[48]Various explanations of the underlying reasons for industrial stagnation during 1966–1979 have been summarised in Varshney (1984).

[49]Elaborated explanations of these factors can be found in Varshney (1984).

Table 2.8 India's industrial growth rates: 1959–1960 to 1978–1979 (Per cent Per annum)

	Value added		Value of output	
	1959–1960 to 1965–1966	1966–1967 to 1978–1979	1959–1960 to 1965–1966	1966–1967 to 1978–1979
(A) Use-based classification				
Total	8.0	5.7	8.8	6.5
(1) Basic goods	11.0	6.0	12.2	7.2
(2) Intermediate goods	5.7	4.4	9.4	6.1
(3) Capital goods	15.4	6.8	15.8	7.3
(4) Consumers goods	4.7	5.6	5.9	6.2
(a) Durables	11.5	11.5	12.3	12.6
(b) Non-durables	4.2	4.9	5.7	5.7
(B) Input-based classification				
(1) Agro-based	3.7	4.1	5.9	5.1
(2) Metal-based	14.1	6.6	14.6	7.1
(3) Chemical-based	8.2	8.4	11.3	11.2

Source: Ahluwalia (1983)

It is often argued that the above industrial deceleration of all industry-groups except the consumer goods (durable and non-durable such as electrical goods, cars, and motor cycles.) was the result of rising inequality in consumer expenditure towards the late 1970s. As can be seen from Table 2.9, percentage share in consumer expenditure of the middle 40% of rural households had increased from 33.7 to 35.3, while that of the top 30% of urban households increased from 54.3 to 55.4 during the period from 1972–73 to 1977–1978. Both inequalities did, however, reverse during the early 1980s. The same trend can alternatively be evident from Table 2.10 which shows that inequality in consumer expenditure sharply increased in both rural area as a whole (with Gini coefficient increasing from 0.27 in 1973–1974 to 0.336 in 1977–1978) and urban area as a whole (with Gini coefficient increasing from 0.30 to 0.355 during the same period) before they reversed in 1983. Of the two types of consumer goods, durable and non-durable, the very high double-digit growth rates of consumer durables compared to relatively low single-digit growth rates of consumer non-durables during 1959–1979 (Table 2.8) (sectoral disarticulation) thus testify the fact that the impact of underlying inequitable income distribution between the rich and the poor in both rural and urban areas had certainly some bearing on the deceleration of the overall industrial growth through the demand factor (social disarticulation).

Table 2.9 Distribution of household by consumer expenditure (%)

Year	Rural			Urban		
	Bottom 30%	Middle 40%	Top 30%	Bottom 30%	Middle 40%	Top 30%
1961–1962	14.7	33.2	52.1	12.9	31.4	55.7
1965–1966	15.1	34.3	50.6	13.6	31.9	54.7
1970–1971	15.4	35.1	49.5	13.7	31.8	54.5
1972–1973	15.4	33.7	50.9	13.8	31.9	54.3
1977–1978	14.3	35.3	50.4	13.4	31.2	55.4
1983	15.2	33.9	50.9	13.9	32.8	53.3

Source: Agrawal and Varma (1996, Table 4.12 based on Sixth Five-Year Plan 1980–1985 and NSS Report No. 319)

2.5.2 *Widening Development Disparity among the States (1960–1980)*

Part XI of the Constitution of India defines the division of function-areas[50] and financial powers between the federal government (the Centre) and the State governments in India. *Vertical* and *horizontal* imbalances are, however, common features of most federations including India. *Vertical* imbalances result when the States face shortage of financial resources raised from the sources assigned to them. *Horizontal* imbalances result across States due to factors including historical backgrounds, differential endowment of resources, and capacity to raise financial resources. Unlike most other federations, differences in the developmental levels in Indian States are very acute. In an explicit recognition of *vertical* and *horizontal* imbalances, the Indian Constitution embodies various enabling and mandatory provisions to address them through the transfer of resources from the Centre to the States under the category of tax-sharing (Articles 268 & 269), statutory grants-in-aid (Articles 275) and other grants and loans for any public purpose (Articles 282 & 293). Total transfers from the centre to the States as a percentage of a state's total expenditure increased from 42.7 in the First Plan to 53.9 during the Annual Plans, but then declined to 42.1 in the Fifth Plan before slightly increasing

[50]In the seventh schedule of the Constitution of India, there are three lists: Union List, State List and Concurrent List. The Union List consists of 97 areas (original) assigned to the Central government (such as defence, foreign affairs, communications, currency and coinage, and banking and insurance.). The state legislatures have exclusive authority to make laws in relation to 66 items (original) listed in the State List (such as police, public health, land, roads and bridges, agriculture and irrigation, forest and fisheries, and trade and industry.). In addition, there was a Concurrent List of 47 items (original) of common interest such as education, planning and social security, labour welfare, industrial disputes, electricity and newspapers for which the Parliament and state legislatures can both make laws. In fact, education has been transferred from the state to the *concurrent list* by the 42nd amendment to the Constitution of India in November 1976 during the State of Emergency declared by the then Prime Minister Indira Gandhi.

Table 2.10 Inequality in consumer expenditure: 1960–1961 to 1983 (Gini coefficient)

Year	Rural	Urban
1960–1961	0.32	0.34
1965–1966	0.29	0.33
1970–1971	0.28	0.33
1973–1974	0.27	0.30
1977–1978	0.336	0.355
1983	0.297	0.325

Source: Agrawal and Varma (1996, Table 4. based on NSS Reports)

to 44.8 in 1979–1980 (revised). The States' fiscal dependence had thus remained in a narrow range between 42.1% and 53.9% of their total expenditures during 1951–80 (Table 2.11). It is also noteworthy that percentages of grants had been relatively stable within a narrow range throughout the period from 1951 to 1980. However, loans had constituted a significant part of the total transfers to the States and remained within a high range between 49.2% and 55.9% in the earlier Plans during 1951–1969, when their share in taxes had increasingly fallen. This early trend had certainly placed an unduly large burden on the States because it had accentuated their indebtedness.

Until very recently, two commissions—the *Planning Commission*[51] and the *Finance Commission*—were responsible for transfers of financial resources from the Centre to the States and Union Territories. One of their major goals in allocating central assistance to the States was balanced regional development. Both these *Commissions* had been the arenas in which interstate disputes over the allocation of resources used to be resolved by the use of formulas. While the *Finance Commission* operates through a more automatic, formula-based transfer mechanism, the Planning Commission had some limited option to allocate resources through discretionary loans and grants. For example, the prevailing method of allocating assistance to the states used by the *Planning Commission* was the so-called Gadgil Formula,[52] which provided for only 10% of 'central assistance to the states' in the Plans to be distributed according to backwardness.[53] As can be

[51]The *Planning Commission* has been replaced by the *National Institution for Transforming India* (NITI) Aayog (Commission) on 1 January 2015. The new body's acronym-based name 'NITI Aayog' means 'Policy Commission'.

[52]This had been noted in the *Sixth Five Year Plan: 1978–83—Draft* (p. 110). When the original Gadgil Formula for the distribution of central assistance for State Plans was approved by the National Development Council in September 1968, it was agreed that the requirements of Assam, Jammu and Kashmir and Nagaland should first be met out of the total pool of central assistance. The Gadgil Formula was first applied for the Fourth Plan (1969–1974). When the Fifth Plan was formulated, this list was extended to include Himachal Pradesh, Manipur, Meghalaya, Sikkim and Tripura, making eight states in all. It is only since 1980 that the share of special category states was predetermined at 30 per cent. In 1990, the number of special category states was increased to 10 with the inclusion of Arunachal Pradesh and Mizoram (WG-SFR 2012, p. 17).

[53]Brass (1982, pp. 233–34).

Table 2.11 Transfer of resources from the centre to the states through different sources (Rs. Crores)

Plan and period	Share in Taxes	Grants	Loans	Total Transfers	Total Expenditures of State Governments	(4) as Percentage of (5)
	(1)	(2)	(3)	(4)	(5)	(6)
First Plan (1951–1956)	344 (24.0)	288 (20.1)	799 (55.9)	1,431 (100)	3,352	42.7
Second Plan (1956–1961)	668 (23.3)	789 (27.5)	1,411 (49.2)	2,868 (100)	5,846	49.1
Third Plan (1961–1966)	1,196 (21.4)	1,304 (23.3)	3,100 (55.3)	5,600 (100)	10,720	52.2
Annual Plans (1966–1969)	1,282 (24.0)	1,389 (26.0)	2,676 (50.0)	5,347 (100)	9,912	53.9
Fourth Plan (1969–1974)	4,562 (30.0)	3,831 (25.4)	6,708 (44.4)	15,101 (100)	28,551	52.9
Fifth Plan (1974–1979)[a]	8,337 (33.0)	8,135 (32.2)	8,810 (34.8)	25,282 (100)	60,081	42.1
1979–1980 (Revised)	3,346 (40.8)	2,254 (27.5)	2,593 (31.6)	8,193 (100)	18,272	44.8

Notes: (i) This table has been adapted from Bhargava (1984, Table 1) and (ii) Figures in parentheses are percentages of total

[a]The Fifth Five-Year Plan in fact terminated one year earlier on 31 March, 1978

seen from Table 2.12, there had been a long-term shift in the sources of funds transferred from the centre to the States through two Commissions. The Planning Commission distributed a higher percentage of the total resources transferred to the States prior to the Fourth Plan, but afterwards, the Finance Commission had a relatively greater part in distributing the resources to the States during 1969–1980.

In 1979, the Planning Commission, however, adopted the IATP (income adjusted total population) formula for a substantial part of plan assistance and utilised discretionary assistance for the benefit of the poorer states. And, the 1980 modification of the Gadgil formula has also assisted these states. A bias in favour of the relatively 'backward' states was a welcome development. However, an examination of the per capita expenditure on centrally sponsored projects on a state-by-state basis during 1974–1978 shows that the relatively developed states have already benefited more.[54] This can be evident from Table 2.13 which underlines the large area of disparities which exited in both 1960–1961 and 1979–1980 for all States. In 1960–1961, when the Indian development process had just gathered momentum, several States' per capita incomes were below the All-India average of Rs. 306 (measured at current prices).

Among the States, Manipur had the lowest per capita income (Rs. 154) followed by Bihar (Rs. 215), Orissa (Rs. 216), Kerala (Rs. 259), Madhya Pradesh (Rs. 260),

[54]Bhargava (1984, p. 684).

Table 2.12 Transfer of resources from the centre to the states through different sources (Rs. crores)

Plan and period	Finance commission	Planning commission	Other transfers	Total
First Plan (1951–1956)	447 (31.2)	880 (61.5)	104 (7.3)	1,431 (100.0)
Second Plan (1956–1961)	918 (32.0)	1,344 (46.9)	606 (21.1)	2,868 (100.0)
Third Plan (1961–1966)	1,590 (28.4)	2,738 (48.9)	1,272 (22.7)	5,600 (100.0)
Annual Plans (1966–1969)	1,782 (33.3)	1,917 (35.9)	1,648 (30.8)	5,347 (100.0)
Fourth Plan (1969–1974)	5,421 (35.9)	4,731 (31.3)	4,949 (32.8)	15,101 (100.0)
Fifth Plan (1974–1979)[a]	11,168 (44.2)	10,353 (40.9)	3,761 (14.9)	25,282 (100.0)
1979–1980 (Revised)	3,888 (47.5)	3,408 (41.6)	897 (10.9)	8,193 (100.0)

Notes: (i) This table has been adapted from Bhargava (1984, Table 2) and (ii) Figures in parentheses are percentages of total
[a]The Fifth Five-Year Plan in fact terminated one year earlier on 31 March, 1978

and a number of other States. Maharashtra was at the top (Rs. 409) followed by West Bengal (Rs. 390), Punjab (Rs. 366), Gujarat (Rs. 362), Himachal Pradesh (Rs. 359), and Tamil Nadu (334). These figures were all in current prices. Translated into indices (with All-India Average Per Capita Income = 100), the ranking of the States remained very much the same. But, these initial rankings of 1960–1961 had, however, changed over the successive periods to 1979–1980. Excluding smaller States and Union Territories, the range of disparity between the highest and the lowest indices has also grown steadily—from 63.4 in 1960–1961 to 112.7 in 1979–1980. It is often argued that due to ‘a significant element of innate dynamism present in Punjab, Haryana, Gujarat and Maharashtra’, these Northern States had experienced faster progress in per capita income. The progress in four Southern States—Andhra Pradesh, Karnataka, Kerala and Tamil Nadu—had been comparatively stable, although Tamil Nadu had faced a sharp decline between 1960–1961 and 1965–1966. The so-called North–South regional disparity in terms of these eight States’ indices used to be often noted in the political debate on unequal development. Among the remaining States, Bihar, Orissa, Uttar Pradesh and Madhya Pradesh had suffered a moderate decline, although the former pair had started with low indices and the latter pair had started with relatively higher indices.

Two States in the Eastern part of India—Assam and West Bengal—had lost ground moving down from 102.9 to 82.3 and from 127.5 to 101.1, respectively during the period from 1960–1961 to 1979–1980, although Assam had recovered a bit during 1978–1980. This moderate/sharp decline in the States of the Eastern part of India (including some of the new Eastern States) compared to the rest of India

Table 2.13 Widening disparity among the Indian States: 1960–1961 to 1979–1980

State/Union Territory	Estimates of per capita net state domestic product (= State income) (at current prices)				Index with national (= All-India) Average per capita income = 100			
	1960–1961	1970–1971	1975–1976	1979–1980	1960–1961	1970–1971	1975–1976	1979–1980
A. States								
1. Andhra Pradesh	275	586	895	1136	89.9	92.6	87.4	89.4
2. Assam	315	539	789	1083	102.9	85.2	77.1	82.3
3. Bihar	215	402	661	795	70.3	63.5	64.6	60.4
4. Gujarat	362	829	1239	1658	118.3	131.0	121.0	126.0
5. Haryana	327	870	1333	1867	106.9	137.4	130.2	141.9
6. Himachal Pradesh	359	678	1078	1288	117.3	107.1	100.3	97.9
7. Jammu & Kashmir	269	548	928	1254	87.1	86.6	90.6	95.3
8. Karnataka	296	685	1005	1246	96.7	108.2	98.1	94.7
9. Kerala	259	557	892	–	84.6	88.0	87.1	–
10. Madhya Pradesh	260	484	781	877	85.0	76.5	76.3	66.6
11. Maharashtra	409	784	1385	2021	133.7	123.9	135.3	153.0
12. Manipur	154	396	807	822	50.3	62.6	78.8	62.5
13. Meghalaya	–	–	–	–	–	–	–	–
14. Orissa	216	482	715	843	70.6	76.1	69.8	64.1
15. Punjab	366	1030	1597	2278	119.6	162.7	156.0	173.1
16. Rajasthan	284	620	857	1011	92.8	97.9	83.7	76.8
17. Tamil Nadu	334	581	839	1274	109.2	91.8	81.9	96.8
18. Tripura	249	502	813	–	81.4	79.3	79.4	–
19. Uttar Pradesh	252	486	730	994	82.4	76.8	71.3	75.5
20. West Bengal	390	735	1120	1330	127.5	116.1	109.4	101.1
B. Union Territories (UTs)								
1. Delhi	668	1186	2018	2498	218.3	187.4	197.1	189.8
2. Goa, Daman & Diu	–	916	1615	2426	–	144.7	157.7	184.3
3. Pondicherry	–	844	1593	2747	–	133.3	155.6	208.7
All-India (Per capita net national product at factor cost)	**306**	**633**	**1024**	**1316**	**100.0**	**100.0**	**100.0**	**100.0**
Maximum disparity (Range)								
Excluding Smaller States & UTs	194	628	936	1483	63.4	99.2	91.4	112.7
Including Smaller States & UTs	514	790	1357	1952	168.0	124.8	132.5	148.3

Source: IIPO (1982, Table III, p. 16)

seemed to have an irreversible path dependence effect in the coming years, unless sufficient economic and political measures are taken to counter this disparity. It is also noteworthy that high population density in the States of Uttar Pradesh, Bihar, Madhya Pradesh and West Bengal is an additional contributing factor for disparity.

Chapter 3
Economic Liberalisation and Structural Dualism (1980–2017)

3.1 Introduction

The first non-Congress, Janata Government came to power at the Centre for about two and a half years of duration in late 1970s (1977–79).[1] In spite of successive bumper harvests, huge food stocks, and large foreign exchange reserves, the Janata Government was not able to give the required push to the economy in order to make some major dent in poverty and unemployment. Its liberal economic policy essentially strengthened the elite group of big and small business groups as well as the rich peasantry at the expense of the socially deprived and depressed sections of urban workers and the landless labour in particular.[2]

Although the Sixth Five-Year Plan (1980–85) was originally scheduled by the Janata Government for the period of 1978–83, but it was actually launched after Indira Gandhi came back to power as Prime Minister in January 1980. 'New Industrial Growth with Direct Measures for Poverty Eradications' was the development strategy of this Plan.

According to one of the Directive Principles of State Policy in the Indian Constitution:

> (The) State will promote with special care the educational and economic interests of weaker sections of the people, and in particular, of the scheduled castes and scheduled tribes and shall protect them from social injustice and all forms of exploitation.[3]

---

[1]Prime Minister Morarji Desai ruled from March 1977 to 15 July 1979. Later on, due to factional dispute within the Janata coalition, Charan Singh became prime minister on 18 July 1979 with the support of his former political enemy, Indira Gandhi, who had imprisoned him during the state of emergency of 1975–77. Within less than a month, Mrs. Gandhi withdrew her support to Singh's government, and he thenceforth headed a caretaker government until Mrs. Gandhi was returned to power in the elections of January 1980.
[2]Dutta (1989, Footnote 4, p. 130).
[3]The Sixth Five-Year Plan (1980–85, p. 417).

D. Dutta, *Development under Dualism and Digital Divide in Twenty-First Century India*, Dynamics of Asian Development, https://doi.org/10.1007/978-981-10-6344-2_3

However, the Sixth Five-Year Plan (1980–85, p. 417) claimed that the Directive had been reflected in the Five-Year Plans which had sought to raise the socio-economic levels of all the people including the weaker sections, but it acknowledged that:

> … three decades of development have not had the desired impact of these socially, economically and educationally handicapped groups.

Ironically, it also blames the poor:

> Continuing to pursue traditional occupations, they are unable to avail of the fruits of economic growth and participate fully in the process of modernization.

Hence, the Sixth Five-Year Plan felt the urgent necessity to stress special emphasis on measures to solve poverty by direct measures. The major direct measures for poverty eradications during the Sixth Plan (1980–85) were: *Integrated Rural Development Programme* (IRDP), *National Rural Employment Programme* (NREP) and *Rural Landless Employment Guarantee Programme* (RLEGP). Although IRDP was launched in 1978, it extended throughout India by 1980. The NREP was launched in October 1980 and became a regular Plan programme from April 1981. The RLEGP, being introduced on 15 August 1983, soon became a popular direct measure financed by the Central Government and implemented by the States and Union Territories.

3.2 Policy Changes during Pre- and Post-Comprehensive Liberalisation in India

For analytical purposes, India's experiences with economic liberalisation and its effects on economic development will be divided into additional three phases:

Phase III: Policy changes *towards* liberalisation in India (1980–90);
Phase IV: Policy changes *towards* comprehensive liberalisation (1991–2004); and
Phase V: Policy initiatives *under* comprehensive liberalisation (2005–17).

3.2.1 Phase III: Policy Changes towards Liberalisation (1980–90)

Just before the Sixth Five-Year Plan document was published, a new *Industrial Policy Statement* was issued by Mrs. Gandhi's government in July 1980. In fact, this *Statement* was a special effort to stimulate and accelerate industrial growth against the background of India's slower growth/stagnation in the industrial sphere during the late sixties and the seventies. The *Statement* emphasised the necessity of 'a set of pragmatic policies which will remove the lingering constraints to industrial production and, at the same time, act as catalyst for faster growth in coming decades'.[4] Although no special designation was given to the 'directional changes' that the *Statement* was pushing forward, in retrospect, the shift was in favour of 'liberalisation' and 'export promotion'—two thrusts of industrial policy. After the assassination of Prime Minister Indira Gandhi on 31 October 1984, Rajiv Gandhi immediately assumed power as Prime Minister and ruled until 2 December 1989. This Government explicitly recognised the relevance of the two thrusts of Mrs. Gandhi's industrial policy.

During the regime of the Rajiv Gandhi's government, a number of steps were, however, taken to reform the overall industrial policy in such a way that it could become more conducive to the promotion of competition, modernisation and cost efficiency. The reform measures had three basic objectives, namely to facilitate capacity creation, to facilitate output expansion and to remove procedural impediments.[5] Support for these policy reforms is also reflected in the underlying development strategy of the Seventh Five-Year Plan (1985–90)—'Industrial Growth and Liberalisation'.

Some of the major industrial policy changes that resulted from the *New Industrial Policy Initiatives* were: delicensing of a wide range of industries, expansion of asset ceiling of the big monopoly houses and the MRTP companies,[6] liberalisation of depreciation provisions, reduction in both corporate and personal tax rates, drastic import liberalisation, extension of *broad-banding*[7] to a larger number of industries, elimination of many of the existing government controls, etc. The main objective of the industrial policy under the Rajiv Government was thus to encourage economic growth led by the private sector, with the public sector playing more and more of a subordinate role. In fact, the modernisation programme through technological rationalisation and managerial competence had been, since the independence, a very drastic one without any social cost consideration. As the Rajiv Government had complete faith in the 'trickle down' approach of economic growth and development, the direct programmes for poverty eradication of the previous Plan were no longer an important preoccupation of Rajiv Gandhi's regime in power from 31 October 1984 to 2 December 1989.

---

[4]Quoted from the *Industrial Policy Statement* made in the Parliament by the Minister of State for Industry on 23 July 1980.

[5]*Economic Survey: 1988–89*, pp. 46–48.

[6]After the *Monopolies and Restrictive Trade Practices* (MRTP) Act was effective in June 1970, the firms with assets of Rs. 25 Crore or more were put under the obligation of taking permission from the government of India, and they were called MRTP companies. This upper limit of Rs. 25 Crore was known as MRTP limit. It was later relaxed to Rs. 50 crore in 1980, Rs. 100 Crore in 1985 and in 1991 this limit was removed. Now only companies having more than 25% market share are called Monopolies.

[7]The facility of *broad banding* is presumed to enable manufacturing enterprises to adjust their product mix in line with changing market conditions and also to facilitate better capacity utilisation.

According to *Economic Survey 1988–89*—the official annual report of the Government of India—industrial production during 1980–87 grew at a compound annual rate of 7.6% and during 1987–88 grew at 7.5% as against that of 4.2% per annum during 1971–80. There had been a number of infrastructural developments in the Indian capital market during the second half of the eighties.[8] In spite of the various positive developments on the industrial front, the regime started experiencing some disturbing trends since 1987–88. Besides the monsoon failures, there had been a substantial decline in industrial licences, especially for the backward areas, virtual stagnation of employment growth in the *organised* segment, the increasing incidence of industrial sickness, increasing foreign debt, etc. There had been evidence of a marked slowing down of the rate of growth of industrial production since the first quarter of the year of 1989–90. During the short period of about 18 months from December 1989 to June 1991, when two non-Congress governments[9] were in power, the liberalisation process was also slowed down.

3.2.2 Phase IV: Policy Changes towards Comprehensive Liberalisation (1991–2004)

After the assassination of Rajiv Gandhi on 21 May 1991, a minority Congress government of the Prime Minister P.V. Narasimha Rao came to power on 21 June 1991. Because India was in a state of near bankruptcy because its foreign exchange reserves were extraordinarily low, the Rao government hastily introduced the New Economic Policy (NEP) in early July 1991.

The Indian economy underwent substantial change under NEP and almost all areas of the economy have been gradually opened to both domestic and foreign private investment, import licensing restrictions on intermediates and capital goods have been virtually eliminated, tariffs have been significantly reduced, and full convertibility of foreign exchange earnings has been established for current account transactions. Financial markets have been liberalised to a greater extent, and international standards of regulation have been introduced in the financial sector. As a result of the general election in April 1996, the Congress government of

[8]The major examples of such developments include institutions including the *Stock Holding Corporation of India*, *Credit Rating Information Services of India Ltd.*, *Securities and Exchange Board of India*, new mutual funds subsidiaries of nationalised banks, new venture capital companies, venture capital funds.

[9]Of the two non-Congress governments, the first one was the *National Front government* (December 1989–November 1990) led by the Prime Minister V.P. Singh, and the second one was the *Janata Dal* (Samajwadi) government (November 1990–June 1991) of the Prime Minister Chandra Shekhar.

Narasimha Rao was replaced by a number of non-Congress governments,[10] but reforms process went on, although at a slower pace. After the government of Atal Behari Vajpayee's *National Democratic Alliance* (NDA) government was voted to power on 13 October 1999, economic reforms continued. The EXIM Policy announced in March 2001 completed the process of removal of Quantitative Restrictions (QRs) on Balance-of-Payment (BOP) grounds by dismantling restrictions on the remaining 715 items. A host of measures were adopted by the successive governments to further the reform process in general and liberalise the foreign direct investment (FDI) regime in particular as a part of the ongoing effort from 1991 onwards.

State-owned public sector enterprises (PSEs), initially established to enable the economy to achieve 'commanding heights', have been affected by the liberalisation programmes. In order to offer more functional autonomy to the PSEs and remove Government's interference in their management at the microlevel, 696 guidelines, issued for PSEs over the last three decades of the twentieth century, had been withdrawn. Although legal obstacles in the process of disinvestment had been resolved with the Supreme Court decision in the Bharat Aluminum Company Limited (BALCO) case in December 2001,[11] political obstacles to the disinvestment programme of PSEs had then resurfaced in relation to privatisation of Hindustan Petroleum Corp. Ltd. (HPCL) and Bharat Petroleum Corp. Ltd. (BPCL), and disinvestment through public offerings of 10–25% in Indian Oil Corporation (IOC), Oil and Natural Gas Corporation (ONGC), Gas Authority of India Ltd. (GAIL), Bharat Sanchar Nigam Ltd. (BSNL) and National Thermal Power Corp. Ltd. (NTPC). The Cabinet Committee on Disinvestment (CCD) therefore put aside all decisions on privatisation and disinvestment until December 2002.[12]

On 9 December 2002, the Vajpayee's NDA Government gave a clear direction of privatisation policy by announcing that 'the main objective of disinvestment would be to put national resources and assets to optimal use and in particular to unleash the productive potential inherent in our public sector enterprises'.[13] In order to improve competition as a tool for disciplining firms, fostering allocative

---

[10]Firstly, Atal Behari Vajpayee's Hindu Nationalist *Bharatiya Janata Party* (BJP) was voted to power as a caretaker government in May 1996 for only two weeks (16 May–1 June 1996). H.D. Deve Gowda's *United Front* coalition government of 13 parties came in power in June 1996, which lasted until April 1997. Then I.J. Gujral's *United Front* coalition of 16 parties formed the government in April 1997. After its collapse in less than a year, Atal Behari Vajpayee's BJP government ruled from March 1998 to April 1999. After its collapse, it stayed as a caretaker government until Vajpayee's *National Democratic Alliance* (NDA) of a 23-party coalition founded in 1998 was voted to power on 13 October 1999.

[11]As a result of the disinvestment decision of 51% of Government held equity in BALCO on 2 March 2001 in favour of Sterlite Industries (India) Limited for Rs. 551.50 crore, three writ petitions were filed against this decision in the Delhi and Chattisgarh High Courts. These petitions were subsequently transferred to the Supreme Court, which in its order dated 10 December 2001, validated BALCO disinvestment and dismissed the petitions.

[12]*Anon* (2002).

[13]A summary of the disinvestment policy is available in *Economic Survey 2002–2003*, p. 150.

efficiency, and contain the distortions caused by monopoly power, the Competition Act 2002 had also been enacted in December 2002 in order to replace the *Monopolistic and Restrictive Trade Practice* (MRTP) Act.

3.2.3 Phase V: Policy Initiatives under Comprehensive Liberalisation (2005–16)

After the 2004 general election,[14] the *United Progressive Alliance* (UPA), a Congress-led coalition government led by Manmohan Sigh, came to power on 22 May 2004 with external support from the Left Front. The UPA government's overall policies focused on a common minimum programme were, therefore, generally perceived as 'centre-left'. A major development related to trade policy during the early years of the UPA-I government[15] was the operationalisation of the Special Economic Zone (SEZ) Act 2005. SEZ Act and SEZ Rules were notified on 10 February 2006 to give transparency and stability to the policy.[16] The main objectives of the SEZ Act were 'generation of additional economic activity, promotion of exports of goods and services, promotion of investment from domestic and foreign sources, creation of employment opportunities and development of infrastructure facilities'. Various incentives and facilities were offered to both units in SEZs for attracting investments into SEZs (including foreign investment) as well as for SEZ developers. Various issues relating to setting up of SEZs raised by various political parties were being addressed by the Empowered Group of Ministers. The SEZ Rules also provided for 'simplified procedures for development, operation and maintenance of the SEZ, setting up units in SEZs, single window clearance both relating to Central as well as State Governments for setting up of an SEZ and units in a SEZ, and simplified compliance procedures/documentation with emphasis on self-certification'. A Board of Approval had been constituted by Government exercising the powers conferred

[14]The Vajpayee government remained in power from 13 October 1999 to 22 May 2004 for less than a full 5-year term. In fact, the NDA called a general election in early 2004, 6 months ahead of schedule, based around the slogan 'India Shining' which presumed that the NDA government had made a rapid economic transformation of the country. The election result, however, turned out to be disaster for the NDA winning only 186 Parliamentary seats compared to 222 seats won by the UPA. According to some commentators, the NDA had failed to reach out to rural Indians, while others had pointed to its 'divisive' policy agenda as the reason.

[15]In fact, after the UPA government came back to power with Manmohan Singh as its Prime Minister in May 2004, it continued for the next two terms: UPA-I & UPA-II (May 2004–May 2014).

[16]Special Economic Zones (SEZs) India was one of the first in Asia to recognize the effectiveness of the Export Processing Zone (EPZ) model in promoting exports, with Asia's first EPZ set-up in Kandla in 1965. However, the EPZs were not able to emerge as effective instruments for export promotion on account of multiplicity of controls and clearances, absence of world-class infrastructure and an unstable fiscal regime (*Economic Survey 2006–07*, Box 6.6, p. 123).

under the SEZ Act. It was expected that these incentives and facilities would trigger a large flow of foreign and domestic investment in SEZs, in infrastructure and productive capacity, leading to generation of additional economic activity and creation of employment opportunities. However, a major concern had been expressed regarding acquisition of agricultural land for setting up SEZs. Even the State Governments had been 'advised that in land acquisition for SEZs, first priority should be for acquisition of waste and barren land and if necessary single crop agricultural land could be acquired for the SEZs'. If perforce a portion of double-cropped agricultural land had to be 'acquired to meet the minimum area requirements, especially for multi-product SEZ, the same should not exceed 10% of the total land required for the SEZ'.[17] But, the land acquisition issue has remained till today to be dealt with appropriately.

A comprehensive review of the FDI policy was also undertaken in 2006 in order to consolidate the ongoing liberalisation and further rationalise the FDI policy governing various activities. The major policy initiatives as summarised in *Economic Survey 2006–2007*, p. 154, were as follows:

(i) ***Change of route***: FDI has been allowed up to 100% under the automatic route for distillation and brewing of potable alcohol, manufacture of industrial explosives, manufacture of hazardous chemicals, manufacturing activities located within 25 km of the Standard Urban Area limits requiring industrial license under the IDR(Act) 1951, setting up of greenfield airport projects, laying of natural gas/LNG pipelines, market study and formulation and investment financing in the petroleum sector, and cash and carry wholesale trading and export trading.

(ii) ***Increase in equity caps***: FDI caps have been increased to 100%, and automatic route extended to coal and lignite mining for captive consumption, setting up of infrastructure relating to marketing in petroleum and natural gas sector and exploration and mining of diamonds and precious stones.

(iii) **FDI in new activities**: FDI has been allowed up to 100% on the automatic route in power trading and processing and warehousing of coffee and rubber. FDI has also been allowed up to 51% for 'single-brand' product retailing which requires prior approval of Government. Specific guidelines have been issued for governing FDI for 'single-brand' product retailing.

(iv) ***Removal of restrictive conditions***: A mandatory divestment condition for Business-to-Business e-commerce has been dispensed with.

(v) ***Procedural simplification***: The transfer of shares from resident to non-resident including acquisition of shares in an existing company has been placed on the automatic route subject to sectoral policy on FDI.

Although implementation of reforms was very slow because of significant disagreements over important policy areas among the coalition partners of the UPA government, it came to a virtual standstill in 2008 after the Left Front parties

---

[17] *Economic Survey 2006–07*, pp. 122–23.

withdrew their external support for the UPA government in their opposition to the civil nuclear agreement with the USA. On 22 July 2008, the UPA government narrowly survived a vote of confidence in the Parliament brought on by the Left Front, although the Congress Party leaders along with then Samajwadi Party leader Amar Sigh were accused of buying votes with cash bribery to a number of Members of Parliament to save the UPA government. Subsequently, the UPA became closely aligned with the neoliberal factions and returned to power with an increased mandate in the 2009 general election. Manmohan Sigh retained the Prime Ministership and formed the second UPA government on 22 May 2009.

Although India's economy grew rapidly under the UPA governments within a range between 9.5% and 6.7% of real GDP during 2005–12, it subsequently slowed down to a range between 4.5% and 4.7% of the same during 2012–14 (Table 1.2). Lower growth rates during 2012–14 reflect drastic decline in the growth rates of almost all four components of the industrial sector: (i) mining and quarrying, (ii) manufacturing, (iii) electricity, gas and water supply and (iv) construction. Although an investor-friendly FDI policy had gradually been put in place, it had been further liberalised in 2014 partly to enhance economic growth. FDI up to 49% through the *government route* had been permitted in the defence industry. Higher FDI had also been allowed on a case-to-case basis. FDI up to 100% through the *automatic route* had been permitted in most sectors/activities including construction, operation, and maintenance of identified railway transport infrastructure. Norms related to minimum land area, capitalisation and repatriation of funds for FDI in construction development projects had also been further liberalised.[18]

During Singh's second term, the UPA-II government faced a number of corruption charges—over the mismanagement of the 2010 Commonwealth Games,[19] the 2G-spectrum allocation[20] and the allocation of coal blocks.[21] These corruption

[18]*Economic Survey 2014–15*, p. 96.

[19]Charges over the mismanagement of the 2010 Commonwealth Games include serious corruption by its organizing committee members that led to infrastructural compromise, delays in the construction of main Games' venues, and failure to sufficient ticket sales before the events.

[20]The mismanagement of the 2G-spectrum allocation known as 2G-spectram scam was leveled against the UPA government for undercharging 'mobile telephone companies for frequency allocation licenses, which they then used to create 2G spectrum subscriptions for cell phones.' On 2 February 2012, the Supreme Court of India ruled on a public interest litigation (PIL) related to this scam and declared the allotment of spectrum 'unconstitutional and arbitrary'. It cancelled the 122 licenses issued in 2008 by accusing the primary official—A. Raja, then Minister of Communications and IT—that he wanted 'to favour some companies at the cost of the public exchequer' and 'virtually gifted away important national asset[s]'.

[21]The mismanagement of the allocation of coal blocks known as 'coalgate' was a major political scandal concerning the Indian government's allocation of the nation's coal deposits to public sector entities (PSEs) and private companies. In a draft report issued in March 2014, the *Comptroller and Auditor General of India* (CAG) office accused the Government of India for allocating coal blocks in an inefficient manner during the period 2004–2009. 'The essence of the CAG's argument is that the Government had the authority to allocate coal blocks by a process of competitive bidding, but chose not to.' In response to the lodgement of a complaint made by the opposition BJP, the Supreme Court of India 'decided in July 2014 to set up a special CBI court to

allegations against the 'UPA-II' government along with the economic stagnation during the later period of its term had certainly gone against it in the general election that was held from 7 April to 12 May in 2014. It lost the election, and the victorious *National Democratic Alliance* (NDA) replaced the *Indian National Congress* (INC)-led 'UPA-II' government by assuming office on 26 May 2014 with Narendra Modi of the *Bharatiya Janata Party* (BJP)[22] as its Prime Minister and based on a general guiding principle of 'minimum government and maximum governance'.

Right after the NDA came to power in May 2014, the new Modi government undertook a number of additional reform measures. It was argued that their cumulative impact could be substantial. These reform measures noted in *The Economic Survey 2014–15* (vol. 1, Box 1.2, p. 9) included:

- Deregulating diesel prices, paving the way for new investments in this sector;
- Raising gas prices from US$ 4.2 per million British thermal unit to US$ 5.6, and linking pricing, transparently and automatically, to international prices so as to provide incentives for greater gas supply and thereby relieving the power sector bottlenecks;
- Taxing energy products to have positive environmental impact. Taking advantage of declining oil prices, the excise tax on diesel and coal had been increased four times;
- Replacing the cooking gas subsidy by direct transfers on a national scale;
- Instituting the Expenditure Management Commission, which has submitted its interim report for rationalising expenditures;
- Passing an ordinance to reform the coal sector via auctions;
- Securing the political agreement on the goods and services tax (GST) that will allow legislative passage of the constitutional amendment bill;
- Increasing FDI caps in defence;
- Eliminating the quantitative restrictions on gold;
- Passing an ordinance to make land acquisition less onerous, thereby easing the cost of doing business, while ensuring that farmers get fair compensation;
- Facilitating Presidential Assent for labour reforms in Rajasthan, setting an example for further reform initiatives by the states, and consolidating and making transparent a number of labour laws;

(Footnote 21 continued)

try cases arising from coal block allocation scam.' On 24 September 2014, the Court 'decided to cancel 214 out of 218 coal blocks allocated since 1993.' Apart from the cancellation, operational mines were directed to pay 'a penalty of Rs. 295 for every tonne of coal extracted since they started'.

[22]The *Bharatiya Janata Party* (BJP) emerged as a historic winner with 282 of 543 parliamentary seats, which allowed the Prime Minister Narendra Modi to form a government without any need for having to broker a post-election coalition. While submitting the total number of supports to the President Pranab Mukherjee, the Modi government claimed for a total of 335 seats won by the NDA coalition.

- Passing an ordinance increasing the FDI cap in insurance to 49%. Commencing a program of disinvestments under which 10% of the government's stake in Coal India was offered to the public, yielding about Rs. 22,500 crore, of which Rs. 5,800 crore was from foreign investors;
- Passing the Mines and Minerals (Development and Regulation) (MMDR) Amendment Ordinance, 2015 is a significant step in revival of the hitherto stagnant mining sector in the country. The process of auction for allotment would usher in greater transparency and boost revenues for the States.

In order to realise India's full growth potential, the immediate tasks that the Modi government has identified are to ease the cost of doing business, exploit India's *demographic dividend*[23] and refocus on India's agricultural sector from which nearly 42% of Indian households derive bulk of their income. On the Modi government's 'reform-to-transform' agenda, a number of measures, 'each incremental but collectively meaningful', as the *Economic Survey 2015–16* (vol. 1, p. 1) put them, have been enacted. The Modi government has been undertaking a 'number of initiatives such as introducing a new bankruptcy law, rehabilitating stalled projects and considering guidelines for public–private partnerships that can help facilitate exit, thereby improving the efficiency of the economy'. Since the early 1980s, the Indian economy has made progress in increasing entry by dismantling industrial licensing, diluting public sector monopolies, privatising some public sector assets and reducing trade barriers. It is noted that this progress has helped the Indian economy to move from 'socialism with limited entry to "marketism" without exit'. It is argued that a market economy also 'requires exit so that resources are forced or enticed away from inefficient and unsustainable uses'. The current government's initiatives in relation to exit include the new bankruptcy law, rehabilitation of stalled projects and proposed changes to the *Prevention of Corruption Act*.[24] Although there are many ways to measure the exit problem, the Modi government characterises it using some simple metrics. Accordingly, a partial list of the exit problem is provided in Table 3.1, which presents a measure of employment, inefficiency and potential solutions.

As noted in the *Economic Survey 2015–16* (vol. 1, p. 38), two caveats are, however, in order as follows:

> First, focusing on the exit problem does not mean that the challenges of entry have been fully addressed. The Government's reform agenda, including liberalising FDI and launching the start-up India and Entrepreneurship initiatives are noteworthy endeavours to further facilitate entry.

[23]Currently, India has roughly 60% of its population in the age group of 15–59, with the mean age close to 27 years (Das and Kar 2016). This lower share of population in higher- and lower-age brackets together makes the *dependency ratio* significantly lower than that of many countries of the developed world with high percentage of ageing population. The core of the idea of 'demographic dividend' is that such a large share of working age population has the potential to usher high economic growth.

[24]A detailed analysis related to the exit issues is available in *Economic Survey: 2015–2016*, vol. 1, chap. 2.

Table 3.1 Charactersing the exit problem

Sector	Employment	Inefficiency measure/cost[1]	Solution
Public sector			
Fertilisers (inefficient firms)	15,619	Estimated subsidy based on economic cost of production was Rs. 23,013 crore in 2013–14	Progress being made with neem-coating which reduces diversion and decanalisation
Civil aviation	25,047[2]	In 2013–14, the total loss was about Rs. 2400 crore —7th straight year of loss	Strategic approach needs to be taken
Public sector banks (a few banks)	86,744	Capital infusion between 2009–10 and 2015–16 (First half) was Rs. 1.02 lakh crore	Consolidate; Strategically disinvest; 4 R's for the non-performing asset (NPA) problem: *Recognition*, *Recapitalisation*, *Resolution* and *Reform*. Changing *Prevention of Corruption ACT* (PCA) of 1988
Discoms (States' major loss-making electricity distribution companies)	2.6 lakh	Accumulated losses over 2008–09 and 2013–14 about Rs. 2.3 lakh crores	Tying structural improvements with debt relief. Create 'one market' in power
Central public-sector enterprises	2.5 lakh (sick CPSEs, 2013–14)	Accumulated losses of sick units as of 2013–14 was Rs. 1.04 lakh crore	Allow sick CPSEs to exit. Leverage the land and capital unlocked to promote new investment
Administrative schemes	N/A	Number of central sector and centrally sponsored schemes increased from 908 in 2006–07 to 1086 in 2014–15	Rationalisation of schemes as done in 2014–15. Regular evaluations
Regulatory bodies	N/A	The average age of their heads is about 60	Administrative reform to bring in young, professional talent
Private sector			
Agriculture cereals and sugar)	N/A	Over-intensive cultivation of water-intensive crops has led to water tables declining at a rate of 0.3 m per year	Incentivise pulses over water-guzzling crops; facilitate use of *drip irrigation*; highlight social costs and benefits of crop production
Steel	N/A	Cost of production 50–75% higher for few inefficient firms in comparison with global norms	Bankruptcy code

(continued)

Table 3.1 (continued)

Sector	Employment	Inefficiency measure/cost[1]	Solution
Infrastructure (few large groups)	N/A	As of FY15, the average interest cover is about 0.3	Kelkar (PPP) Committee recommendations, bankruptcy code. Changing PCA
Small savings	N/A	Implicit subsidy to well off: Rs. 11,900 crore	Rationalise schemes to benefit the small savers. Make transparent true beneficiaries
Economy wide			
Trade liberalisation	N/A	Nearly highest restrictions on imports; gains from liberalisation of goods and services estimated at 1% of GDP[3]	Safety nets to tackle transitory costs of greater trade liberalisation and competition
Labour	N/A	Not enough big firms and too many small and inefficient firms	Employee-centric regulations; provision of greater choice to employees

Source: Adapted from *Economic Survey: 2015–2016*, vol. 1, Chap. 2, pp. 40–41
1. Unless otherwise specified, numbers are inflation-adjusted
2. Air India Annual Report 2012–13
3. The World Bank (http://www.wds.worldbank.org/external/default/WDSContentServer/WDSP/IB/2015/03/10/090224b082bf51e6/1_0/Rendered/PDF/Economic0impli0nd0the0United0States.pdf)

> Second, there are sectors in which exit is not a first-order problem, for example IT services and e-commerce, evidenced most recently in the dynamism displayed in relation to start-ups in India. The case studies suggest that the [exit] challenge is more a feature of the relatively traditional sectors of the economy but is not restricted to the public sector—indeed; impeded exit in the private sector is becoming a major challenge.

3.3 Evaluation of India's Planned Socio-Economic Development (1980–2014)

During more than six decades (1951–2014) of planned development in independent India, average annual growth rates of net national income (NNI) and per capita NNI (both at 2004–05 prices) were at moderate rates of 4.9% and 2.8%, respectively (Table 3.2), as against the average population growth rate of 1.91% per annum[25]

[25]The average annual population growth rate of 1.91 during 1951–2011 is calculated as simple average of the five average annual growth rates in 1951, 1961, 1971, 1981, 1991, 2001 and 2011 obtained from Table 3.2.

roughly during the same period (1951–2011). India's annual average growth rates (by both the measures) under individual Sixth to Eleventh Plans during the post-reform period since 1980 were however consistently above the 1951–2014 average. While India's industrial base had become more diversified during the pre-reform period, many of its industries were reported to be inefficient by the international standard. Although the import substitution strategy of the earlier decades had been successful to a certain extent, many industries had failed to maintain an appropriate technological standard, and as a result, they required the importation of technology all over again. While India's emphasis on public sector growth might have helped contain expansion of some large private monopolies, it is often argued that many inefficient public monopolies during the pre-reform are responsible for the low average growth rate, both Gross and National Incomes (GNI and NNI) measured at 2004–05 prices, except during the Second Five-Year Plan period (1956–61). All the growth rates are shown in Table 3.2. During the early reform period of 1980s coincided with the Sixth and the Seventh Five-Year Plan period (1980–90), the average growth rates (at 2004–05 prices) were moderate within a range between 5.5 and 5.6%. During the post-comprehensive-reform period, the real growth rates started to accelerate during the Eighth Five-Year Plan (1992–97), although it was followed by a somewhat lower growth rate during the Ninth Five-Year Plan period (1997–2002). These growth rates exceeded 7.5% during the Tenth and Eleventh Plan periods (2002–2012) when the comprehensive economic liberalisation seemed to have taken a strong hold in Indian economy. Note that during India's planned development (1951–2014), India's overall annual average growth rates have been 4.9% of both GNI and NNI at factor cost and measured at 2004–05 prices.

It is also interesting to point out that India's average annual population growth rate has, according to the census years, moderately declined from 2.22% during the decade of 1981–90 to 2.14% during 1991–2000 and then sharply to 1.64% during 2001–2011 as is evident from Table 3.3. This fact has also partly helped to increase India's per capita NNI from 4.6% in the Eighth Plan (1992–97) to 6.3% in the Eleventh Plan (2007–12) (see Table 3.2).

Social Implications of the Policy of Economic Liberalisation during 1990s

In response to the contemporary globalisation process,[26] economic liberalisation has been taking place in India—a labour surplus dualistic economy—since the mid-1980s, although more so since its adoption of comprehensive economic reforms in July 1991. Many argue that Indian liberalisation policy has been, in many ways, erratic, hasty and unplanned at least during the early years of 1990s.

[26]Two phases of globalisation are often compared in the literature: the first one is during the last quarter of the nineteenth century that culminates until the beginning of the First World War, and the second one is during the last quarter of the twentieth century. For details, one can see Hoogvelt (1997) and Nayyar (1997).

Table 3.2 India's annual average growth rate

Plan period		GNI at factor cost		NNI at factor cost		Per capita NNI at factor cost	
		At current prices	At 2004–05 prices	At current prices	At 2004–05 prices	At current prices	At 2004–05 prices
First Plan	1951–56	1.8	3.7	1.9	4.2	0.0	2.4
Second Plan	1956–61	9.5	4.2	9.6	4.2	7.4	2.2
Third Plan	1961–66	9.6	2.8	9.5	2.6	7.1	0.3
Annual Plan	1966–69	12.2	3.9	12.2	3.7	9.8	1.5
Fourth Plan	1969–74	11.1	3.4	10.8	3.2	8.4	0.9
Fifth Plan	1974–79	10.7	4.9	10.4	4.9	8.0	2.6
Annual Plan	1979–80	9.4	−5.0	8.4	−5.9	5.8	−8.2
Sixth Plan	1980–85	15.3	5.4	15.3	5.4	12.8	3.1
Seventh Plan	1985–90	14.1	5.6	13.8	5.5	11.4	3.3
Annual Plan	1990–91	16.3	5.1	16.3	4.9	13.9	2.7
Annual Plan	1991–92	15.1	1.4	14.2	0.8	12.0	−1.2
Eighth Plan	1992–97	16.4	6.6	16.6	6.7	14.2	4.6
Ninth Plan	1997–02	10.9	5.7	10.7	5.5	8.7	3.6
Tenth Plan	2002–07	12.7	7.6	12.7	7.5	11.0	5.9
Eleventh Plan	2007–12	16.2	8.0	16.3	7.8	14.7	6.3
Twelfth Plan	2012–13	1.5	4.1	11.0	3.4	9.7	2.1
	2013–14	12.3	4.9	11.9	4.2	10.4	2.8
Average	1951–2014	11.8	4.9	11.7	4.9	9.6	2.8

Source: *National Accounts Statistics 2014*, Central Statistics Office, Government of India, Table 17(a)

Table 3.3 India's population growth (1951–2011)

Census years	Population (in millions)	Decadal growth (%)	Average annual growth (%)	Density (per km^2)	Sex ratio (females per 1000 males)
1951	361.09	13.31	1.25	117	946
1961	439.23	21.64	1.96	142	941
1971	548.16	24.80	2.20	177	930
1981	683.33	24.66	2.22	216	934
1991	846.39	23.86	2.14	267	927
2001	1027.02	21.34	1.93	324	933
2011[a]	1210.19	17.64	1.64	382	940

Source: *Economic Survey 2001–2002*, Government of India, Table 10.14
[a]*Census 2011* (www.census2011.co.in and http://censusindia.gov.in/2011-prov-results/data_files/india/Final_PPT_2011_chapter3.pdf)

According to the earlier critics, it eroded the role of the planning process[27] and aggravated the social problems of unemployment and poverty, and also increased India's external vulnerability.

As to the long-run social implications of the policy of economic liberalisation adopted most strongly since the middle of 1991, there was immediate concern that some of India's stabilisation and structural reforms might had led to the erosion of living standards of the poor;[28] increased its regional disparities in terms of industrial benefits[29]; reduced employment generation; and created greater casualisation, feminisation and deskilling of the workforce (Kurien 1996, p. 67). Some Indian economists were also concerned that the economy was experiencing a distorted development process, and the service sector had bypassed the industry sector in the order. The distortion in the development process was not because the industry sector lagged behind, but because the service sector grew at a higher rate. There was a positive side though—a buoyant service sector was expected to add to industry's growth potential. However, there was a fear that if industry would fail to grow at a

[27]India's Planning Commission has eventually been dissolved in 2015 by the Narendra Modi-led National Democratic Alliance (NDA) government and replaced it with *Niti Aayog* focused on cooperative federalism.

[28]Release of preliminary National Sample Survey (NSS) data for 1993–94 had produced a spate of articles that forcefully argued that the poor had been hurt at least in the initial reform period (Papanek 1996, p. 1). Although it was debatable (see Gupta, 1995), both the official source (*Economic Survey: 1995–96*, p. 13) and the World Bank Country Study on India (1996, p. 28) suggested that economic reforms had begun to help the poor.

[29]Although economic liberalisation had accelerated industrial development, but some argued that benefits had not been evenly distributed across states. Ghuman (1997, p.13) noted that Gujarat, Maharashtra and Tamil Nadu had initially gained the most from liberalised policy initiatives; other beneficiaries were West Bengal, Karnataka and Orissa; the remaining states had either gained moderately or had suffered losses.

required rate, not only would the growth of the service sector suffer, but also it would drag down the GDP growth too (Mahanti 2000).

In a study on manufacturing sector of urban India for the decade between 1983 and 1993–94, Pais (2002, p. 651) had found a significant decline in casualisation, specifically in manufacturing industries based on agricultural inputs, while incidence of casual labour in construction and agriculture had increased. In fact, casual labour, according to this study, dominated the construction industry. It is noteworthy that only two sectors in India's unorganised segment—construction and transportation—had an increasing trend in their share of net domestic product; but this upward trend in construction sector had been relatively much higher. Deaton and Dréze (2002) had, however, noted several related adverse trends such as growing uncertainty and hidden hardships associated with patterns of economic changes, particularly for impoverished sections of India's unorganised segment as well as generally for impoverishment among specific regions or social groups in the country as a whole.[30]

As the Ninth Five-Year Plan (1997–2002) document argued, the Government recognised that high growth of incomes was by itself not enough to improve the quality of life of the poor which is organically related to India's unorganised segment. It went on adding the following:

> If the growth is sourced upon those sectors of the economy or those activities which have a natural tendency to involve the poor in their expansion, such growth helps poverty eradication. Therefore, it is important to source a large part of economic growth in agriculture, in rural non-agricultural activities and in productive expansion of the informal sector which all have high employment elasticities, as well as in an export strategy based on labour intensive exports.[31]

On the basis of several other studies across different states in India, social scientists did not seem to be very optimistic about the possibility for implementing appropriate strategy of any credible food or employment security for the poor in the near future. For example, Rao (1998, p. 1954) argued that given the ruling elite groups formulating and implementing the strategy for the poorer stratum among the poor, the policies shaped by them lacked responsiveness to the aspirations and needs of the large *unorganised* masses including the poor. Perhaps, the former President's 'safe pedestrian crossings for the unempowered of India across the three-way fast lane of liberalisation, privatisation and globalisation' hopefully partly lie in the poor people's direct involvement in the then revamped Panchayati Raj Institutions (PRI).[32] Unfortunately, instead of evolving as 'institutions of

[30]Deaton and Dréze (2002, p. 3742) note, for example, of localised impoverishment in the poorer districts of Orissa, deep recession in power loom sector, serious crisis in edible oil industry as a result of slashing import tariffs, periodic waves of bankruptcy among cotton growers, displacement of traditional fishing sector by commercial shrimps farms and a number of sectoral crises associated with the abrupt lifting of quantitative restrictions on imports in mid-2001.

[31]*Ninth Five Year Plan* (Sect. 2.1.3).

[32]The real spirit of *Panchayati Raj Institutions* (PRI) is devolution of power from Central and State governments to a third tier of self-government at village, intermediate and district levels.

self-government', the PRI had been, as Aiyar (2002, p. 3296) argued, 'reduced to functional impotence and the corruption which arises out of chairpersons (*prad-hans*) exercising their authority without the involvement and sanction of the members of the panchayat at all levels and of the *gram sabha* at the village level'.

3.3.1 Diminished Role of the Planning Commission

As expected, the role of the Planning Commission has largely diminished with the programme of comprehensive economic liberalisation until it has eventually been dissolved by the NDA government in 2015 and replaced with *Niti Aayog* focused on cooperative federalism. In order to keep pace with the liberalisation policy, the Eighth Five-Year Plan (1992–97) had therefore redefined the role of the Planning Commission as an instrument for *indicative* planning. However, it duly recognised 'human development' as the core of all developmental effort, and it realised the essential need to involve people in the process of development. Similarly, the Ninth Five-Year Plan (1997–2002) recognised the integral link between rapid economic growth and the quality of life of the masses. It also recognised the need to combine high-growth policies with the pursuit of the ultimate objective of improving policies that were pro-poor and aimed at the correction of historical inequalities. Thus, the focus of the Ninth Plan was: 'Growth with Social Justice and Equity'. The development strategy of the Ninth Plan was oriented to enabling India's broad-based and varied private sector to reach its full potential for raising production, creating jobs and raising income levels in society. A vigorous private sector, operating under the discipline of competition and free markets, was expected to encourage efficient use of scarce resources and ensure rapid growth at minimum cost.[33] The government's role is, according to the Ninth, and subsequent Tenth (2002–2007) and Eleventh (2007–2012) Five-Year Plan documents, assumed to design government policies that must create an *environment* encouraging this outcome.

The Tenth Five-Year Plan document had highlighted the need for bringing about dramatic improvements in the functioning of India's 'administrative, judicial and internal security systems' in order to foster a dynamic and vibrant market economy by removing numerous barriers to interstate, and even intra-state, trade and commerce. It also wanted to introduce effective delivery of basic social services to the people by empowering the *Panchayati Raj Institution* (PRI) so that it could become the cutting edge of India's three-tier political structure and the focal point of democratic decentralisation. The main objectives of the Tenth Five-Year Plan (2002–2007) of India in a nutshell were:

[33]Dutta (2011).

- Introducing more investor-friendly reforms in the industrial sector;
- Increasing and optimising the mobility of all the available financial resources;
- Setting up of a state-of-the-art infrastructure for all the existing industries;
- Encouraging the initiative of capacity building within the Indian industrial sector;
- Creating a friendly, amiable and pleasant investment environment;
- Encouraging sufficient transparency in the corporate sectors of India; and
- Following a regional approach rather than sectoral approach to bring down regional inequalities.

The Eleventh Five-Year Plan (2007–2012) outlined the new priorities for the public sector. These related to 'reviving dynamism in agriculture and building the necessary supportive infrastructure in rural areas, expanding access to health and education, especially in rural areas, undertaking programmes for improving living conditions for the weaker sections and for improving their access to economic opportunity'. It also included a major thrust for infrastructure development in general. The major goals were:

- Rapid and inclusive growth in agriculture, industry and services sectors at 4%, 10% and 9%, respectively;
- Emphasis on social sector and delivery of service therein;
- Empowerment of the weaker section of people through education and skill development;
- Reduction in gender inequality; and
- Environmental sustainability.

The Twelfth Five-Year Plan (2012–17) had decided for the growth rate at 8.2%, but the National Development Council (NDC) on 27 December 2012 approved 8% growth rate during its plan period because of the deteriorating global economic situation. The government intended to reduce poverty by 10% during the Twelfth Five-Year Plan. Mr. Montek Singh Ahluwalia, the then Deputy Chairman of the Planning Commission, said, 'We aim to reduce poverty estimates by 9% annually on a sustainable basis during the Plan period'. Earlier, addressing a conference of State Planning Boards and Planning departments, he also said the rate of decline in poverty doubled during the Eleventh Plan. The Commission had said, while using the Tendulkar poverty line, the rate of reduction in the 5 years (from 2004–05 to 2009–10) was about 1.5% points each year, which was twice that when compared to the period (from 1993–95 to 2004–05). The Plan aimed towards the betterment of the infrastructural projects of the nation avoiding all types of bottlenecks. The document presented by the Planning Commission was aimed to attract private investments of up to US$1 trillion in the infrastructural growth during the Twelfth Five-Year Plan. It was expected to ensure a reduction in subsidy burden of the government to 1.5% from then 2% of the GDP.

Table 3.4 Estimates of poverty in India

Year	Number of poor (million)			Poverty ratio (%)		
	Rural	Urban	Total	Rural	Urban	Total
1973–74	261	60	321	56.4	49.0	54.9
1977–78	264	65	329	53.1	45.2	51.3
1983	252	71	323	45.7	40.8	44.5
1987–88	232	75	307	39.1	38.2	38.9
1993–94*	328.6	74.5	403.1	50.1	31.8	45.3
2004–05	326.3	80.8	407.1	41.8	25.7	37.2
2009–10	278.2	76.5	354.7	33.8	20.9	29.8
2011–12	216.5	52.8	269.3	25.7	13.7	21.9

*Poverty estimates from 1993–94 have been updated/calculated by using Tendulkar Method, and therefore, the earlier estimates are not strictly comparable

Sources: *Economic Survey 2001–02* (Table 10.5), *Economic Survey 2012–13* (Table 13.5) and *Economic Survey 2013–14* (Table 13.4)

3.3.2 *Trend in Poverty*

In spite of having more than self-sufficiency in food-grain production and considerable increase in industrial production, about 21.9% of India's population was, even according to the official source, still below the poverty level during 2011–12 (Table 3.4).[34] Although the poverty ratio has steadily declined over time, one must not, however, ignore the fact that rural–urban and interstate disparities in terms of poverty ratio are still very much visible.

In order to give a big dent on poverty, the recent annual publication of the Government of India, *Economic Survey 2016–17* (Chap. 9), has proposed an alternative option of introducing a Universal Basic Income (UBI) scheme for a serious public deliberation.

> Universal Basic Income is a radical and compelling paradigm shift in thinking about both social justice and a productive economy. … It is premised on the idea that a just society needs a guarantee to each individual a minimum income which they can count on, and which provides the necessary material foundation for a life with access to basic goods and a life of dignity. …It promotes equality by reducing poverty. It promotes efficiency by reducing waste in government transfers. …An unconditional cash transfer treats them as agents, not subjects. A UBI is also practically useful. The circumstances that keep individuals trapped in poverty are varied; the risks … and the shocks they face also vary. The state is not in the best position to determine which risks should be mitigated and how

[34]Poverty at the national level is estimated as the weighted average of state-wise poverty levels. The latest poverty ratio, on a 30 day recall basis, has been estimated from the state-specific poverty lines, and the distribution of persons by expenditure groups obtained from the latest large sample 55th Round Survey (July 1999–June 2000) conducted by the *National Sample Survey Organisation* (NSSO).

priorities are to be set. UBI liberates citizens from paternalistic and clientelistic relationships with the state. By taking the individual and not the households as the unit of beneficiary, UBI can also enhance agency, especially of women within households.[35]

3.3.3 Trend in Employment

One can now look at the trend of two important macro-variables namely investment and employment, in order to have a better picture of the post-reform period. On the basis of disaggregated data published in different issues of *National Accounts Statistics*, although one could find that real investment in 1990s has expanded slowly in agriculture and its allied sub-sectors, but that in non-agricultural sector has been unstable, more so during the post-1995 years. There has been an overall steep decline in the growth rate of total investment from 5.48% per annum during 1983/1993–94 to 3.90% per annum during 1993–94/1999–2000, or equally seriously, from 5.97% to 3.90% in the case of the non-agricultural sector (Chadha and Sahu 2002, pp. 2020–22).

In order to have a better picture of the post-reform period's impact on poverty, let us now have a look at the trend in employment—a very important macro-variable related to the incidence of poverty. Firstly, annual average growth rate of overall employment (in both the organised and unorganised segments) was 2.73% per annum during the period from 1972–73 to 1977–78, which declined to 1.54% per annum over the period from 1983 to 1987–88 (Table 3.5). Although the growth rate of overall employment increased to 2.43% per annum during 1987–88 to 1993–94, it sharply dropped to 1.08% per annum in the subsequent period from 1993–94 to 1999–2000. Growth in organised sector employment has been slowing down as can be seen from Table 3.6. This is mainly due to falling employment growth in the public sector from an average increase of 2.16% per annum during 1983–88 to that of 0.99 during 1988–94 followed by a decline of −0.03% per annum during 1994–2000. In the post-reform phase, a natural attrition of excess labour is occurring as industry restructures. While the private sector has dismissed workers with increased competition, the public sector seems to be relying more on voluntary retirement schemes (Venu 2000).

The sector-wise employment trends (Table 3.7) indicate that the deceleration of overall annual average employment growth rate during the period from 1983–1994 to 1994–2000 has been primarily due to slower growth in agricultural employment, with the absolute number of persons employed in agriculture showing a decline for the first time. On the contrary, employment in some of the service-related sectors (such as trade, construction, financial services, transport, storage, communication as well as manufacturing) has grown faster than the average; also, share of these

[35] *Economic Survey: 2016–17*, Government of India, pp. 173–74.

Table 3.5 Rates of population growth, labour force and employment[a] in India during 1972–2012

Period	Rate of growth of population (% per annum)	Rate of growth of labour force (% per annum)	Rate of growth of employment (organised and unorganised) (% per annum)
1972–73 to 1977–78	2.27	2.94	2.73
1977–78 to 1983	2.19	2.04	2.17
1983 to 1987–88	2.14	1.74	1.54
1987–88 to 1993–94	2.10	2.29	2.43
1993–94 to 1999–2000	1.95	1.16	1.08
1999–2000 to 2004–05	1.64	2.93	2.91
2004–05 to 2009–10	1.45	−0.01	0.05
2004–05 to 2011–12	1.42	0.44	0.46
2009–10 to 2011–12	1.36	1.58	1.50

[a]The NSS gives the percentage distribution across industries of each of the four categories of workers. This distribution is applied to the absolute numbers of workers of each category for each year and adds up the four categories in each industry to derive estimates of total workers in each industry. The total employment figures are on Usual Status basis, i.e. Usual Principal plus Subsidiary Status (UPSS) of measuring an individual's employment-related activities

Sources: *Economic Survey 2001–2002* (Table 10.6). *Economic Survey 2003–2004* (Table 10.7). *Economic and Political Weekly*, vol. 50, no. 16 (18 April, 2015, p. 91)

sectors in total employment has increased. These trends reflect explicit structural changes in product markets in the post-reform (comprehensive) period.[36]

During the initial years of the post-reform (comprehensive) period, the real investment (i.e., real gross capital formation as a percentage of real GDP at market prices) had moved in an opposite direction to that of the movement in real GDP growth (RBI 1999). Both these trends suggest that productivity increase may have

[36]*Economic Survey: 2000–2001*, Government of India, Sect. 10.11.

Table 3.6 Total employment and organised sector employment in India during 1983–2012

Total/Sectoral	Employment (Million)							CAGR (%)					
	1983	1988	1994	2000	2005	2010	2012	1983–88	1988–94	1994–2000	2000–05	2005–10	2010–12
Total population	718.2	790.0	895.1	1004.1	1089.0	1170.0	1202.0	1.92	2.53	1.93	1.64	1.45	1.36
Total labour force	308.6	333.5	381.9	406.1	469.0	468.8	483.7	1.56	2.29	1.03	2.92	−0.01	1.58
Total employment	302.8	324.3	374.5	397.0	457.9	459.0	472.9	1.38	2.43	0.98	2.90	0.05	1.50
Organised sector employment	24.0	25.7	27.4	28.0	26.5	28.3	29.3	1.38	1.05	0.45	−1.10	1.32	1.75
Public sector	16.4	18.3	19.5	19.3	18.0	17.5	17.3	2.16	0.99	−0.03	−1.38	−0.56	−0.57
Private sector	7.6	7.4	7.9	8.7	8.5	10.8	11.9	−0.47	1.18	1.56	−0.46	4.91	4.97

Notes:
[a]Total employment figures are on Usual Status basis, i.e. Usual Principal and Subsidiary Status (UPSS)
[b]Organised sector employment figures are as reported in the Employment Market Information System of Ministry of Labour and pertain to 1st March of 1983, 1988, 1994 and 1999
[c]Rate of growth of total employment and organised sector employment are compound rates of growth
Sources: *Economic Survey 2001–2002*, Table 10.7. *Economic and Political Weekly*, Statistics on Countrywide Employment and Unemployment, 18 April 2015, vol. 50, no. 16, p. 91

Table 3.7 Growth of employment by sectors in India during 1983–2000

Sector	Employed workers[a] (Million)			Annual average employment growth rate (%)	
	1983	1993–94	1999–2000	1983–94	1994–2000
Agriculture	207.23	242.46	237.56	1.51	−0.34
Mining and quarrying	1.76	2.70	2.27	4.16	−2.85
Manufacturing	34.03	42.50	48.01	2.14	2.05
Electricity, gas and water supply	0.85	1.35	1.28	4.50	−0.88
Construction	6.78	11.68	17.62	5.32	7.09
Trade	19.22	27.78	37.32	3.57	5.04
Transport, storage and communication	7.39	10.33	14.69	3.24	6.04
Financial Services	1.70	3.52	5.05	7.18	6.20
Community, social and personal services	23.80	35.13	33.20	2.90	0.55
Total employment	**302.76**	**374.45**	**397**	**2.04**	**0.98**

[a]The total employment figures are on Usual Status basis, i.e. Usual Principal and Subsidiary Status (UPSS)

Source: Adapted from Papola and Sahu (2012, Table 1, p. 5)

played an important role in the growth process during the post-reform period.[37] What is, however, apparent is a strong structural shift in the composition of the GDP and in favour of the services sector since the 1980s. According to the Reserve Bank of India's 1998–99 *Report on Currency and Finance*, the services sector's contribution had been more pronounced—its share grew from an average 42.2% of GDP in the 1980s to that of 46.6% in the 1990s (*RBI* 1999a). The Report also added that it was the growth in the services sector that helped GDP growth. More importantly was the contribution of services to India's software exports, despite industrial sluggishness especially during 1998–99. Meanwhile, India had witnessed some political instability[38] during the second half of the 1990s particularly after the Congress Government under the Prime Minister of Narasimha Rao lost power in May 1996. Notwithstanding several structural improvements resulted after the adoption of comprehensive economic liberalisation, attention of the Governments in 1990s had been drawn to the importance of urgently addressing the remaining

[37]An earlier analysis of India's registered manufacturing sector by Chaudhuri (2002, p. 160) suggested that labour productivity increased steadily between 1990–91 and 1995–96, but had stagnated afterwards; capital productivity increased marginally until 1995–96 followed by a decline. He also noted that both labour and capital productivities increased in only 70 product groups, accounting for about 37% of the value added.

[38]After a number of short-lived coalition governments, the newly formed *National Democratic Alliance* (NDA) led by the Bharatiya Janata Party formed a stable government with Atal Behari Vajpayee as its Prime Minister in October 1999, who remained in power until May 2004.

Table 3.8 Growth of employment (UPSS) by sectors in India from 1999–2000 to 2009–2010

Sector	Annual average employment growth rate (%)			
	1993–94/1999–00	1999–00/2004–05	2004–05/2009–10	1999–00/2009–10
Primary sector (agriculture and allied)	**0.05**	**1.40**	**−1.63**	**−0.13**
Secondary sector	**2.44**	**5.83**	**3.46**	**4.64**
Mining and quarrying	−2.11	2.41	3.00	2.70
Manufacturing	1.62	5.06	−1.06	1.95
Utilities (electricity, gas and water supply)	−5.89	3.22	1.02	2.11
Construction	6.38	8.18	11.29	9.72
Tertiary sector	**2.85**	**4.08**	**1.59**	**2.83**
Trade, hoteling etc.	6.28	4.01	1.10	2.54
Transport and Communication etc.	5.09	5.23	2.14	3.68
Financing, insurance, Real Estate and Business Services	5.28	9.62	5.77	7.68
Community, social and personal services	−1.48	2.71	0.99	1.85
All non-agricultural (Secondary + Tertiary sectors)	**2.68**	**4.81**	**2.41**	**3.61**
Total	**1.04**	**2.81**	**0.22**	**1.50**

Source: Adapted from Papola and Sahu (2012, Table 1, p. 5)

structural constraints to higher growth. Chief among them were reducing the country's chronically high fiscal deficits;[39] removing the remaining investment and trade restrictions, particularly in agriculture; averting a crisis in the supply of infrastructure; and strengthening the country's human capital base (*World Bank Country Study on India 1996*, p. vii).

The most noticeable fact has been a sharp rise in employment growth of 2.81% during the period from 1999–2000 to 2004–05 (Table 3.8) over that of 0.98% during 1994–2000 (Table 3.7). Note that this employment growth includes both the organised and unorganised segments' employment. The Government's official interpretation of this upturn in employment growth at the beginning of the new millennium is that the economic reforms along with the ongoing globalisation forces have started to bear fruits. The fact is that the organised segment's employment growth experienced an absolute decline (−1.10%) during 2000–05 (Table 3.6), which implies most employment growth came from the economy's unorganised or informal segment.

[39]After the fiscal deficit was reduced from 8.3% of GDP in 1990–91 to 6% in 1991–92, the Central Government had relaxed its fiscal deficit targets. For example, this figure not only had been well above the target of 3%, but had also been increasing during the 1990s.

(a) **LOW INCOMES OF RURAL HOUSEHOLDS**

Households (%) highest earner of more than Rs. 10,000/month	Households (%) highest earner in the range of Rs. 5,000-10,000/month	Households (%) highest earner less than Rs. 5,000/month
8.29	17.18	74.49

Note: Adapted from *Anon.* (2015)

(b) **SIX REASONS WHY RURAL INCOMES ARE SO LESS**

Reason 1 — **LACK OF SKILLS (% of landless households dependent on casual labour)**

All India:	38.27
Tamil Nadu:	55.80
Bihar:	54.33
Jharkhand:	22.94
Karnataka:	22.26

Reason 2 — **LOW LEVEL OF NON-FARM ACTIVITY (% of households with non-farm enterprise)**

All India:	2.73
Gujarat:	8.07
Haryana:	7.57
Madhya Pradesh:	0.82
Chhattisgarh:	0.57

Reason 3 — **MISSING PRIVATE SECTOR JOBS (% of households in private sector jobs)**

All India:	3.57
Himachal Pradesh:	9.43
Uttarakhand:	9.23
Madhya Pradesh:	0.93
Chhattisgarh:	0.67

Reason 4 — **LANDED HIGHLY DEPENDENT ON RAINS (% of households, All India)**

Owning unirrigated land:	38.27
Owning irrigated land:	54.33
Owning irrigation equipment:	22.26

Reason 5 — **GOVT & PUBLIC SECTOR NOT DOING TOO WELL (% of households, All India)**

Government Jobs:	5.00
Public Sector Jobs:	1.11

Reason 6 — **HIGH LEVELS OF ILLITERACY (% of total rural population)**

Illiterate:	35.73
Below primary:	13.97

Note: Adapted from *Anon.* (2015)

Fig. 3.1 **a** Low incomes of rural households, **b** Six reasons why rural incomes are so less

Subsequently, total employment growth rate has suffered a further setback, when it declined to 0.22% during the period 2004/05–2009/10 (Table 3.8). If one looks at the sectoral and sub-sectoral employment performance of different activities, employment growth rates of all the three sectors have been very low and even negative for the *primary* sector (−1.63%), *secondary* sector (3.46%) and *tertiary* sector (1.59%). Under *secondary* sector, only its construction sub-sector has maintained a high employment growth along with a moderate growth rate of its sub-sector of mining and quarrying. Under *tertiary* sector, although the financial services sub-sector has a fairly moderate growth rate, it seems that the other sub-sectors with the possible exception of community, social and personal services have high potential for employment generation, which can be envisaged from their employment growth rates during 1999/00–2009/10 (Table 3.8).

3.3.4 Major Reasons for Low Rural Income

The first socio-economic and caste Census 2011 of the independent India was released by the government in July 2015. The findings of its socio-economic survey as summarised[40] in *The Economic Times* on 6 July, 2015 show a clear picture of struggling rural India with few non-farm jobs, low incomes, excessive dependence on land, lack of basics, etc. Of the 17.91 crore rural households surveyed, a majority of 74.49% report the monthly income of their highest earning member is less than Rs. 5,000 compared to only 8.29% of rural households with highest earning member with income of more than Rs. 10,000 per month (Fig. 3.1a). Figure 3.1b identifies six major reasons for low income of rural households: lack of skills, high level of illiteracy, few non-farm jobs (in both public and private sectors of the modern segment) and high dependence on rains for agricultural production.

3.4 Implications of Economic Liberalisation for Unorganised Segment Employment

Although the share of the organised segment in net domestic product/gross value added (at factor cost in current prices) has increased sharply from 30% during 1980–81 to 39.7% during 1995–96, and then moderately to 44.7% during 2012–13 (see Table 3.9), its share in employment has continuously declined from 9.18% of total workers in 1983 to only 5.70% in 2005 before it started slowly increasing to 6.27 in 2012 (see Table 3.10). As a result, the unorganised segment continues to contain over 93% of India's labour force (mostly as disguised underemployed as well as unemployed labours), in spite of the decline in its share in net domestic

[40] *Anon*. (2015).

Table 3.9 Share of organised and unorganised segments in India's net domestic product/gross value added (at factor cost in current prices) (%)

Year	Organised	Unorganised
1980–81	30.0	70.0
1985–86	35.2	64.8
1990–91	36.2	63.8
1995–96	39.7	60.3
2000–01	39.6	60.4
2004–05	43.7	56.3
2005–06	44.7	55.3
2006–07	45.1	54.9
2007–08	45.0	55.0
2008–09	44.8	55.2
2009–10	45.6	54.4
2010–11	44.8	55.2
2011–12	43.9	56.1
2012–13	44.7	55.3

Source: *National Accounts Statistics* 1993 (pp. 203–04), 1998 (pp. 198–99), 2000 (p. 180), 2007 (pp. 182–83) and 2014 (pp. 208–09)

product from 70.0% during 1980–81 to 60.9% during 1998–99 (Table 3.11 based on old series of data) and then its further decline though very slowly from 56.3% during 2004–05 to 55.3% during 2012–13 (Table 3.12 based on new series of data).

3.4.1 Employment Growth in Rural and Urban Areas during the Post-Reform Period

As often rural and urban areas are interchangeably used for unorganised and organised segments of a dualistic economy, one must not forget that urban areas may contain urban informal segment consisting of say, urban slums and self-employed petty shops, while a part of the organised segment involving public- and private-sector institutions is certainly situated in rural areas. Data availability on growths of rural and urban employment is therefore expected to shed some light on the dynamics of the rural non-farm or non-agricultural activities and therefore India's dualism especially during the post-reform period. As is evident from Table 3.13, there has been an increase in rural non-agricultural employment during the post-reform period from 1993–94 to 2009–10. The distribution in terms of shares of employment between the secondary (industrial) and tertiary (services) sectors has been tilted more towards the former. The share of construction (29.32%) in rural non-agricultural employment has overtaken that of manufacturing (22.32%) in 2009–10. Among services, trade has maintained roughly 20% of share of rural non-agricultural employment. While the share of rural employment in community, social and personnel services has sharply declined from 24.96% in 1993–94 to

Table 3.10 Estimates of employment in organised and unorganised segments in India (in millions)

Year	Organised[a]	Unorganised[b]	Total labour force[c]	Share of organised segment employment
1983	24.00[d]	237.33	261.33[e]	9.18
1990	26.35	304.36	330.71	7.97
1991	26.73	311.94	338.67	7.89
1992	27.06	319.74	346.80	7.80
1993	27.18	327.94	355.12	7.65
1994	27.38	335.62	363.00	7.54
1995	27.53	342.26	369.79	7.45
1996	27.94	349.33	377.27	7.41
1997	28.25	355.94	384.19	7.35
1998	28.17	362.99	391.16	7.20
1999	28.11	370.05	398.16	7.06
2000	27.96	377.23	405.19	6.90
2001	27.79	389.36	417.15	6.66
2002	27.21	401.39	428.60	6.35
2003	27.00	413.21	440.21	6.13
2004	26.44	425.50	451.94	5.85
2005	26.46	438.04	464.50	5.70
2006	26.99	438.47	465.46	5.80
2007	27.28	438.75	466.03	5.85
2008	27.55	438.68	466.23	5.91
2009	28.17	438.73	466.90	6.04
2010	28.71	437.68	466.39	6.16
2011	29.00	440.81	469.81	6.17
2012	29.58	442.55	472.13	6.27

[a]Estimates of employment in organised public and private sectors (in Million persons as on 31 March) obtained from Statistical Appendix's Table: Estimates of Employment in Organised Public and Private Sectors in various issues of *Economic Survey*, GOI

[b]Potential employment (including disguised, part-time and full-time) in unorganised segment is derived as total labour force minus employment in organised segment

[c]Data from 1990 and onwards on total labour force are taken from *World Development Indicator*, online data, World Bank [http://data.worldbank.org/indicator/SL.TOTL.IN/countries?page=4] accessed on 12 May 2015

[d]From *Economic Survey 1994–95*, pp. S-54–S-55

[e]From *Economic Survey 2002–2003*, p. 218

14.89% in 2009–10, transport has gained an improvement from 6.71% to 9% during the same period.

Because the *primary sector* which is predominantly agricultural accounts for a very high share in rural economy and growth in employment in primary sector has been very low or even sometimes absolute negative (e.g. −1.65% and −0.19% per annum during 2004–05/2009–10 and 1999–00/2009–10, respectively), rural

Table 3.11 Share of unorganised segment in India's net domestic product by economic activity (old series at current prices) (%)

Sectors	80–81	89–90	90–91	91–92	92–93	93–94	94–95	95–96	96–97	97–98	98–99
Agriculture, forestry and fishing	95.2	95.7	96.2	96.4	96.5	96.5	96.6	96.0	96.4	96.5	97.0
Mining and quarrying	9.6	7.2	7.7	9.4	9.2	7.3	6.9	8.2	7.2	7.4	7.0
Manufacturing	46.3	38.5	39.1	38.3	39.8	36.6	34.9	35.1	34.5	37.8	38.9
Electricity, gas and water supply	6.0	4.7	3.6	3.4	2.8	7.2	5.9	5.6	6.4	5.8	5.2
Construction	48.0	54.8	55.5	53.4	55.2	51.1	52.2	50.0	51.9	56.0	57.4
Trade, hotels and restaurants	89.6	93.1	91.9	89.7	88.4	88.8	87.6	85.8	85.1	83.4	82.2
Transport, storage and communication	45.2	49.1	52.3	54.8	54.5	42.7	44.4	43.2	46.3	47.4	49.1
Financial, insurance, real estate and bus services	65.0	43.0	40.6	35.1	36.7	50.7	48.7	44.1	44.1	42.5	42.2
Commercial, social and personal services	25.9	19.6	19.4	20.0	20.3	19.0	19.4	19.1	19.2	18.0	17.3
Total (at factor cost)	**70.0**	**63.7**	**63.8**	**63.3**	**63.5**	**63.1**	**62.5**	**60.4**	**61.3**	**60.6**	**60.9**

Source: *National Accounts Statistics* 1997 (pp. 250–51), 1998 (pp. 198–99), 2000 (pp. 180–81) and 2001 (p. 192)

employment growth has been consistently lower than that in urban areas. As can be seen from Tables 3.14 and 3.15, the rural and urban areas recorded employment growth rates of 0.67% and 2.30% per annum, respectively, during the post-reform period of 1993–94/1999–2000. But subsequently these growth figures increased to 2.29% and 4.44%, respectively, during the quinquennium of 1999–00/2004–05 before reversing to their worst figures of −0.34 and 1.78, respectively, during 2004–05/2009–10. It is, however, interesting to note that the rural areas did better in employment performance of their *secondary sector* activities continuously over the period from 1993–94 to 2009–10. As far as the employment growth rate of non-agricultural activities (i.e., *secondary* plus *tertiary* activities) is concerned, the rural areas did better performance compared to the urban areas, although only during 1999–00/2009–10 (Tables 3.14 and 3.15).

Table 3.12 Share of unorganised segment in India's gross value added by economic activity (new series at current prices) (%)

Sectors	2004–05	2005–06	2006–07	2007–08	2008–09	2009–10	2010–11	2011–12	2012–13
Agriculture, forestry and fishing	94.2	94.4	94.3	94.7	94.7	94.3	94.6	94.6	94.7
Mining and quarrying	8.7	10.3	12.7	13.2	12.9	12.6	11.8	12.6	13.2
Manufacturing	35.5	33.8	32.7	32.8	31.4	30.2	29.6	28.4	28.2
Electricity, gas and water supply	3.1	3.0	2.8	2.7	2.8	2.5	2.9	2.8	2.6
Construction	63.4	54.3	53.3	52.9	62.3	59.9	58.7	63.5	60.2
Trade, hotels and restaurants	77.2	75.4	74.7	74.0	74.6	75.7	77.2	80.3	78.3
Transport, storage and communication	55.7	57.2	58.2	59.0	60.5	60.4	63.0	64.8	65.9
Financial, insurance, real estate and business services	49.1	48.2	46.8	47.0	45.8	46.7	46.1	45.0	44.2
Commercial, social and personal services	24.7	24.7	25.2	25.2	23.9	22.7	23.1	23.7	24.2
Total (at factor cost in current prices)	**56.3**	**55.3**	**54.9**	**55.0**	**55.2**	**54.4**	**55.2**	**56.1**	**55.3**

Source: Author's compilation using *National Accounts Statistics* 2013 (pp. 198–201) and 2014 (pp. 206–09)

3.4.2 Employment Growth in Unorganised Manufacturing Sector across the States

It is also to be noted that the relatively vast and diverse unorganised manufacturing sector at the national level and across a number of Indian states plays an important role in India's industrial sector employment. According to Saikia and Goswami (2017, footnote 2), this sector accounts for about 99.5% of India's manufacturing enterprises and over 80% of its manufacturing employment during 1994–95/2010–11. India's unorganised manufacturing sector's employment comes predominantly from a group of agro-based as well as resource-based industries such as food products, textiles, wood products and chemicals. It also includes a small share of

Table 3.13 Composition of rural employment (UPSS) by sectors from 1993–94 to 2009–10 (%)

Sector	1993–94	1999–00	2004–05	2009–10
Rural agricultural employment	**78.43**	**76.23**	**72.58**	**67.93**
Rural non-agricultural employment	**21.57**	**23.77**	**27.42**	**32.07**
Distribution within rural non-agriculture (secondary plus tertiary) employment				
Secondary sector	**47.12**	**47.74**	**49.53**	**54.08**
Mining and quarrying	2.58	2.09	1.79	2.01
Manufacturing	32.46	31.15	29.47	22.32
Utilities (electricity, gas and water supply)	1.06	0.55	0.47	0.43
Construction	11.02	13.96	17.81	29.32
Tertiary sector	**52.88**	**52.26**	**50.47**	**45.92**
Trade, hoteling, etc.	19.86	21.59	22.62	20.33
Transport and communication etc.	6.71	8.66	9.11	9.00
Financing, insurance, real estate and business services	1.36	1.52	1.76	1.70
Community, social and personal services	24.96	20.49	16.98	14.89

Source: Adapted from Papola and Sahu (2012, Table 7, p. 13)

Table 3.14 Growth of rural employment (UPSS) by sectors in India from 1993–94 to 2009–10

Sector	Annual average employment growth rate (%)			
	1993–94/1999–00	1999–00/2004–05	2004–05/2009–10	1999–00/2009–10
Primary sector (Agriculture and allied)	**0.20**	**1.29**	**−1.65**	**−0.19**
Secondary sector	**2.55**	**6.03**	**4.65**	**5.34**
Mining and quarrying	−1.25	2.11	5.21	3.65
Manufacturing	1.62	4.09	−2.74	0.62
Utilities (Electricity, gas and water supply)	−8.29	1.83	1.19	1.51
Construction	6.44	10.50	13.61	12.04
Tertiary sector	**2.12**	**4.52**	**0.90**	**2.70**
Trade, hoteling etc.	3.76	6.23	0.66	3.41
Transport and communication etc.	6.75	6.33	2.58	4.44
Financing, insurance, real estate and business services	4.27	8.41	2.07	5.20
Community, social and personal services	−0.99	1.38	0.16	0.77
All non-agricultural (Secondary + Tertiary sectors)	**2.32**	**5.25**	**2.83**	**4.03**
Total	**0.67**	**2.29**	**−0.34**	**0.96**

Source: Adapted from Papola and Sahu (2012, Table 4, p. 9)

Table 3.15 Growth of urban employment (UPSS) by sectors in India from 1993–94 to 2009–10

Sector	Annual average employment growth rate (%)			
	1993–94/1999–00	1999–00/2004–05	2004–05/2009–10	1999–00/2009–10
Primary sector (Agriculture and allied)	**−3.48**	**4.47**	**−1.17**	**1.61**
Secondary sector	**2.32**	**5.60**	**2.01**	**3.79**
Mining and quarrying	−3.69	3.00	−1.87	0.53
Manufacturing	1.63	6.05	0.45	3.21
Utilities (Electricity, gas and water supply)	−4.16	4.05	0.93	2.47
Construction	6.29	4.68	6.60	5.64
Tertiary sector	**3.37**	**3.78**	**2.06**	**2.92**
Trade, Hoteling etc.	8.08	2.53	1.43	1.98
Transport and communication etc.	3.94	4.36	1.77	3.06
Financing, insurance, real estate and business services	5.59	9.96	6.67	8.30
Community, social and personal services	−1.87	3.75	1.58	2.66
All non-agricultural (Secondary + Tertiary sectors)	**2.99**	**4.44**	**2.06**	**3.23**
Total	**2.30**	**4.44**	**1.78**	**3.10**

Source: Adapted from Papola and Sahu (2012, Table 5, p. 10)

Table 3.16 Share of major industry groups in unorganised manufacturing employment across the states

Industry groups	1994–95	2005–06	2010–11
Food products	20.13	17.43	13.74
Tobacco products	7.73	11.53	8.84
Textiles	22.45	30.96	35.55
Leather products	1.64	1.30	0.93
Wood products	14.96	11.15	8.12
Paper and printing	1.86	2.10	2.38
Chemical products	10.99	9.61	11.23
Metal and metal products	4.55	4.86	5.60
Machinery and electrical	3.05	2.47	3.07
Transport and transport equipments	0.42	0.60	0.39
Furniture and other manufacturing	12.21	7.98	10.14
Total	**100.00**	**100.00**	**100.00**

Source: Adapted from Saikia and Goswami (2017, Table 3)

Table 3.17 Pattern of unorganised manufacturing enterprises across the Indian States

States	Percentage share in employment			Per capita gross value added[a]		
	1994–95	2005–06	2010–11	1994–95	2005–06	2010–11
Andhra Pradesh	7.62	8.07	8.90	67	76	109
Arunachal Pradesh	0.03	0.01	0.01	54	51	37
Assam	1.86	1.74	1.21	44	62	54
Bihar	7.41	6.60	3.88	46	37	28
Delhi	2.11	1.26	2.14	409	198	293
Gujarat	5.75	5.08	9.21	214	149	245
Haryana	0.88	1.49	1.34	111	154	106
Himachal Pradesh	0.46	0.45	0.44	65	113	88
Jammu and Kashmir	0.21	0.87	0.97	19	146	111
Karnataka	5.63	5.42	4.33	84	127	98
Kerala	2.10	3.82	2.80	63	133	141
Madhya Pradesh	3.72	6.03	5.41	54	50	39
Maharashtra	7.09	7.96	9.23	149	171	141
Manipur	0.23	0.22	0.17	79	70	53
Meghalaya	0.13	0.25	0.11	55	121	50
Mizoram	0.03	0.03	0.02	53	54	36
Nagaland	0.06	0.04	0.03	45	33	15
Odisha	9.92	5.56	3.63	71	65	52
Punjab	1.39	1.65	2.20	119	115	123
Rajasthan	2.45	3.56	3.50	56	80	79
Sikkim	0.00	0.02	0.01	17	85	64
Tamil Nadu	9.01	9.25	10.07	185	164	219
Tripura	0.39	0.40	0.32	73	179	100
Uttar Pradesh	17.45	14.9	15.48	89	70	59
West Bengal	13.85	15.09	14.36	122	127	118
All India	**100**	**100**	**100**	**100**	**100**	**100**

Note: [a]The states per capita gross value added is expressed to the all India average
Source: Saikia and Goswami (2017, Table 2)

employment from capital goods industries such as metal and machinery and electrical products, metal products, transport and transport equipment. Table 3.16 shows share of major 11 two-digit industry groups in India's unorganised manufacturing employment for 1994–95, 2005–06 and 2010–11. Over these periods, increase in the share of employment has been substantial in textiles followed by a small increase in metal and metal products. Employment shares of food, wood and leather products have sharply declined during the same periods. However, only a few states have high concentration of such unorganised manufacturing enterprises (Table 3.17). Such states as have high percentage share in employment in these enterprises during the post (comprehensive) liberalisation period (1994–95/2010–11) include Uttar Pradesh, West Bengal, Tamil Nadu, Maharashtra, Gujarat and

Andhra Pradesh. All these states except Uttar Pradesh and Andhra Pradesh have, however, continuously higher per capita gross value added than the national average over the same period.

3.4.3 Informal Segment as a Subset of the Unorganised Segment

Under the Sect. 2.2 above, there have been very general definitions of the 'organised' and the 'unorganised' segments of a dual economy. Lately, there has been a conscious attempt under National Commission for Enterprises in the Unorganised Sector (NCEUS) for reviewing the definitional, methodological and statistical issues involved for the estimation particularly of the unorganised segment GDP/NDP and its employment. Until this review process started, the words 'unorganised' and 'informal' used to be interchangeably applied. In fact, an NCEU *Task Force on Definitional and Statistical Issues Relating to the Unorganised Sector* defines the unorganised or informal segment as the one that 'consists of all unincorporated private enterprises owned by individuals or households engaged in the sale and production of goods and services operated on a proprietary or partnership basis and with less than ten total workers'. The NCEUS accepted not only this definition, but also the definition of informal employment as (i) the unorganised workers consisting of those working in the unorganised segment or households, excluding regular workers with social security benefits provided by the employers and (ii) the workers in the organised or formal segment without any employment and social security benefits provided by the employers.[41]

As reported in NCEUS (2008), Ramesh Kolli and Suvendu Hazra of the Central Statistical Organisation (CSO) estimate the share of the informal segment (as a subset of the unorganised segment) in the net domestic product (NDP) by applying a Method of Apportioning. The definitions used in apportioning are as follows:

(i) Informal segment enterprises consist of unorganised segment's all own account enterprises (i.e., unincorporated private enterprises owned by individuals or households) as well as its other enterprises with at least one hired worker or having five or less workers;
(ii) Among the informal segment enterprises identified above, the following ones are excluded:

 (a) registered under the Companies Act;
 (b) employing processes that require high degree of technical know-how;
 (c) franchises of organised or formal segment units;
 (d) non-profit organisation; and

[41]NCEUS (2008, Footnote 1, p. 3).

Table 3.18 Share of informal and unorganised segments in NDP: 2001–02 (%)

Industry group	Informal	Others	Unorganised	Organised	Total
Agriculture, forestry and fishing	25.5		25.5	0.9	26.4
Mining and quarrying	0.2		0.2	1.8	2.0
Manufacturing	1.6	3.4	5.0	8.4	13.4
Electricity, gas and water supply	0.1		0.1	1.0	1.0
Construction	3.9		3.9	2.5	6.4
Trade, hotels and restaurants	9.3	2.5	11.9	3.8	15.6
Transport and communication	3.3	0.6	3.9	2.8	6.7
Real estate, financial services and ownership of dwellings	2.6	2.9	5.4	7.6	13.0
Community, social and personal services	1.3	1.3	2.6	12.8	15.4
Total	**47.7**	**10.7**	**58.5**	**41.5**	**100.0**

Source: NCEUS (2008, Table 1, p. 3)

(e) not covered under production boundary of the System of National Accounts (SNA).

Accordingly, the sector-wise details under different segments' (*informal, unorganised* and *organised*) shares in NDP as estimated by Kolli and Hazra for 2001–02 are given in Table 3.18. It is to be noted that the unorganised segment's only manufacturing component under secondary sector and all services under tertiary sector have been split into two separate categories of *informal* and *others*. The resulting contribution of *informal* segment to NDP becomes 47.7% as compared to the conventional *unorganised* segment's estimate of 58.5%. Subsequently, a modified Method of Apportioning has been applied to compare similar estimates of gross value added (GVA) for the years 1999–2000 and 2004–05. The share of informal segment in total GVA reduced by 5.48% points in aggregate between these two years.[42] It seems that the downsizing of the unorganised segment to the level of *informal* segment[43] and thereby its counterpart of the *formal* segment is essentially an *expanded organised* segment, which by definition implies the lower level of *dualism*.

During the same period (1999–00/2004/05), the overall employment elasticity[44] of *informal* segment was as high as 0.71 as compared to 0.36 in the *formal* or

[42]*Ibid.* (p. 6).

[43]Recently, Nagaraj (2016) questions the methodology applied in the new *National Accounts Statistics* (NAS) for 2011–12 that shows household (*informal* or *unorganised*) segment output has shrunk by 22% in absolute size, or by 11% points of GDP, compared to the old series with 2004–05 as the base year.

[44]*Employment elasticity* is a measure of how employment varies with economic growth. If it is, say, 0.05%, it means that for every 1% growth in GDP, employment increases by 0.05%.

organised segment and 0.48 for the entire economy. Among different industries, *informal* segment agriculture had an employment elasticity of 1.50 as against 0.19 in the *formal* segment. In the case of manufacturing industries, the *informal* segment elasticity was 1.04 as against 0.58 in their *formal* segment. Real estate, renting and business services activities in the *informal* segment had an abnormally high employment elasticity of 3.09. Elasticity was also considerably high in the case of private households with paid employees which are entirely in the *informal* segment.[45] All this boils down to the fact that there was a shift of jobs to the *informal* segment.

During the period from 2004–05 to 2009–10, there has been a reduction in the number of workers employed in agriculture, which is, as Chakravarty (2012) notes, a good thing, if, of course, the secondary and tertiary segments can absorb surplus workers from agriculture. In fact, the employment elasticity in the manufacturing sector too was negative, at −0.31 compared with 0.76 in the first half of the first decade of the new millennium.[46] If employment in the manufacturing sector contracted, where did people find jobs? The total net increase in employment between 2004–05 and 2009–10 was 2.72 million. But the increase in informal employment during the period was 4.62 million. That means not only were the new jobs all created in the informal sector, but there was some shrinkage in formal sector employment as well, with jobs continued shifting to the informal sector. Indeed, in the decade 1999–2000 to 2009–10, formal sector jobs shrunk by two million, and the entire job growth was in the informal sector. Nearly 93% of the workforce in 2009–10 was in informal employment, compared with 91% in 1999–2000. Not only are jobs hard to get, their quality too has worsened.[47]

Many of the new jobs in the informal sector were in the construction industry. Between 2004–05 and 2009–10, there was a reduction of 14 million jobs in agriculture and five million in manufacturing. Most of the persons displaced found jobs in construction, where employment went up by 18 million. And since most of the construction industry is in the informal sector, the trend explains the growing share of informal employment.

A caution that has been made in *Economic Survey 2014–15* (Vol. I, p. 11) is the following:

> Regardless of which data source is used, it seems clear that employment growth is lagging behind growth in the labour force. For example, according to the Census, between 2001 and 2011, labor force growth was 2.23 percent (male and female combined). This is lower than most estimates of employment growth in this decade of closer to 1.4 percent. Creating more rapid employment opportunities is clearly a major policy challenge.

---

[45]NCEUS (2008, p. 9).

[46]Before comprehensive liberalisation, between 1983 and 1987–88, the employment elasticity of manufacturing was 0.59. The Planning Commission explained this by saying there had been a substitution of labour by capital-intensive technology.

[47]Chakravarty (2012).

In addition to this major policy challenge related to the employment scenario, the *Economic Survey 2016–17* (p. 161–62) stresses also on job quality and labour reform measures:

> The growth in employment by category reflects increase in both casual and contract workers. This has adverse implications on the level of wages, stability of employment, social security of employees owing to the 'temporary' nature of employment. It also indicates preferences by employers away from regular/formal employment to circumvent labour laws.
>
> The multiplicity of labour laws and the difficulty in their compliance have been an impediment to the industrial development and employment generation. At present, there are 39 Central labour laws which have been broadly proposed to be grouped into four or five Labour Codes on functional basis with the enactment of special laws for small manufacturing units. In a major initiative for bringing compliance in the system, catalysing the need of job creation and to ensure ease of doing business while ensuring safety, health and social security of every worker, the Government has put forth a set of labour reform measures.

3.5 Demonetisation and Goods and Services Tax (2016–2017): Implications for Dualism

Demonetisation

On 8 November 2016, the Modi Government suddenly announced an unconventional monetary policy of demonetising two highest denomination currency notes (Rs. 500 and Rs. 1,000) with immediate effect. These two currency notes which together constituted 86% of the cash[48] in circulation ceased to be legal tender except for a few specified purposes such as paying utility bills. Converting cash into deposits was allowed till 30 December 2016 and then was legally restricted under the Specified Banknote (Cessation of Liabilities) Ordnance, although conversion of the banned notes was still allowed thereafter at select Reserve Bank of India (RBI) counters till 31 March 2017. The fourfold aims of the demonetisation were to curb (i) corruption; (ii) counterfeiting; (iii) the use of high denomination notes for terrorist activities; and (iv) the accumulation of 'black money' generated by income that has not been declared to the tax authorities and therefore maintained as unaccounted private wealth in the form of cash.[49] The fourth aim of demonetisation has direct implication for dualism.

India's informal economy that is estimated to be nearly half of its overall economy depends heavily on cash transactions. The cash-intensive informal segment has certainly borne the inconvenience and hardship especially its workers who

---

[48]The terms 'cash' and 'currency' will be used interchangeably.

[49]It is noteworthy that although income from corruption is by definition black money, most black money is earned through perfectly legal activities. However, in most cases, income becomes 'black' solely because of tax evasion, i.e., by not declaring this income to the tax authorities.

have lost income and employment. While demand for formal segment's consumer goods may have been temporarily dampened, some participants in the informal economy may have adopted formal payment systems.

> These costs are transitory, and may be minimised in recorded GDP because the national income accounts estimate informal activity on the basis of formal sector indicators, which have not suffered to the same extent. … At the same time, demonetisation has the potential to generate long-term benefits in terms of reduced corruption, greater digitalisation of the economy, increased flows of financial savings, and greater formalisation of the economy, all of which could eventually lead to higher GDP growth, better tax compliance and greater tax revenues.[50]

On 1 July 2017, Prime Minister Narendra Modi informs that data mining during the post-demonetisation period shows over 3 lakh registered companies have indulged in suspected dealing to hide black money. He reveals that the government has already cancelled registration of over 1 lakh companies in a single stroke, and more than 37,000 shell firms have been identified for strong action to be taken against. So, it is expected that demonetisation has the potential for integration of a part of the unorganised segment into the organised segment and thereby expanding the size of the latter segment. The overall effect of demonetisation is, therefore, very likely to be a reduction in the degree of dualism.

Goods and Services Tax (GST)

Both the UPA and NDA Governments in the recent years have been working on the transformational reforms for sometimes to create 'One India, One Market, One Tax' via the long-awaited Goods and Services Tax (GST). It is expected that the 'GST will create a common Indian market, improve tax compliance and governance and boost investment and growth; it is also a bold new experiment in the governance of India's cooperative federalism'.[51]

After the passage of the Constitutional amendment for GST in the Parliament on 8 August 2016 and its ratification by more than 15 states during early September 2016, the GST Council, consisting of representatives from the Centre and the states, approved a four-rate GST structure[52]: the lowest rate of 5% for common use items, two standard rates of 12% and 18% for goods and services, and a highest tax slab of 28% applicable to items currently taxed at more than 30% (excise duty plus value-added tax). With a view to keep inflation under control, essential items including food, which presently constitute roughly half of the consumer inflation basket, will be taxed at zero rate. Luxury cars, tobacco and aerated drinks would also be levied with an additional cess on top of the highest tax rate.[53] There has

[50]*Economic Survey 2016–17*, p. 2.

[51]*Ibid.*, p. 1.

[52]Many experts, as quoted in Sikarwar (2017), have questioned the four-rate structure arguing that it undermines the basic tenet of the GST—a simple structure with at most two rates.

[53]*Anon.* (2016).

been the successful passage of four GST Bills[54] for their enactment in the Lower House of the Parliament (Lok Sabha or House of People) on 29 March 2017 and in its Upper House (Rajya Sabha or Council of States) on 6 April 2017.

With its implementation from 1 July 2017, it is noteworthy of what GST is expected to bring with it[55]:

- GST is a destination-based tax that will replace the current Central taxes and duties such as Excise Duty, Service Tax, Counter Veiling Duty (CVD), Special Additional Duty of Customs (SAD), central charges and cesses and local state taxes, i.e. Value Added Tax (VAT), Central Sales Tax (CST), Octroi, Entry Tax, Purchase Tax, Luxury Tax, Taxes on lottery, betting and gambling, state cesses and surcharges and Entertainment tax (other than the tax levied by the local bodies).
- It will be a dual levy with State/Union territory GST and Central GST. Moreover, interstate supplies would attract an Integrated GST, which would be the sum total of CGST and SGST/UTGST.
- Petroleum products, i.e. petroleum crude, high-speed diesel, motor spirit, aviation turbine fuel, natural gas, will be brought under the ambit of GST from such date as may be notified by the Government on recommendation of the Council. Alcohol for human consumption has been kept outside the purview of GST.
- A well-designed GST in India is expected to simplify and rationalise the current indirect tax regime, eliminate tax cascading and put the Indian economy on high-growth trajectory. The proposed GST levy may potentially impact both manufacturing and services sector for the entire value chain of operations, namely procurement, manufacturing, distribution, warehousing, sales and pricing. It will also stimulate the need to relook at internal organisation and IT systems.

On 18 May 2017, the GST Council finalised 5 broad tax slabs: 0, 5, 12, 18 and 28%, the majority of a total of 1,211 items being under 18% slab. As it was expected, the list was subject to further vetting afterwards before it is rolled on 1 July 2017. In fact, following representations from industry, and as per discussions thereafter in the 16th GST Council Meeting held on 11 June 2017, earlier rates on 66 items have been revised. An updated list of selected items under five tax slabs is shown in Table 3.19.[56]

Note that gold and rough diamonds do not surprisingly fall under any of the five GST slabs and will be taxed only at 3% and 0.25%, respectively. In fact, after going through a prolonged industrial action organised by the jewellery sector's India Bullion and Jewellers Association (IBJA), the sector has welcomed GST of 3% on

---

[54]The four GST Bills are: Central GST (CGST), Integrated GST (IGST), Union Territory GST (UTGST) and the Bill for Compensation to States. The State GST (SGST) laws are supposed to be passed through individual state assemblies. IGST is essentially the sum total of CGST and SGST/UTGST.

[55]http://www.ey.com/in/en/services/ey-goods-and-services-tax-gst (accessed on 13 April, 2017).

[56]*Anon.* (2017).

Table 3.19 A list of selected items under five tax slabs

Rates	Goods	Services
0%	No tax is imposed on a number of food items such as fresh meat, fish, chicken, eggs, milk, butter milk, curd, natural honey, fresh fruits and vegetables, flour, besan, bread, all kinds of salt, jaggery and hulled cereal grains Also bindi, sindoor, kajal, palmyra, human hair, bangles, stamps and judicial papers, printed books, drawing or colouring books, newspapers, jute and handloom, bones and horn cores, hoof meal, horn meal, bone grist, bone meal, etc., are also included in this category of tax exemption	Hotels and lodges with tariff below Rs. 1,000 do not attract any tax under GST, which implies that a low-budget holiday may even get cheaper compared to pre-GST price Grandfathering service has also been exempted under GST
5%	Food items such as fish fillet, packaged food items, cream, skimmed milk powder, branded paneer, frozen vegetables, coffee, tea, spices, pizza bread, rusk, sabudana, cashew nut, cashew nut in shell, raisin, ice and snow Also in this slab included are apparel below Rs. 1000, footwear below Rs. 500, bio gas, kerosene, coal, medicine, insulin, stent, agarbatti (incense sticks), kites, postage or revenue stamps, stamp-post marks, fertilisers, first-day covers and lifeboats	Small restaurants will be under the 5% category, so will be transport services (railways, air transport), because their main input is petroleum, which is outside GST ambit
12%	Edibles like frozen meat products, butter, cheese, ghee, dry fruits in packaged form, animal fat, sausage, fruit juices, numkeen, ketchup and sauces; Cutlery items like spoons, forks, skimmers, cake servers, fish knives and tongs; Utility items like tooth powder, umbrella, sewing machine and spectacles; Indoor games items like playing cards, chess board, carom board, and ludo; Ayurvedic medicines, all diagnostic kits and reagents; Cellphones, apparel above Rs. 1000, etc.	Non-AC hotels, business class air ticket, state-run lottery, work contracts, etc.
18%	Another set of consumables like biscuits, flavoured refined sugar, pasta, cornflakes, pastries and cakes, preserved vegetables, jams, sauces, soups, ice cream, instant food mixes, curry paste, mayonnaise and salad dressings, mixed condiments and mixed seasonings and mineral water; Footwear costing more than Rs. 500;	AC hotels that serve liquor, branded garments, telecom services, IT services, and financial services

(continued)

Table 3.19 (continued)

Rates	Goods	Services
	Printed circuits, cameras, speakers and monitors, printers (other than multi-function printers), electrical transformers, CCTV, optical fiber, etc.; Other items like bidi patta (leaves), tissues, envelopes, sanitary napkins, note books, steel products, kajal pencil sticks, headgear and its parts, aluminum foil, weighing machinery (other than electric or electronic weighing machinery), bamboo furniture, swimming pools and padding pools	
28%	The residuary set of edibles which include chewing gum, molasses, chocolate not containing cocoa, waffles and wafers coated with chocolate, pan masala, aerated water; An array of personal care items like deodorants, shaving creams, after shave, hair shampoo, dye, sunscreen; Other items like bidi, paint, wallpaper, ceramic tiles, water heater, dishwater, weighing machine, washing machine, ATM, vending machines, vacuum cleaner, shavers, hair clippers, automobiles, motorcycles, and aircraft for personal use	5-star hotels, race club betting, private lottery and movie tickets above Rs. 100

gold and gold jewellery products as a win-win outcome. In fact, with the earlier 10% import duty remaining, consumers will have to pay an effective duty of 13% on gold jewellery, up from 12.5% (10% import duty, 1% value-added tax, 1% excise duty and 0.5% of cess). Rough precious and semi-precious stones will attract GST rate of 0.25%. The Gem & Jewelry Export Promotion Council (GJEPC) has been disappointed with the 0.25% tax rate on rough diamond because almost 95% of rough diamond is used for exports, but claiming its refund is time-consuming. According to Finance Minister Arun Jaitley, it is simply meant for audit trail.

The GST threshold of annual turnover is Rs. 20 lakh. Many small entrepreneurs with turnover less than this threshold may feel that they can bypass the GST regime's registration formalities. It is warned that this exemption comes with its own set of problems. For example, it is very likely that the unregistered businesses will find their business clients are switching to GST-registered vendors in order to avoid any related burden/loss that may arise. Also, the government may use the Compliance Rating Score (CRS) in future in order to identify businesses with poor score, which may lead to their loss. It is also noteworthy that all e-commerce businesses, irrespective of their turnover level, require to be registered under the GST regime.

Although all the handwritten ledgers, accounting books and notepads will become history, but GST regime requires a very high level of compliance; everything will instead be online and needs to be updated regularly. A business will have to file 37 returns in a year (three returns per month and one annual return) per state. If it does business from offices in more than one state, the number of returns will go up accordingly. A business with offices in, say, three states will now have to file 111 tax returns in a year. However, the GST provides some relief for smaller outfits that may not be able to meet these stiff requirements. An enterprise with an annual turnover of less than Rs. 50 lakh can opt for the *composition scheme*, which levies a presumptive tax of 0.5–2.5% on the turnover. However, this option is not open to everybody; only manufacturers and specific service providers (restaurants) can opt for this *composition scheme*. Although the *composition scheme* requires lesser GST compliance, it has several drawbacks such as: (i) only businesses which operate within a particular state can opt for this, and (ii) this scheme also breaks the chain of seamless input tax credit. The scheme disallows any credit of input tax to a purchaser of inputs from a composition dealer as well as to any composition dealer purchasing inputs from even a registered seller.[57]

Over all, by creating a common Indian market, the interstate trade barriers will certainly be removed; tax compliance and governance are also expected to be improved. The resulting efficiency gain and thereby cost reduction are likely to boost investment and finally the overall economic growth. Unlike demonetisation with fourfold aims, the fiscal efficiency gain from the GST is the prime objective and confined primarily within the organised/formal segment's fiscal reform process. But behind this prime objective, there is also compulsion for the small entrepreneurs in unorganised/informal segment to be registered under the GST regime. Therefore, the implication of this segment's integration into the organised/formal segment seems to have high potential, although there is no doubt that the transition to the GST regime will be initially disruptive while the large unorganised/informal segment and consumers slowly adjust to the new tax system.

[57]Zaidi (2017).

Chapter 4
Role of Social Sector Development Programmes during 1980–2016

4.1 Introduction

Since the very early years of the independent India, cooperatives assumed a significant role in its socio-economic development via poverty alleviation programme and economic growth particularly in rural areas. With the advent of planning process, cooperatives became an integral part of the Five-Year Plans. There had been substantial growth of the cooperatives in diverse areas of the economy during the second half of the twentieth century. The number of all types of cooperatives increased from 1.81 lakh in 1950–51 to 4.53 lakh in 1996–97. The total membership of cooperative societies increased from 1.55 crore to 20.45 crore during the same period. The cooperatives have been operating in various areas of the economy such as credit, production, processing, marketing, input distribution, housing, dairying and textiles. In some of the areas of their activities like dairying, urban banking and housing, sugar and handlooms, the cooperatives had achieved success to an extent but there were larger areas where they had not been so successful.

> The failure of cooperatives in the country is mainly attributable to dormant membership and lack of active participation of members in the management of cooperatives. Mounting overdues in cooperative credit institution, lack of mobilisation of internal resources and over-dependence on Government assistance, lack of professional management, bureaucratic control and interference in the management, political interference and over-politisation have proved harmful to their growth. Predominance of vested interests resulting in non-percolation of benefits to a common member, particularly to the class of persons for whom such cooperatives were basically formed, has also retarded the development of cooperatives.[1]

Meanwhile, after the Fourth Five-Year Plan (1969–74), and more specifically since the Sixth Five-Year Plan (1980–85), 'Direct Measures for Poverty Eradication' in terms of several special employment programmes have been in operation targeting

[1]http://pib.nic.in/feature/fe0299/f1202992.html.

D. Dutta, *Development under Dualism and Digital Divide in Twenty-First Century India*, Dynamics of Asian Development, https://doi.org/10.1007/978-981-10-6344-2_4

Table 4.1 Pattern of Five-Year Plan outlays on social services (Rs. Crore)

Plan and period	Outlay	Actuals
Sixth Plan 1980–85	14,035 (14.4)	15,917 (14.5)
Seventh Plan 1985–1990	31,545 (17.5)	34,960 (16.0)
Eighth Plan 1992–97	79,012 (18.2)	88,807 (18.3)
Ninth Plan 1997–2002	1,83,273 (21.3)	1,94,529 (20.6)
Tenth Plan 2002–2007	3,47,391 (22.8)	4,36,529 (27.0)
Eleventh Plan 2007–12	11,02,327 (30.2)	11,97,576 (32.6)
Twelfth Plan 2012–17	26,64,843 (34.7)	NA

Note: figures in brackets indicate percentage to total plan outlay
Source: Kaur et al. (2013, Table 1)

both the rural and urban poor. Public sector outlays on social services (both planned projection and actual realisation) have substantially increased since the Sixth Five-Year Plan (1980–85). As a proportion of total plan outlays, they have more than doubled from 14.4% in the Sixth Plan to 30.2% in the Eleventh Plan and were projected at 34.7% in the Twelfth Plan (Table 4.1).

4.2 Direct Measures for Poverty Eradication and Social Sector Development Programmes

4.2.1 1980–90

As 'Direct Measures for Poverty Eradication', an earlier special programme called *Integrated Rural Development Programme* (IRDP) was initially launched by the Government of India during 1978–79. IRDP with its two sub-programmes: *Training for Rural Youth for Self-Employment* (TRYSEM) and *Development of Women and Children in Rural Areas* (DWCRA) had been extended throughout India in 1980. The programme covered small and marginal farmers, agricultural workers and landless labourers and rural craftsmen and artisans and virtually all the families of about five persons with an annual income level below Rs. 3500. The main aim of IRDP was to raise the below poverty line (BPL) families in the rural areas above the poverty line on a lasting basis by giving them income generating assets and access to credit and other inputs. The programme was meant to be implemented by District Rural Development Agency (DRDA) with the assistance from block level machinery.[2]

Subsequently, two wage employment programmes, *National Rural Employment Programme* (NREP) [launched in 1980] and *Rural Landless Employment Guarantee Programme* (RLEGP) [introduced in 1983], had also been noteworthy. These two latter programmes had, however, been merged to form the *Jawahar Rozgar Yojana* (JRY) in 1989–90. While IRDP's purpose was to 'promote self-employment by providing productive assets and inputs to the rural poor through a mix of subsidy and bank credit', TRYSEM was meant to provide 'training in technical skills to poor rural youth to enable them to take up self-employment or wage employment'; DWCRA's goal was to promote 'economic activities among groups of rural women'. JRY was designed to 'generate additional gainful employment for the rural unemployed and underemployed by taking up works for creating productive economic assets'. During the Seventh Plan period (1985–90), the Government report claimed that '18.2 million families were assisted under IRDP, and the wage employment programmes (NREP/RLEGP and JRY) generated 3,947 million man-days of employment'.[3]

For the urban poor, three major programmes were initiated during the 1980s. The *Scheme for Self-Employment to the Educated Urban Youth* (SEEUY) 'was launched during the year 1983–84 of the Sixth Plan (1980–85), with the objective of promoting self-employment among the educated youth age between 18 and 35 years belonging to families with income not exceeding Rs. 10,000/– per annum'. It covered areas other than cities with a population of more than one million. The Central Government provided a capital subsidy of 25% of the loan provided by the banks. During the Seventh Plan (1985–90), one of the two other major programmes launched in September 1986 was *Self-Employment Programmes for the Urban Poor* (SEPUP), which covered 'all cities and towns with a population of 10,000 and above and areas not covered by IRDP'. Under the SEPUP scheme, loans up to Rs. 5,000/– were provided by banks to the urban poor for taking up useful economic ventures with Central Government providing a capital subsidy of 25% of the total loan. The third programme *Nehru Rojgar Yojana* (NRY) was launched in October 1989 in order to improve the living conditions of the urban poor.

In spite of the increase in per capita income, reduction in poverty level and the continual decline of the unorganised segment's share in NDP since the early 1980s, the fact that the unorganised segment continues to contain more than 90% of India's labour force has a deeper implication from the viewpoint of the progress of their 'total way of life' or simply 'social development'.

---

[2]PEO (1985, p. 1).

[3]*Economic Survey 1991–92*, Part II, p. 135.

4.2.2 1991–96

After the P.V. Narasimha Rao's government (21 June 1991–16 May 1996) introduced drastic liberalisation policy in order to overcome an economic crisis of unprecedented dimensions, the planning process became more of an indicative and supportive one in nature rather than being a directive one as before. In the Planning Commission's Annual Report 1991–1992, it was clearly stated:

> [T]he Planning Commission would now work on building a long-term strategic vision of the future. The concentration would be on anticipating future trends and evolving integrated strategies for achieving the highest possible level of development of the country in keeping with the competitive international standards.[4]

The new approach to development would, according to this report, be based on 'a re-examination and reorientation of the role of the government, harnessing the latent energies of the people through people's involvement in the process of nation building, creating an environment which encourages and builds up people's initiatives rather than their dependence on the government and which sets free the forces of growth and modernisation'. It, however, claimed to remain committed to play a major role on 'protecting the interests of the poor and the underprivileged'. Keeping these things in view, the objectives which the Eighth Five-Year Plan (1992–97) sought to give priority were 'adequate employment generation, containment of population growth, universalisation of elementary education, generation of agricultural surpluses for export and strengthening of infrastructure'.[5]

More importantly, the Government of India's official annual report *Economic Survey 1991–92* (Part II: Sectoral Development) included for the first time a new chapter on the development of *Social Sectors* covering education, health and family welfare, water supply, sanitation, housing, rural development, social welfare, nutrition and minimum basic services. In the *Introduction* of this chapter (Ch. 9, p. 125), it notes:

> Human capital is a basic input for planning and its successful implementation. Hence, the development of social sectors has been one of the major objectives of our Plans. Proper utilization of human resources, on the other hand, provides the key to the economic and social development. … The major areas, which contribute in this direction, are education, health and family welfare, poverty alleviation programmes, housing and training etc. The programmes directed towards women and children have also assumed special importance in this context. Similarly, water supply, sanitation, labour and labour welfare and special employment programmes have been included in the thrust areas.

The Rao Government, the architect of India's comprehensive liberalisation, also committed to expand the scope and coverage of direct poverty reduction

[4]http://planningcommission.nic.in/reports/genrep/area9099/index.php?repts=ar91-92.htm.
[5]*Ibid.*

programmes. One of the seven major areas of policy reforms[6] was human resource development:

> The people must be helped to enhance their own capabilities. They should have considerably better access to education and training, and opportunities to use them in productive work. Renewed efforts are necessary to expand health care and to improve its quality. Social and economic uplift of women must be given special emphasis. Not only is the potential of the women capable of being more fully exploited, but their advancement is essential for moderating population growth.[7]

Recognising that proper utilisation of human resources provides the key to economic and social development, the Rao Government took several additional measures and launched new schemes for improvement in social sectors. The major programmes in social sectors contributing towards the goals of improving the quality of life, reducing poverty and ensuring social justice are identified in the field of education, health and family welfare, housing, water supply, sanitation and employment generation.

The *Economic Survey 1992–93* had, however, acknowledged that the social development had also not been uniform across various States. Table 4.2 shows wide variations that existed in the early 1990s in terms of social indicators for major States, *viz* estimated infant mortality (126 in Odisha, while 17 in Kerala), birth rate (35.8 in Madhya Pradesh, while 18.1 in Kerala), death rate (13.8 in Madhya Pradesh, while 6.0 in Kerala), literacy (38.5 in Bihar, while 89.8 in Kerala) and population below poverty line (40.8 in Bihar, while 7.2 in Punjab).

In 1992–93, the Rao Government launched three schemes: *Scheme of Urban Enterprises* (SUME) to 'provide support to the urban poor in upgrading their skills and setting up microenterprises in all urban settlements along the line of IRDP'; *Scheme of Urban Wage Employment* (SUWE) for providing wage employment through provision of basic amenities to the poor in all urban settlements with a population of less than one lakh; and the *Scheme of Housing and Shelter Upgradation* (SHASU) for providing employment through housing and shelter upgradation in urban settlements with population between one and 20 lakh with relaxation in the lower population limit in certain specified locations.[8] The existing programme SEPUP was merged with the SUME under NRY from 1992–93. The redesigned NRY, therefore, consisted of three sub-schemes, namely SUME, SUWE and SHASU.

In order to give a fillip to employment generation, two additional programmes had been launched in 1993–94: *Employment Assurance Scheme* (EAS) for providing 100 days of unskilled manual work to the rural poor seeking employment during the lean agricultural season; *Prime Minister's Rozgar Yojana* (PMRY) for the Educated Unemployed Youth covering initially only urban areas and then both

---

[6]The seven major policy reforms that emerged were related to areas of fiscal, trade, industrial, financial, agricultural, poverty alleviation and human resource.

[7]*Economic Survey 1991–92*, Part I, p. 26.

[8]*Economic Survey 1992–93*, p. 217.

Table 4.2 Selected indicators of social development for major states in early 1990s[a]

States	Infant mortality rate (per 1000 live births)	Birth rate (per 1000)	Death rate (per 1000)	Literacy (per cent)	Population below poverty line (per cent)
1	2	3	4	5	6
Andhra Pradesh	73	26.0	9.7	44.1	31.7
Assam	81	30.9	11.5	52.9	22.8
Bihar	69	30.5	9.8	38.5	40.8
Gujarat	69	27.5	8.5	61.3	18.4
Haryana	68	33.1	8.2	55.9	11.6
Karnataka	77	26.8	9.0	56.0	32.1
Kerala	17	18.1	6.0	89.8	17.0
Madhya Pradesh	122	35.8	13.8	44.2	36.7
Maharashtra	60	26.2	8.2	64.9	29.2
Odisha	126	28.8	12.7	49.1	44.7
Punjab	53	28.6	8.0	58.5	7.2
Rajasthan	77	34.3	9.8	38.6	22.4
Tamil Nadu	57	20.7	8.8	62.7	32.8
Uttar Pradesh	93	35.1	11.1	41.1	35.1
West Bengal	70	26.7	8.1	57.7	27.6
All India	80	29.3	9.8	52.2	29.9

Source: *Economic Survey 1992–93*, Government of India, Table 9.3, p. 198
[a]Major States are States with population of 10 million and above as per 1991 Census
Notes: (i) Column 2, 3 and 4 are based on Sample Registration System estimates for 1991
(ii) Column 5 is based on final population totals of 1991 Census excluding Jammu and Kashmir in all India
(iii) Column 6 is based on the draft report of 43rd Round of N.S.O data on household consumer expenditure relating to population as on 1 March 1988

rural and urban areas. From 1994–95 onwards, a provision was made that the existing scheme for *Self-Employment for Educated Unemployed Youth* (SEEUY) would be integrated into PMRY.

Recognising the strategic importance of the social sectors' development for achieving the primary objectives of economic growth and equity, the Rao Government increased investment in human capital development. This was reflected in the substantial increase in the Central Plan allocations for social sectors and poverty alleviation programmes during 1993–96.[9] Also, five new social welfare schemes had been launched in 1995–96: *National Social Assistance Programme*

[9]These increased allocations for social sectors and poverty allocation programmes had been reported in *Economic Survey 1995–96*, Table 10.1, p. 168.

(NSAP), *Mid-Day Meal Programme*, *Rural Group Life Insurance Scheme* (RGLIS), *Indira Mahila Yojana* (IMY) and *Prime Minister's Integrated Urban Poverty Eradication Programme* (PMIUPEP).[10]

For better implementation of various employment generation and poverty alleviation programmes, special attention had been given by the Rao Government. Effective involvement of the *Panchayati Raj Institutions* (PRIs) and *non-governmental organisations* (NGOs) had been emphasised especially because these programmes are focused on disadvantaged sections of the population. Apart from dovetailing the programmes with sectoral and area development programmes, proper planning for identifying thrust areas at grass root level, selecting viable projects within the management capacities of poor families and effective tying up of forward and backward linkages with credit and marketing had been increasingly emphasised with a view to bringing about qualitative improvements of the programmes.[11]

4.2.3 1997–2002

Because of the lack of political stability during the period from May 1996 to October 1998,[12] there had been no new major programmes as such were launched. Instead, only the existing special employment and poverty alleviation programmes for both the rural and urban areas had been restructured and fine-tuned to increase their effectiveness and sustainability. However, substantial increase in the

---

[10]The targets and achievements of various special employment and poverty alleviation programmes are provided in *Ibid.* (Table 10.13, p. 183).

[11]*Ibid.*, p. 184.

[12]The outcome of India's general election in 1996 was a hung parliament with neither of the top two leading political parties—*Indian National Congress* (INC) and *Bharatiya Janata Party* (BJP)—was able to secure a mandate, although the BJP's Atal Behari Vajpayee managed to form a government, but it was short-lived (16 May 1996 to 1 June 1996). Afterwards, the newly formed *United Front* (UF), consisting of non-Congress and non-BJP parties, secured support from 332 members out of the 545 seats in the Lok Sabha (House of the People)—the lower house of India's Bicameral-Parliament. The UF government with H.D. Deve Gowda from the *Janata Dal* as its Prime Minister formed the government. Subsequently, the INC which was supporting the UF government from outside decided to withdraw this support, which led to its collapse in April 1997. To avoid mid-term elections, a compromise was reached; the INC agreed to support another UF government under a new leader. As a result, the UF elected I.K. Gujral as its new leader, who was sworn in as Prime Minister on 21 April 1997. But, again India had to go to a general election in 1998 as a result of withdrawal of the INC's support to the Gujral government. Another newly formed *National Democratic Alliance* (NDA) led by the BJP's Atal Behari Vajpayee formed the government in May 1998, but it also collapsed in late 1998, when *All India Anna Dravida Munnetra Kazhagam* (AIADMK) party withdrew its support.

Table 4.3 Estimates of poverty in rural and urban India: 1973–74 to 1999–2000 (percentage poor)

Year	Rural	Urban	Total
1973–74	56.4	49.0	54.9
1977–78	53.1	45.2	51.3
1983	45.7	40.8	44.5
1987–88	39.1	38.2	38.9
1993–94	37.3	32.4	36.0
1999–2000[a]	27.1	23.6	26.1

[a]Because the methodology used for the poverty estimate in 1999–2000 is different from that used in the earlier estimates, they are not strictly comparable (*Economic Survey 2000–2001*, Government of India, p. 194)

Source: *Economic Survey 2001–2002*, Government of India, Table 10.4, p. 238

availability of funds by the Central Government for the State-level social programmes gave the signal that the States' involvement was crucial not only for their effective implementation, but also in evolving various innovative programmes, which are likely to benefit the poor directly.[13]

After winning the 1999 election with a larger majority, the newly formed *National Democratic Alliance* (NDA) led by the Bharatiya Janata Party (BJP) formed the government with Atal Behari Vajpayee as its Prime Minister on 13 October 1999. Although the Vajpayee Government found that both the external and internal economic environments were conducive to higher economic growth,[14] but one of the daunting challenges that India had been facing was to provide employment not only for the additions to the labour force, but also to reduce the backlog of unemployment accumulated from the past. In addition to these positive economic conditions, there had been a rapid decrease in the proportion of people living below poverty line (BPL) from 36% to 26.1% during the period between 1993–94 and 1999–2000 as claimed by the government's official figures on the poverty estimates (Table 4.3).

Although there had been a steady decline of the incidence of poverty at the national level and State/UTs levels over the last three decades of the twentieth century, but rural–urban and interstate disparities were still visible (Table 4.4):

[13]*Economic Survey 1996–97*, p. 196.

[14]Among the positive signs of the internal economic environment were industrial recovery from the cyclical downturn of the earlier two years, accelerated growth of the construction sector, markedly improved of the performance of infrastructure sectors and dropping of the inflation rate to international levels of 2–3% for the first time in decades. On the external environment side, the balance of payments survived the twin shocks of the East-Asian financial crisis that began in July 1997 and the post-Pokhran-II sanctions (as a result of India's nuclear bomb testing in May 1998) with a low current account deficit and sufficient capital inflows (*Economic Survey: 1999–2000*, p. 1).

Table 4.4 Estimates of poverty at the state level in rural and urban India (1973–74 to 1999–2000) (Percentage poor)

States and Union Territories	Rural			Urban			Total		
	1973–74	1993–94	1999–2000	1973–74	1993–94	1999–2000	1973–74	1993–94	1999–2000
Andhra Pradesh	48.41	15.92	11.05	50.61	38.33	26.63	48.86	22.19	15.77
Arunachal Pradesh	52.67	45.01	40.04	36.92	7.73	7.47	51.93	39.35	33.47
Assam	52.67	45.01	40.04	36.92	7.73	7.47	51.21	40.86	36.09
Bihar	62.99	58.21	44.30	52.96	34.50	32.91	61.91	54.96	42.60
Goa	46.85	5.34	1.35	37.69	27.03	7.52	44.26	14.92	4.40
Gujarat	46.35	22.12	13.17	52.57	27.89	15.59	48.15	24.21	14.07
Haryana	34.23	28.02	8.27	40.18	16.38	9.99	35.36	25.05	8.74
Himachal Pradesh	27.42	30.34	7.94	13.17	9.18	4.63	26.39	28.44	7.63
Jammu and Kashmir	45.51	30.34	3.97	21.32	9.18	1.98	40.83	25.17	3.48
Karnataka	55.14	29.88	17.38	52.53	40.14	25.25	54.47	33.16	20.04
Kerala	59.19	25.76	9.38	62.74	24.55	20.27	59.79	25.43	12.72
Madhya Pradesh	62.66	40.64	37.06	57.65	48.38	38.44	61.78	42.52	37.43
Maharashtra	57.71	37.93	23.72	43.87	35.15	26.81	53.24	36.86	25.02
Manipur	52.67	45.01	40.04	36.92	7.73	7.47	49.96	33.78	28.54
Meghalaya	52.67	45.01	40.04	36.92	7.73	7.47	50.92	37.92	33.87
Mizoram	52.67	45.01	40.04	36.92	7.73	7.47	50.32	25.66	19.47
Nagaland	52.67	45.01	40.04	36.92	7.73	7.47	50.81	37.92	32.67
Odisha	62.28	49.72	48.01	55.62	41.64	42.83	66.18	48.56	47.15
Punjab	28.21	11.95	6.35	27.96	11.35	5.75	28.15	11.77	6.16
Rajasthan	44.76	26.46	13.74	52.13	30.49	19.85	46.16	27.41	15.28
Sikkim	52.67	45.01	40.04	36.92	7.73	7.47	50.86	41.43	36.55
Tamil Nadu	57.43	32.48	20.55	49.40	39.77	22.11	54.94	35.03	21.12
Tripura	52.67	45.01	40.04	36.92	7.73	7.47	51.00	39.01	34.44
Uttar Pradesh	56.53	42.28	31.22	60.09	35.39	30.89	57.07	40.85	31.15
West Bengal	73.16	40.80	31.85	34.67	22.41	14.86	63.43	35.66	27.02
Andaman and Nicobar Island	57.43	32.48	20.55	49.40	39.77	22.11	55.56	34.47	20.99
Chandigarh	27.96	11.35	5.75	27.96	11.35	5.75	27.96	11.35	5.75
Dadra and Nagar Haveli	46.85	51.95	17.57	37.69	39.93	13.52	46.55	50.84	17.14
Daman and Diu	N.A.	5.34	1.35	N.A.	27.03	7.52	N.A.	15.80	4.44

(continued)

Table 4.4 (continued)

States and Union Territories	Rural			Urban			Total		
	1973–74	1993–94	1999–2000	1973–74	1993–94	1999–2000	1973–74	1993–94	1999–2000
Delhi	24.44	1.90	0.40	52.23	16.03	9.42	49.61	14.69	8.23
Lakshadweep	59.19	25.76	9.38	62.74	24.55	20.27	59.68	25.04	15.60
Pondicherry	57.43	32.48	20.55	49.40	39.77	22.11	53.82	37.40	21.67
All India	**56.44**	**37.27**	**27.09**	**49.01**	**32.36**	**23.62**	**54.88**	**35.97**	**26.01**

Notes: *N.A.* Not Available
(i) Poverty estimates on a 30-day recall basis are for 1999–2000
(ii) Poverty Ratio of Assam is used for Sikkim, Arunachal Pradesh, Meghalaya, Mizoram, Nagaland and Tripura
(iii) Poverty Line of Maharashtra and expenditure distribution of Goa are used to estimate Poverty Ratio of Goa
(iv) Poverty Line of Himachal Pradesh and expenditure distribution of Jammu and Kashmir are used to estimate Poverty Ratio of Jammu and Kashmir
(v) Poverty Ratio of Tamil Nadu is used for Pondicherry and Andaman and Nicobar Island
(vi) Urban Poverty Ratio of Punjab used for both rural and urban poverty of Chandigarh
(vii) Poverty Line of Maharashtra and expenditure distribution of Dadra and Nagar Haveli are used to estimate Poverty Ratio of Dadra and Nagar Haveli
(viii) Poverty Ratio of Goa is used for Daman and Diu
(ix) Poverty Ratio of Kerala is used for Lakshadweep
(x) Urban Poverty Ratio of Rajasthan may be treated as tentative
Source: *Economic Survey 2001–2002*, Government of India, Table 10.5, p. 239 (based on Planning Commission's report)

> The rural poverty ratio was still relatively high in Orissa (now Odisha), Bihar and the North Eastern States. In Orissa, Madhya Pradesh, Bihar and Uttar Pradesh, the urban poverty ratios were in the range of 30.89 to 42.83 per cent in 1999–2000. The combined rural and urban poor made up 47.15 per cent of Orissa and 42.60 per cent of Bihar. For the states of Madhya Pradesh, Sikkim, Arunachal Pradesh and Assam the combined poverty ratios in 1999–2000 were in the range of 33.47 to 37.43 per cent. There had been a significant reduction in poverty during the period in Kerala, Jammu & Kashmir, Goa, Lakshdweep, Delhi, Andhra Pradesh, Gujarat, Tamil Nadu, Karnataka, West Bengal and Andaman and Nicobar Islands. Thus, while some states such as Punjab and Haryana had succeeded in reducing poverty by following the path of high agricultural growth, others had focused on particular areas of development e.g. Kerala had focused on human resource development, West Bengal on vigorous implementation of land reform measures and empowerment of Panchayats, and Andhra Pradesh on direct public intervention in the form of public distribution of food grains.[15]

The NDA Government gave a special attention to agriculture and rural development as a vehicle for enhancing employment that would accelerate the growth of the overall economy. The rural area programme IRDP and its allied ones such as TRYSEM, DWCRA and MWS had been restructured into a single self-employment programme called the *Swarnajayanti Gram Swarozgar Yojana* (SGSY) from April

[15]*Economic Survey 2001–2002*, p. 238.

1999 with the objectives of (a) giving a focused approach to poverty alleviation; (b) capitalising advantages of group lending; and (c) overcoming the problems associated with multiplicity of programmes. The SGSY was conceived as a holistic programme of microenterprises covering all aspects of self-employment which included organising rural poor into *self-help groups* (SHGs). It integrated various agencies—District Rural Development Agencies, banks, line departments, Panchayati Raj Institutions, non-governmental organisations and other semi-government organisations. The objective of SGSY was to bring the existing poor families above the poverty line by providing them income generating assets through a mix of bank credit and government subsidy and to ensure that an assisted family has a monthly net income of at least Rs. 2000. The existing wage employment programme, JRY, after being restructured and streamlined for providing employment to below poverty line (BPL) families, had been renamed as *Jawahar Gram Samridhi Yojana* (JGSY) in April 1999. The primary objective of JGSY was 'creation of demand driven village infrastructure including durable assets at the village level to enable the rural poor to increase the opportunities for sustained employment'. While there was no sectoral earmarking of resources under JGSY, 22.5% of the annual allocation was allocated for the beneficiary schemes for scheduled castes/scheduled tribes (SC/ST); 3% of annual allocation was for the creation of barrier free infrastructure for the disabled.[16] In order to improve the quality of life of the village people through State intervention in the form of targeted anti-poverty programmes, *Pradhan Mantri Gramodaya Yojana* (PMGY) was launched by the Vajpayee government in Budget 2000–01. Its focus was on village-level development in five critical areas: health, primary education, drinking water, housing and rural roads.

As to the urban employment and anti-poverty programmes, the existing PMRY scheme set up during the Eighth Plan (1992–97) continued in the Ninth Plan (1997–2002) with certain modifications. But the other existing urban poverty programmes viz., NRY and PMIUPEP including the *Urban Basic Services for the Poor* (UBSP), were subsumed in a new programme called *Swarna Jayanti Shahari Rozgar Yojana* (SJSRY) during the Vajpayee government. It sought to provide employment to the urban unemployed or underemployed poor living below the poverty line (BPL) and educated up to IX standards through encouraging the setting up of self-employment ventures or the provision of wage employment. The scheme gives special impetus to empower and uplift the poor women and launches a special programme, namely *Development of Women and Children in Urban Areas* (DWCUA) under which groups of urban poor women setting up self-employment ventures are eligible for subsidy up to 50% of the project cost.[17] The DWCUA scheme for the urban area became the counterpart scheme of the existing DWCRA scheme for the rural area.

[16]*Economic Survey 1999–2000*, p. 169.

[17]*Ibid.* (pp. 169–70).

4.2.4 2004–2013

After the United Progressive Alliance (UPA-I) government came to power at the Centre with Dr. Manmohan Singh as its Prime Minister in May 2004, it continued for the next two terms until May 2014. Major programmes[18] for the development of social sector during 2004–05 include:

- Launching of National Food for Work Programme on 14 November 2004 in 150 most backward districts to intensify generation of supplementary wage employment and provision of food security through creation of need-based economic, social and community assets in these districts.
- Introduction of National Rural Employment Guarantee Bill, 2004, in Parliament on 21 December 2004 to provide for enhancement of livelihood security of the poor in rural areas by providing at least 100 days of guaranteed wage employment in every financial year to every household whose adult members volunteer to do unskilled manual work.
- Additional Rs. 10,000 crore of Gross Budgetary Support (GBS) for Plan programmes like Food for Work, Sarva Shiksha Abhiyan, mid-day cooked-meal scheme, basic healthcare, accelerated irrigation benefit programme, drinking water and roads.
- Increase in coverage of Antyodaya Anna Yojana from 1.5 crore to 2 crore families.
- Strengthening of public distribution system.
- Allocation of Rs. 1, 180 crore for programmes concerning the scheduled castes and Rs. 1, 146 crore for scheduled tribes.
- Additional allocation of Rs. 50 crore for the National Minorities Development and Finance Corporation.
- Indicative target of credit linking 5.85 lakh self-help groups (SHGs) during the period up to March 2007.
- Imposition of a cess of 2% on Union taxes and duties to yield Rs. 4000 crore–Rs. 5000 crore in a full year, with proceeds earmarked for education including cooked mid-day meal.
- Launching of a programme for upgrading 500 Industrial Training Institutes (ITIs) over the next five years.
- A new universal health insurance scheme for the poor.
- A special group insurance scheme of Rs. 10, 000 at a premium of only Rs. 120 per person.

In its first term, the UPA-I government also executed several key projects and legislations, including the National Rural Health Mission (NRHM) (2005), National Rural Employment Guarantee (NREG) Act (2005), Right to Information (RTI) Act (2005) and Unique Identification Authority of India (2006). The NRHM was meant for mobilising community health workers across the country.

---

[18]*Economic Survey 2004–05* (Box 10.1, p. 225).

The goal of the RTI Act, that has proved crucial in India's fight against corruption, was to

> provide for setting out the practical regime of right to information for citizens to secure access to information under the control of public authorities, in order to promote transparency and accountability in the working of every public authority, the constitution of a Central Information Commission and State Information Commissions and for matters connected therewith or incidental thereto.

Originally conceived in 2006, the Planning Commission of India created the *Unique Identification Authority of India* (UIDAI) in 2008, and then it was elevated to a cabinet ministerial level post in 2009 with Nandan Nilekani, former Chairman of Infosys, as its chairperson. The goal of the UIDAI was to provide a unique identity numbers, named 'Aadhaar' initially to the targeted population of the flagship schemes of the UPA government such as NREG scheme, NRHM, the Right to Free and Compulsory Education (RTE) Act, 2009 (*Sarva Shiksha Abhiyan*), and *Bharat Nirman*[19] so that they can easily be verified and authenticated online.

Meanwhile, after the withdrawal of major left parties' support, the UPA government managed to survive a vote of confidence in the Parliament on 22 July 2008, and subsequently came to power with a stronger 'UPA-II' government after the general election held during April–May in 2009. In line with the major objective of the Eleventh Five-Year Plan (2007–2012) namely inclusive economic growth,[20] the newly invigorated 'UPA-II' government capitalised on high average annual economic growth rates of more than 8% during 2005–2011 except in 2008–09 when this growth rate fell to 6.7% due to Global Financial Crisis (GFC) [See Table 1.2 in Chap. 1]. The UPA-II government decided to strike a delicate balance between the twin goals of economic growth and human development. It focused on an inclusive development policy that incorporated social and financial inclusion of many segments of the population like landless agricultural labourers, marginal farmers, schedule castes (SCs), scheduled tribes (STs) and other backward classes (OBCs) who suffer social and financial exclusion. This government implemented a number of social sector programmes under different headings such as poverty alleviation and employment generation, social protection, rural and urban infrastructure development, education and skill development, health, women and child development and welfare and development of marginalised sections of the society.[21] Some social sector programmes are ongoing and some are new initiatives. Among the

---

[19]'Bharat Nirman' was an Indian business plan launched by the UPA-I government in 2005 for creating and augmenting basic rural infrastructure to provide some basic amenities to the rural India. It comprised of projects on irrigation, roads (*Pradhan Mantri Gram Sadak Yojana*), water supply (National Rural Drinking Water Programme), electrification (*Rajiv Gandhi Grameen Vidyutikaran Yojana*) and telecommunication connectivity.

[20]The major emphases of inclusive economic growth are on poverty reduction; delivery of services in social sector through education, skill development and reduction of gender inequality; as well as on environmental sustainability.

[21]*Economic Survey 2013–14*, pp. 240–51.

new initiatives[22] under the Mahatma Gandhi NREGA, the following are noteworthy:

- inter-departmental convergence and collaboration of activities like construction of individual household latrines under the *Nirmal Bharat Abhiyan* (NBA), construction of *anganwadi*[23] centres under the *Integrated Child Development Services* (ICDS) Scheme, construction of village playfields under the *Panchayat Yuva Krida Aur Khel Abhiyan* and watershed management programmes;
- introducing steps to open individual bank/post office accounts for all women workers;
- identifying and providing job cards to widowed, deserted and destitute women;
- taking initiatives for the disabled and other vulnerable persons by fixing schedule of rates (SoR) based on work and time motion study at state level; and
- adding new works to the existing list of permissible works specifically focused on rural livelihood and agricultural activities.

4.2.5 2014–2017

Right after the NDA government led by Narendra Modi came to power in May 2014, the new government undertook a number of additional social sector development related measures in order to bring the marginalised and poor sections of society into main stream. Understanding that social inclusion requires financial inclusion as a necessary condition, and disbursement of benefits needs a systematic channel, the *Pradhan Mantri Jan Dhan Yojana* (PMJDY), the biggest financial inclusion initiative in the world, was launched on 28 August 2014. It aimed to extend the banking services to the vast unbanked population particularly of India's unorganised segment. Another scheme called the RuPay Card became a payment solution. While PMJDY scheme has been started with a target to provide 'universal access to banking facilities' starting with 'basic saving bank account' with an overdraft up to Rs. 5000 subject to satisfactory operation in the account for six months, the RuPay Debit Card has the inbuilt accident insurance cover of Rs. 1 lakh. It is expected that these two schemes together will not only provide financial empowerment, but also make monitoring easier and the local bodies more accountable. On its first anniversary on 28 August 2015, Arun Jaitley, the Finance Minister, proudly notes[24]:

---

[22]*Ibid.* (Box 13.2, p. 240).

[23]*Anganwadi* is a government sponsored childcare and mothercare centre in India. It caters services to children in the 0–6 age group. The word *Anganwadi* means 'courtyard shelter'.

[24]http://pib.nic.in/newsite/PrintRelease.aspx?relid=126439.

> PMJDY has been one of the most vital initiatives towards financial inclusion till date. … Owing to the dedicated efforts of Government and banking institutions, substantial results have been achieved. With close to 18 crore (180 million) bank accounts opened and nearly every household having a bank account, wage payments and subsidies being directly routed to bank accounts, we indeed have come a long way. … I am sure that together we will succeed in empowering the poor of the country in having a financial footprint and remarkably improving their standard of living.

Given the involvement of multiple social sector development programmes to foster inclusive growth, more active role of Panchayati Raj Institutions (PRIs) and urban local governments (ULGs) is critical. According to the current government's assessment, over the years since the 73rd and 74th Constitutional Amendments[25] for decentralised governance in the early 1990s, PRIs and ULGs 'have not been strengthened in terms of functions, finances and functionaries (triple Fs) with regard to preparation of plans and the listed subjects'.[26]

An innovative rural development programme called *Sansad Adarsh Gram Yojana* (SAGY) had been launched by the Prime Minister Narendra Modi on 11 October 2014. Under this scheme, each member of the Parliament can choose one village from its constituency, except its own or in-laws' village and fix parameters and make it a model village or Adarsh Gram by 2016. Thereafter, they can take on two or three more villages and do the same by the time the next general elections come along in 2019, and thereafter, set themselves ten-year-long village or rural improvement projects. Villages will be offered smart schools, universal access to basic health facilities and pucca housing[27] to homeless villagers. Although no new funds are allocated to this scheme, but funds may be raised through (i) the Member of Parliament Local Area Development Scheme (MPLADS); (i) funds from existing schemes such as the Indira Awas Yojana, Pradhan Mantri Gram Sadak Yojana, Mahatma Gandhi National Rural Employment Guarantee Scheme and Backward Regions Grant Fund; (iii) the *Gram Panchayat*'s own revenue; (iv) Central and State Finance Commission Grants; and (v) corporate social responsibility funds.

After consolidating its political and administrative power within a year, the Modi government wanted to further strengthen the existing social infrastructure, particularly education and health, as reflected in its second budget session of 2015–16.

> Social infrastructure like education and health is critical for improving the output productivity of the population. Lack of access to affordable and quality health and educational facilities leads to economic impoverishment and lowers potential human capabilities for

---

[25]The 73rd and 74th Constitutional Amendments were introduced in the Parliament in September 1991 by the government of Prime Minister Narasimha Rao of the Congress (I) party in the form of two separate Bills for rural local bodies (also known as *Panchayats*) and municipalities, which subsequently were passed in December 1992 and then officially enacted as the Constitution (73rd Amendment) Act, 1992 (commonly referred to as the Panchayati Raj Act) effective from 24 April 1993, and the Constitution (74th Amendment) Act (or the Nagarpalika Act) effective from 1 June 1993.

[26]*Economic Survey 2014–15* (Box 9.5, p. 144).

[27]Pucca housing generally refers to dwellings with walls built of material such as brick, cement, stone or timber, while roofs can be made of concrete, tin or tiles.

> many. Economic development needs to be inclusive by involving all sections of society, deprived and marginalized groups like women and children, scheduled tribes, scheduled castes, the differently abled and senior citizens. Additionally, skill gaps in various productive sectors in India are large and will require upscaling of training and skill development to maximize the benefits of its demographic dividend and make India's development trajectory more inclusive and productive. Thus, India has to address the challenges of not just providing employment but of increasing the employability of the labour force, which is correlated to knowledge and skills developed through quality education and training along with ensuring good quality of health.[28]

The government has adopted a multipronged policy approach to enable skill development including but not limited to initiatives such as setting up of SSCs (sector skill councils). This also includes funding initiatives such as the *Standard Training and Assessment Reward* (STAR) scheme, *etc*., which are likely to create a widespread positive impact on the skills ecosystem in India. Besides, under the *Pradhan Mantri Kaushal Vikas Yojana* aiming to offer 24 lakh Indian youth meaningful, industry-relevant and skill-based training, 4.38 lakh persons have successfully completed training throughout India by early 2016.

Acknowledging innumerable challenges in the delivery of efficient health services in India given the paucity of resources and the plethora of requirements in the health sector, the current government has been stressing more on society's basic sanitation level and hygienic environment that are closely related to people's overall health condition.

> The progress in sanitation has witnessed a spurt since the launch of the Swachh Bharat Mission. More than 122 lakh toilets have already been constructed in rural areas since the beginning of the *Swachh Bharat Mission* (Gramin). It is also imperative that the constructed toilets are maintained and utilized by the beneficiaries to reap the benefits of the Swachh Bharat Mission. In order to improve availability of drinking water in rural areas, the National Rural Drinking Water Programme initiated a new World Bank-supported project named the Rural Water Supply and Sanitation Project–Low Income States.[29]

In an evaluation of the current government's big-ticket social welfare schemes, some old and recast, others completely new, Sharma (2017b) notes that the government has been able to reach out to the poorest of the poor and also bring about greater transparency in the operation of social sector. For example, during 2014–17, the government has held 4, 718 camps benefitting 6.40 lakh beneficiaries under Assistance to Disabled Persons for Purchase/Fitting of Aids/Appliances (ADIP), up from a mere 37 camps in 2012–13. There have been several course corrections of the Mahatma Gandhi National Rural Employment Guarantee Scheme (MNREGS) since 2014—the first initiative has been to bring down the number of registers maintained at the *gram panchayat* level from an average of 22 to 7; the biggest initiative has been the verification of 8 crore job cards out of total 13.04 crore in September 2016, which leads to deletion of 93.75 lakh fake cards.

[28]*Economic Survey 2015–16*, (Vol. 2, pp. 26–27).

[29]Ibid. (p. 28).

4.3 Government Expenditure on Socio-Economic Services: Composition, Trend and Impact

Since the comprehensive liberalisation in 1991, India has recorded a growth path of 6–7% annually during the 1990s. But this improved growth rate has continued to elude the poor unemployed/semi-employed masses from accessing basic necessities of life such as education, health care, housing, water, electricity, cooking fuel and sanitation. During the 1990s, the governments tried to provide the poor initially with 'free and easily accessible schools for children, mid-day meals at schools, public health services, cheap public transport and basic sanitation and water supply facilities'. After realising that most of the rural habitations and urban slums may have only limited supply of these facilities, both Plan and Non-Plan expenditure of the Central Government on various social sector services and rural development had quadrupled from Rs. 5,892 crore in 1991–92 to Rs. 23,406 crore in 1999–2000 and then had a substantial increase to Rs. 39,123 crore in 2004–05. As a ratio of GDP at current market prices, expenditure on social and economic services although increased from 1.33% in 1991–92 to 1.70% in 1999–2000 and to 1.93 in 2003–04, but then slightly declined to 1.89 in 2004–05 (Table 4.5).

Because most social sector programs in education, health, rural sanitation and social welfare are implemented by the State Governments, they require focused action at the State level. The Central Government does supplement efforts of the States through release of additional funds for specific programmes. The available figures on the Central and State Governments' combined expenditures on social sector services (as a percentage of GDP measured at current prices) from Table 4.6 indicate both way movements in the range of 5.52–6.9 during 1986–2014, although there have been intermittently declining trends from 6.1 in 1986–87 to 5.52 in 1995–96, from 6.04 in 2001–02 to 5.66 in 2004–05 and again from 6.9 in 2009–10 to 6.5 in 2013–14. Another noteworthy observation from Table 4.6 is that education and health services taken together accounts for around two-thirds of the total social sector expenditures of both the Central and State Governments.[30]

While there has been a steady increase in the share of social sector expenditure in Central Government's total Plan expenditures (Table 4.1), total public sector expenditure on important social sector heads, however, remains low when compared with international standards. As can be seen from Table 4.6, the combined expenditures of the central and state governments in India on education are 3.0 and 3.1 per cent of GDP in 2011–12 and 2013–14, respectively, while those on health are even lower at 1.2% of GDP in both the years. In contrast, some of the other

[30]According to a recent research done by Kaur et al. (2013), it is noteworthy that on a per capita basis, social sector expenditure (in real terms) recorded a threefold increase during the period covered in the study. The increase was about 2.7 times for education expenditure and about 2.3 times for health expenditure on a real per capita basis. A large part of the increase in real per capita social sector expenditure has been achieved in the post-2000 period (Kaur et al. 2013).

Table 4.5 Central Government expenditure (Plan and Non-Plan) on socio-economic services (1991–2005) (Rs. Crore)

Item	1991–92	1995–96	1996–97	1997–98	1998–99	1999–2000	2003–04	2004–05
1. Social services	**5,892**	**11,631**	**13,659**	**15,894**	**19,747**	**23,406**	**32,336**	**39,123**
a. Education, sports and youth affairs	1,755	3,630	3,988	5,012	6,604	7,081	10,928	13,985
b. Health and family welfare	1,382	2,542	2,751	3,174	3,993	5,012	7,195	8,191
c. Water supply, sanitation, housing and urban development	934	1,756	2,957	3,304	4,073	4,465	7,892	9,023
d. Information and broadcasting	417	596	593	898	1,037	1,169	1,300	1,319
e. Welfare of SC/ST and other backward classes (OBC)	419	800	833	725	916	951	1,132	1,322
f. Labour, employment and labour welfare	357	507	587	562	709	845	833	1,002
g. Social welfare and nutrition	628	1,800	1,950	2,219	2,415	3,883	2,343	2,580
h. Other social services							713	1,701
2. Economic services	**2,283**	**6,609**	**7,547**	**8,456**	**9,538**	**9,232**	**16,951**	**14,743**
a. Rural development (including rural employment and poverty alleviation programmes)	2,283	6,609	5,081	5,583	5,854	5,184	12,226	9,516
b. Basic Minimum Services (BMS)[a] including slum development			2,466	2,873	3,684	4,048		
c. (i) Pradhan Mantri Gramodaya Yojana (PMGY)[b]							2,400	2,766
c. (ii) Pradhan Mantri Gram Sadak Yojana (PMGSY)[b]							2,325	2,461
3. Social and economic services (1 + 2)	**8,175**	**18,240**	**21,206**	**24,350**	**29,285**	**32,638**	**49,287**	**53,866**
4. Social and economic services as % of GDP at current prices[c]	**1.33**	**1.54**	**1.56**	**1.60**	**1.70**	**1.70**	**1.93**	**1.89**

Notes:
[a]BMS that came into operation in 1996–97 was gradually merged into PMGY and PMGSY in 2001
[b]Both PMGY and PMGSY were launched by the NDA government in its 2000–01 budgets as new initiatives for basic rural needs. However, PMGY has been discontinued from 2005–06 under the UPA-I government
[c]GDP figures for the years 1991–92 and 1992–93 are based on old series (Base 1980–81) and figures from 1993–94 onwards are based on new series (Base 1993–94) of *National Accounts Statistics* released by the *Central Statistical Organisation* (CSO)
Sources: *Economic Survey 1999–2000* (p. 165), *Economic Survey 2001–2002* (p. 235) and *Economic Survey 2006–2007* (p. 206)

Table 4.6 Trends of social sector expenditure by Central and State Governments combined (1986–2015)

Items	1986–87	1990–91	1995–96	2001–02	2003–04	2004–05	2009–10	2011–12	2013–14	2014–15 (Revised estimate)
(As a percentage of GDP measured at current prices)										
Total expenditure	32.29	28.78	25.55	28.26	28.85	27.82	28.6	27.4	26.2	28.1
Expenditure on social sector	6.1	5.85	5.52	6.04	5.68	5.66	6.9	6.6	6.5	7.0
Education	2.78	3.01	2.72	2.98	2.79	2.74	3.0	3.1	3.0	3.1
Health	1.47	1.29	1.19	1.25	1.26	1.25	1.4	1.2	1.2	1.3
Others	1.85	1.56	1.6	1.81	1.64	1.67	2.5	2.2	2.3	2.6
(As a percentage to total expenditure)										
Expenditure on social sector	18.9	20.3	21.6	21.4	19.7	20.4	24.1	24.0	24.8	24.9
Education	8.6	10.4	10.7	10.6	9.7	9.9	10.6	11.4	11.6	10.9
Health	4.5	4.5	4.7	4.4	4.4	4.5	4.8	4.6	4.6	4.8
Others	5.7	5.4	6.3	6.4	5.7	6.0	8.7	8.0	8.6	9.1
(As a percentage of total social sector expenditure)										
Education	45.6	51.4	49.4	49.4	49.0	48.5	44.11	47.7	46.7	44.0
Health	24.1	22.0	21.6	20.7	22.2	22.1	19.7	19.0	18.6	19.3
Others	30.3	26.6	29.0	29.9	28.8	29.5	36.1	33.3	34.7	36.7

Sources: *Economic Survey 2004–2005* (p. 226), *Economic Survey 2006–2007* (p. 207) and *Economic Survey 2015–2016* (p. 193). Also, the GDP figures at current prices (for 1986–87, 1990–91, 1995–96 and 2001–02) had been obtained by the author from *National Accounts Statistics* (2001, 2004 and 2009)

Table 4.7 Government's expenditure on health and education as a percentage of GDP

Selected asian countries	Health[1]	Education[2]
	2014	Different years as in bracket
China	3.1	3.93 (2011)[3]
India	1.4	3.83 (2012)
Malaysia	2.3	6.09 (2013)
Republic of Korea	4.0	4.62 (2012)
Thailand	5.6	4.13 (2013)

1. Source: http://data.worldbank.org/indicator/SH.XPD.PUBL.ZS (accessed on 9 July 2016)
2. Source: http://data.uis.unesco.org/?queryid=181 (accessed on 9 July 2016)
3. Source: http://news.xinhuanet.com/english/china/2013-01/04/c_132080607.htm (accessed on 9 July 2016)

Asian countries spend higher percentage of their GDP on both health and education as shown in Table 4.7.

4.3.1 Distribution of Central Plan Assistance to the States during 1980–2014

The Planning Commission used to allocate aggregate (normal) plan assistance among the States under a set of criteria called modified Gadgil Formula during the 1980s and then used the Gadgil–Mukherjee Formula since 1991 until the establishment of the NITI Aayog in January 2015. The uniqueness of the Gadgil–Mukherjee Formula was the inclusion, for the first time, of performance criteria for the allocation of Central Plan resources. The performance criteria include tax effort, fiscal management, national objectives and special problems.[31]

The Planning Commission also used to provide *developmental grants* to States as part of an overall assistance package. This package used to be determined as a composite of *loans* and *grants*. The relative shares of *loans* and *grants* were different for the *special category* States as compared to those of the *general category*. For the *general category* States, assistance was 30% grant and 70% loan. For the *special category* States, 90% of assistance was given as grant and 10% as loan. No capital grants as such were envisaged for the *general category* of States in plan

[31]The main weaknesses in the application of the Gadgil–Mukherjee Formula in its various mutations as summarised in WG-SFR (2012, p. 28) were (i) 30% earmarking for the special category states is arbitrary; (ii) shares determined on the basis of tax effort and fiscal discipline indexes were unscaled implying that if a large state like Maharashtra and a small state like Goa had the same tax effort ratio; (iii) the link between plan schemes/projects and plan assistance has been lost, leading to a severing of a link between costs and benefits, and lack of effective project based monitoring; and (iv) the 30:70 grant to loan ratio had long become irrelevant if the 30% grant ratio was meant to cover revenue expenditure on plans.

assistance; it was expected that their all capital expenditures would be met by borrowing and by surpluses on revenue account.[32] The position of the *special category* States was, however, different in the sense that from the 90% that they were getting as grant, 30% could be allocated for the revenue component of the plan, and the balance of 60% could then emerge as a capital grant.

In reality, the relative claim of recurrent (revenue) expenditure continued to increase and has become, on average, 60% of plan outlay in the case of *general category* States; borrowing, thus, basically finances capital expenditure of these States. In fact, not only that there were no capital grants, but also that a substantive part of current expenditures was also being financed by borrowing.

Two other channels of the Central Plan Assistance were *additional central assistance* (ACA) and *external assistance* (EA). Both were given on the same terms and conditions as normal plan assistance prior to a change in the terms and conditions for transmission of external assistance.

After the recommendations of the Twelfth Finance Commission,[33] *external assistance* is passed on to the States, as additional central assistance on back-to-back basis, that is, on the same terms and conditions as the original *external assistance*. Thus, in the dispensation of Central Plan Assistance, plan loans were, after the recommendations, virtually delinked from plan grants. Table 4.8 gives the relative share of States in different components of Plan Transfers namely (i) normal central assistance (NCA), (ii) additional central assistance for externally aided projects (ACA-EAPs), and (iii) additional central assistance for other special programmes (ACA-others). Components (ii) and (iii) are very ad hoc assistances. In the case of the *special category* States, under component (i), Jammu and Kashmir and Assam had the highest shares followed by Himachal Pradesh and Uttarakhand under both Tenth and Eleventh Plan periods. The distributions of component (ii) and (iii) of *ad hoc* assistances show wide range of variation among the States. For example, the highest share of component (iii) has been for Jammu and Kashmir and Uttaranchal (Uttarakhand) under both the Tenth and Eleventh Plan periods. As to the variation among the *general category* States, the ranges across the three components of Plan Transfers are relatively less wide.

---

[32]The expenditure side of State budgets was divided into four parts: (a) non-plan revenue expenditure, (b) plan revenue expenditure, (c) plan capital expenditure, and (d) non-plan capital expenditure. The components (a) and (b) combined to give the revenue account of a State, which pertains to recurrent (revenue) expenditures. Plan assistance was meant for the (b) and (c) components taken together. In the initial stages, when plan assistance was conceived of in terms of an overall package, the expectation was that nearly 30% of the plan assistance would actually be in the nature of recurrent expenditures and 70% would pertain to capital expenditures. In accordance with such an expectation, the grant and loan components were fixed at 30 and 70% of total plan assistance, respectively. It was expected that all capital expenditures would be met by borrowing and by surpluses on revenue account WG-SFR (2012, pp. 25–26).

[33]The Twelfth Finance Commission of India headed by C. Rangarajan was appointed on 1 November 2002 to make recommendations on the distribution of sharable tax revenue between the Centre and the States and Union Territories. The report that covered the period from 2005–2010 was submitted on 30 November 2004.

Table 4.8 [a]Components of Central Plan Assistance (Revenue + Capital Expenditures) share of states (%)

States	Average Tenth Plan Period (2002–2007)				Average Eleventh Plan Period (2007–2012)			
	NCA (i)	ACA-EAPs (ii)	ACA-others (iii)	Total central assistance	NCA (i)	ACA-EAPs (ii)	ACA-others (iii)	Total central assistance
Special category states								
Arunachal Pradesh	7.97	1.16	3.75	5.88	7.94	0.27	8.31	7.34
Assam	19.16	37.82	15.13	18.81	19.56	30.87	12.33	17.20
Himachal Pradesh	9.70	4.46	12.46	10.44	9.59	5.49	6.16	7.51
Jammu and Kashmir	19.23	11.36	31.93	23.66	19.16	12.92	32.04	24.78
Manipur	5.87	7.68	7.40	6.58	5.85	2.59	8.24	6.68
Meghalaya	4.87	3.52	3.72	4.34	4.86	3.62	5.72	5.15
Mizoram	5.62	7.98	2.70	4.63	5.60	7.93	3.20	4.67
Nagaland	5.94	1.42	3.15	4.56	5.92	2.49	5.51	5.37
Sikkim	3.79	2.88	1.79	2.95	3.78	1.39	3.30	3.30
Tripura	8.28	0.55	4.13	6.16	8.19	2.46	5.28	6.19
Uttarakhand	9.58	21.18	13.83	11.99	9.55	29.97	9.90	11.80
Total (11 States)	**100.00**	**100.00**	**100.00**	**100.00**	**100.00**	**100.00**	**100.00**	**100.00**
General category states								
Andhra Pradesh	7.51	20.76	7.68	10.68	6.28	5.17	11.17	10.06
Bihar	10.87	0.06	12.38	9.17	11.26	0.76	10.42	10.06
Chhatisgarh	2.99	1.15	3.00	2.57	2.81	5.77	3.60	3.58
Goa	0.50	0.09	0.54	0.43	0.48	0.00	0.49	0.46
Gujarat	4.00	12.81	6.15	7.20	3.93	2.12	6.67	5.98
Haryana	1.78	0.52	1.41	1.29	1.84	0.30	1.41	1.42
Jharkhand	3.46	0.63	4.57	3.40	3.39	1.55	3.90	3.69

(continued)

Table 4.8 (continued)

States	Average Tenth Plan Period (2002–2007)				Average Eleventh Plan Period (2007–2012)			
	NCA (i)	ACA-EAPs (ii)	ACA-others (iii)	Total central assistance	NCA (i)	ACA-EAPs (ii)	ACA-others (iii)	Total central assistance
Karnataka	4.45	10.77	6.21	6.86	4.40	11.84	5.02	5.28
Kerala	3.45	6.10	2.69	3.66	3.20	5.25	2.43	2.70
Madhya Pradesh	6.88	4.61	6.89	6.36	7.14	14.21	7.82	8.04
Maharashtra	6.91	4.51	10.95	8.52	6.91	5.69	14.04	12.43
Odisha	5.41	8.73	6.74	6.89	5.95	6.56	6.26	6.22
Punjab	2.18	1.10	2.10	1.89	2.23	0.57	2.44	2.31
Rajasthan	5.64	5.69	5.02	5.32	5.91	5.73	4.37	4.69
Tamil Nadu	5.98	5.09	5.28	5.40	5.90	8.94	4.34	4.84
Uttar Pradesh	19.45	8.26	12.39	13.06	20.20	7.51	9.66	11.28
West Bengal	8.55	9.12	5.98	7.30	8.17	18.04	5.96	6.95
Total (17 States)	**100.00**	**100.00**	**100.00**	**100.00**	**100.00**	**100.00**	**100.00**	**100.00**
Share of special and general category states								
SCS	**57.71**	**13.98**	**29.55**	**36.63**	**56.63**	**50.52**	**24.37**	**34.21**
GCS	**42.29**	**86.02**	**70.45**	**63.37**	**43.37**	**49.48**	**75.63**	**65.79**

[a]This table has been adapted from WG-SFR (2012, Table 5, p. 33)

Table 4.9 shows the relative importance of different components of plan assistance to both types of States during the Tenth and Eleventh Plan periods. Comparing the two, it is clear that the ad hoc component in plan assistance has the highest share and its share has increased in the Eleventh Plan compared to the Tenth Plan (except for Himachal Pradesh).

It was often argued that by mixing grants and loans, the Plan assistance mechanism had been combining two modes of resource transfer, which, therefore, needed to be governed by entirely different sets of principles. Grants should have been given consideration of resource deficiencies, and also that for projects with large social benefits but limited direct return like primary education and primary health. On the other hand, loans should have taken into consideration of the capacity of a provincial state to absorb and service the loan especially for the projects with varying returns over different periods of time. By mixing the two together, the centre might have been burdening states with debt that they could not service, but could not afford to forego either, because with it the component of grant also had to be foregone. With large accumulated debt due to the emphasis on plan size, state governments had often asked 'the Finance Commissions to take committed interest payment liabilities as legitimate revenue expenditures as also for writing-off debt'. The artificial dichotomy between Plan and non-Plan expenditures had also induced a number of inefficiencies. The following caution had been made in WG-SFR (2012, p. 29):

> There is an undue emphasis on taking up new schemes, while uncompleted projects of the past Plans and maintenance of assets acquired in the past get little attention. In effect, Plan schemes, as originally envisaged cannot be taken up fully, because the contemplated "balance from current revenues" (BCRs) are often not realized. Plan finances are diverted to non-Plan items, and time overruns increase costs. As a result, many schemes remain half done. While contributing little to output and to non-tax revenues, appointments have already been made, and capital structure has been put in place requiring maintenance and other expenditures. While old assets degenerate fast due to inadequate maintenance, new assets are not ready to contribute to output, the schemes remaining incomplete, thus causing a double blow to the productivity of government expenditures.

4.3.2 Interstate Variation in Social Sector Expenditures during 1990–2013

As Table 4.10 shows, at sub-national level, majority of the 17 non-special category (NSC) States exhibited a decrease in social sector expenditures (including health and education) as a per cent of gross state domestic product (GSDP) during 2000–09 (second sub-period) when compared with 1990s (first sub-period) and an increase during 2010–13 (third sub-period) when compared with 2000s (second sub-period), although their interstate variation (measured in terms of a range, i.e.

Table 4.9 Composition of Central Plan Assistance to states (%)

States	Tenth Plan period (2002–2007)				Eleventh Plan period (2007–2012)			
	NCA	ACA-EAPs	ACA-others	Total central assistance	NCA	ACA-EAPs	ACA-others	Total central assistance
Special category states								
Arunachal Pradesh	73.85	1.28	24.87	100.00	44.62	0.37	55.00	100.00
Assam	55.56	13.12	31.33	100.00	46.88	18.31	34.81	100.00
Himachal Pradesh	50.70	2.79	46.51	100.00	52.68	7.47	39.85	100.00
Jammu & Kashmir	44.30	3.13	52.57	100.00	31.89	5.32	62.79	100.00
Manipur	48.60	7.61	43.79	100.00	36.10	3.96	59.94	100.00
Meghalaya	61.28	5.29	33.43	100.00	38.90	7.18	53.93	100.00
Mizoram	66.09	11.23	22.68	100.00	49.39	17.32	33.30	100.00
Nagaland	71.05	2.04	26.92	100.00	45.43	4.73	49.84	100.00
Sikkim	69.98	6.36	23.65	100.00	47.14	4.30	48.57	100.00
Tripura	73.27	0.58	26.15	100.00	54.51	4.06	41.43	100.00
Uttarakhand	43.56	11.52	44.92	100.00	33.36	25.92	40.73	100.00
Total (11 SC States)	**54.52**	**6.52**	**38.95**	**100.00**	**41.23**	**10.21**	**48.57**	**100.00**
General category states								
Andhra Pradesh	16.24	45.13	38.64	100.00	10.25	2.67	87.08	100.00
Bihar	27.37	0.16	72.48	100.00	18.38	0.39	81.23	100.00
Chhatisgarh	26.87	10.39	62.74	100.00	12.88	8.38	78.75	100.00
Goa	26.97	4.96	68.08	100.00	16.98	0.00	83.02	100.00
Gujarat	12.82	41.30	45.89	100.00	10.78	1.84	87.38	100.00
Haryana	31.95	9.39	58.66	100.00	21.23	1.10	77.67	100.00
Jharkhand	23.50	4.28	72.22	100.00	15.08	2.19	82.73	100.00

(continued)

Table 4.9 (continued)

States	Tenth Plan period (2002–2007)				Eleventh Plan period (2007–2012)			
	NCA	ACA-EAPs	ACA-others	Total central assistance	NCA	ACA-EAPs	ACA-others	Total central assistance
Karnataka	14.99	36.43	48.58	100.00	13.69	11.66	74.64	100.00
Kerala	21.80	38.73	39.47	100.00	19.44	10.10	70.46	100.00
Madhya Pradesh	24.98	16.82	58.19	100.00	14.58	9.18	76.24	100.00
Maharashtra	18.74	12.29	68.97	100.00	9.12	2.38	88.50	100.00
Odisha	18.11	29.40	52.49	100.00	15.70	5.48	78.82	100.00
Punjab	26.71	13.53	59.76	100.00	15.83	1.28	82.89	100.00
Rajasthan	24.47	24.83	50.70	100.00	20.67	6.35	72.98	100.00
Tamil Nadu	25.59	21.88	52.53	100.00	20.04	9.61	70.35	100.00
Uttar Pradesh	34.39	14.67	50.94	100.00	29.39	3.46	67.15	100.00
West Bengal	27.03	28.97	44.00	100.00	19.29	13.49	67.22	100.00
Total (17 GC states)	**23.10**	**23.21**	**53.69**	**100.00**	**16.41**	**5.20**	**78.39**	**100.00**
Total states (28)	**34.61**	**17.10**	**48.29**	**100.00**	**24.90**	**6.91**	**68.19**	**100.00**

Source: adapted from WG-SFR (2012, Table 6, p. 34)

Table 4.10 NSC states' expenditure on social sector, education and health, (as per cent of GSDP at current market prices)

Non-special category states	Social sector			Education			Health		
	1990s	2000s	2010–13	1990s	2000s	2010–13	1990s	2000s	2010–13
Andhra Pradesh	6.5	6.5	7.4	2.3	2.1	2.5	0.8	0.7	0.8
Bihar	12.0	10.5	10.9	5.9	5.1	4.6	1.6	1.1	1.0
Chhattisgarh	NA	8.1	11.5	NA	2.3	4.2	NA	0.6	0.9
Goa	8.2	6.4	7.9	4.0	2.8	3.4	1.6	1.0	1.2
Gujarat	5.4	5.4	5.3	2.6	2.1	2.1	0.7	0.5	0.6
Haryana	4.7	4.7	5.5	2.1	2.0	2.4	0.6	0.4	0.5
Jharkhand	NA	9.8	10.0	NA	3.5	3.6	NA	1.1	0.9
Karnataka	6.5	6.3	7.2	2.8	2.7	2.8	0.9	0.7	0.7
Kerala	5.2	5.5	6.0	2.7	2.7	3.0	0.7	0.8	0.9
Madhya Pradesh	9.5	7.8	9.3	3.6	2.7	3.4	1.1	0.8	0.9
Maharashtra	5.0	5.0	5.3	2.3	2.6	2.5	0.6	0.5	0.5
Odisha	7.7	7.1	8.2	3.3	3.0	3.3	0.9	0.7	0.7
Punjab	4.1	4.0	4.8	2.4	2.1	2.3	0.7	0.6	0.7
Rajasthan	6.9	7.8	7.0	3.1	3.3	3.0	1.0	0.9	0.8
Tamil Nadu	6.4	5.9	6.5	2.8	2.3	2.4	0.9	0.7	0.7
Uttar Pradesh	6.2	7.0	9.3	3.0	3.1	4.0	0.9	1.0	1.1
West Bengal	5.8	5.5	6.9	2.9	2.7	3.1	0.9	0.8	0.8
Total	**6.1**	**6.2**	**7.0**	**2.8**	**2.6**	**2.9**	**0.8**	**0.7**	**0.7**

Source: adapted from Kaur et al. (2013, Table 4.3)

maximum *minus* minimum values) has declined from 7.5 to 6.5 and then to 6.2 during the three sub-periods, respectively. Another point to note is that both the expenditure on education as a per cent of GSDP and its interstate variation have been larger than that on health, although the variation has declined continuously (from 3.8 to 3.1 and then to 2.5) in education during the second and third sub-periods. In the case of health, the interstate variation has declined only in second sub-period (from 1.0 to 0.7) and then remained at the same level in third sub-period. A decline in health expenditure as a per cent of GSDP during the second and third sub-periods over the first sub-period (except in Kerala and Uttar Pradesh) may have been, as Kaur et al. (2013) argue, compensated through higher private-sector expenditure on health during these years. They also make another general point that fiscal consolidation at the state level has been achieved during the period from 1990 to 2013 primarily at the cost of lower health and education spending.

As Kaur et al. (2013) had remarked:

> Apart from the low public sector expenditure levels (relative to international standards), significant disparities persist across states when it comes to expenditure of state governments on social services in India. Available data indicates that the states lagging behind

> with regard to expenditure on social sector have not attempted to catch up with the better-performing states through higher allocations of expenditure for social sector which is a key contributor to human development outcomes. The per capita social sector expenditure in the laggard states remained significantly lower than that of the leading states, resulting in the persistence of disparities in human development indicators (HDI) across states during the 2000s (RBI 2013).

Restricting their panel data analysis for 17 NSC States to the period from 2000 to 2013, Kaur et al. (2013) suggest that India's overall social sector spending is *acyclical* at the State level, i.e. there is no co-movement between social sector spending and GDP growth rates. However, education spending turns out to be *pro-cyclical* with the pro-cyclicality being more pronounced in situations of positive output gaps or upturns (i.e. when GDP growth is above its potential) and for bigger States. As States tend to protect social sector expenditures during negative output gaps or downturns (i.e. when GDP growth is below its potential), it explains their acyclical behaviour. This is also evident from a consistent increase in the share of social sector expenditure in total revenue expenditure of NSC States.

4.3.3 Interstate Comparisons of Selected Socio-Economic Indicators during 2001–2013[34]

The following Table 4.11 provides selected growth rates and socio-economic indicators of India's major states during the recent years: growth rates of *population* (during the decade of 2001–2011) and *average gross state domestic product* (GSDP) (during 2005–06 to 2012–13) as well as *absolute per capita income* in 2012–13, *unemployment rates* and *poverty headcount ratios* in both rural and urban areas (in 2011–12 compared to 2004–05).

Population Growth

Kerala was the best performing state in terms of the lowest decadal growth of population (4.9%) during 2001–11 and was well ahead of other states while Andhra Pradesh was a distant second (11.0%). Bihar was the least performing state with highest decadal growth of population (25.4%) followed by Rajasthan (21.3%), Madhya Pradesh (20.3%) and Uttar Pradesh (20.2%) against the national average of 17.7%.

Income

Bihar had been the best performing state in terms of growth rate of average *gross state domestic product* (GSDP) during 2005–06 to 2012–13 (9.9%) followed by Gujarat (9.7), Tamil Nadu (9.5) and Maharashtra (9.3) against the all India average of 8.0%. However, in terms of *absolute per capita income* in 2012–13, Haryana

[34]This section is adapted from *Economic Survey 2013–14*, Government of India (Ch. 13).

Table 4.11 Selected socio-economic indicators of India's major states in recent years (2001–13)

States	Population growth (2001–2011) (%)	Average GSDP growth (2005–06 to 2012–13) (%)	Absolute per capita income (at current prices) 2012–13 (Rs.)	Unemployment rates (per 1000)[a] 2011–12 (2004–05)		Poverty headcount ratios 2011–12 (2004–05)		
				Rural	Urban	Rural	Urban	Total
Andhra Pradesh	11.0	8.6	78,958	1.2 (0.7)	4.3 (3.6)	11.0 (32.3)	5.8 (23.4)	9.2 (29.6)
Assam	17.1	5.8	40,475	4.5 (2.6)	5.6 (7.2)	33.9 (36.4)	20.5 (21.8)	32.0 (34.4)
Bihar	25.4	9.9	28,774	3.2 (1.5)	5.6 (6.4)	34.1 (55.7)	31.2 (43.7)	33.7 (54.4)
Gujarat	19.3	9.7	96,976	0.3 (0.5)	0.8 (2.4)	21.5 (39.1)	10.1 (20.1)	16.6 (31.6)
Haryana	19.9	8.8	120,352	2.4 (2.2)	4.2 (4.0)	11.6 (24.8)	10.3 (22.4)	11.2 (24.1)
Himachal Pradesh	12.9	8.0	83,899	1.0 (1.8)	4.0 (3.8)	8.5 (25.0)	4.3 (4.6)	8.1 (22.9)
Karnataka	15.6	7.5	77,309	0.9 (0.7)	2.9 (2.8)	24.5 (37.5)	15.3 (25.9)	20.9 (33.3)
Kerala	4.9	8.1	88,527	6.8 (10.7)	6.1 (15.6)	9.1 (20.2)	5.0 (18.4)	7.1 (19.6)
Madhya Pradesh	20.3	8.4	44,989	0.4 (0.5)	2.6 (2.8)	35.7 (53.6)	21.0 (35.1)	31.6 (48.6)
Maharashtra	16.0	9.3	107,670	0.7 (1.0)	2.3 (3.6)	24.2 (47.9)	9.1 (25.6)	17.4 (38.2)
Odisha	14.0	7.7	49,241	2.2 (5.0)	3.5 (13.4)	35.7 (60.8)	17.3 (37.6)	32.6 (57.2)
Punjab	13.9	6.8	86,106	1.9 (3.8)	2.8 (5.0)	7.7 (22.1)	9.2 (18.7)	8.3 (20.9)
Rajasthan	21.3	7.9	59,097	0.7 (0.7)	3.1 (2.9)	16.1 (35.8)	10.7 (29.7)	14.7 (34.4)
Tamil Nadu	15.6	9.5	98,550	2.0 (1.2)	2.7 (3.5)	15.8 (37.5)	6.5 (19.7)	11.3 (29.4)
Uttar Pradesh	20.2	6.9	33,137	0.9 (0.6)	4.1 (3.3)	30.4 (42.7)	26.1 (34.1)	29.4 (40.9)
West Bengal	13.8	6.7	62,509	2.7 (2.5)	4.8 (6.2)	22.5 (38.2)	14.7 (24.4)	20.0 (34.2)
All India	**17.7**	**8.0**	**67,839**	**1.7 (1.7)**	**3.4 (4.5)**	**25.7 (41.8)**	**13.7 (25.7)**	**21.9 (37.2)**

[a]As followed by the *National Sample Survey* (NSS), the total employment figures are on Usual Status basis, i.e. Usual Principal plus Subsidiary Status (UPSS) of measuring an individual's employment related activities

Source: adapted from *Economic Survey 2013–14* (Table 13.7, pp. 236–37)

(Rs. 120,352) and Maharashtra (Rs. 107,670), respectively, were at the top, followed by Tamil Nadu (Rs. 98,550) and Gujarat (Rs. 96,976), all against the national average of Rs. 67,839. It is noteworthy that Bihar (Rs. 28,774) and Uttar Pradesh (Rs. 33,137) are the two states with very high population density that had the lowest and second-lowest *absolute per capita income* in 2012–13, respectively.

Unemployment

Rural unemployment rate as per the usual status (adjusted) was lowest in Gujarat followed by Madhya Pradesh and Rajasthan in both 2011–12 and 2004–05. The rural unemployment rate of 3 per thousand in 2011–12 in Gujarat was much below the 17 per thousand all India average. In the case of urban unemployment also, Gujarat had the lowest rate. Urban unemployment at 8 per thousand in 2011–12 in Gujarat was way below the all India level of 34 per thousand. Maharashtra with 23 per thousand was a distant second. While Kerala's unemployment rate (both urban and rural) was unusually the highest both in 2004–05 and 2011–12, but it had fallen in 2011–12, it was still the highest.[35] After Kerala, Assam followed by Bihar, West Bengal, Haryana and Odisha had high rural unemployment, and Bihar followed by West Bengal, Andhra Pradesh and Haryana had high urban unemployment.

Poverty

Poverty estimates indicate that Odisha had the highest poverty headcount ratio (HCR) of 57.2% in 2004–05, being the result of rural and urban HCRs of 60.8% and 37.6%, respectively. Bihar which had the second-highest HCR of 54.4% in 2004–05 moved to first place in 2011–12 with the HCR at 33.7% relegating Odisha to second place with the HCR at 32.6%. Kerala had the lowest HCR of 7.1% in 2011–12 followed by Himachal Pradesh (8.1%) and Punjab (8.3%). While the all India poverty HCR was 21.9% in 2011–12, states like Madhya Pradesh (31.6%), Assam (32.0) and Uttar Pradesh (29.4), besides Bihar and Odisha, had above all India poverty levels in 2011–12. However, in terms of rural poverty in 2011–12, both Odisha and Madhya Pradesh (35.7%) were at the top followed by Bihar (34.1%) and Assam (33.9%).

The selected social indicators of and programmes participation/achievement in the major States in India are summarised in Table 4.12.

Health

Infant mortality rate (IMR) in 2012 was lowest in Kerala (12) and highest in Madhya Pradesh (56) followed by Assam (55), Odisha and Uttar Pradesh (53 each) against an all India IMR of 42. Birth rate was also lowest in Kerala (14.9) and highest in Bihar (27.7) followed by Madhya Pradesh (26.6) and Rajasthan (25.5) as

[35]According to the explanation given in *Economic Survey 2013–14* (p. 238), the highest unemployment rate in Kerala in both 2004–05 and 2011–12 is very likely due to unemployment of educated particularly women who are in search of the right job. This is also indicated in the lower labour force participation rate (LFPR) of females in the age group 15–59 years, with the LFPR of rural females being lower than the all India average.

Table 4.12 Selected social indicators and programmes in India's major states in recent years (2010–14)

States	Health (2012)			Education (2010–11)		Participation in and achievement of key social sector programmes (2013–14)		
	Infant mortality rate (per 1000 live births)	Birth rate (per 1000)	Death rate (per 1000)	Gross enrolment ratio (GER[a]) (6–10 years)	Gross enrolment ratio (GER[a]) (11–13 years)	Average person days per household under NREGA	Women's share in employment under NREGA	Achievement of *Indira Awas Yojana* (IAY) against target of house constructed (%)
Andhra Pradesh	41	17.5	7.4	99.5	80.1	50	58.7	83.3
Assam	55	22.5	7.9	94.3	67.9	24	24.8	36.0
Bihar	43	27.7	6.6	127.7	64.6	42	34.9	43.0
Gujarat	38	21.1	6.6	120.3	85.7	40	44.0	25.8
Haryana	42	21.6	6.4	94.9	83.5	36	41.7	20.0
Himachal Pradesh	36	16.2	6.7	109.2	113.8	52	62.6	17.1
Karnataka	32	18.5	7.1	104.7	90.7	50	46.6	82.6
Kerala	12	14.9	6.9	91.4	103.9	57	93.4	97.7
Madhya Pradesh	56	26.6	8.1	135.2	101.4	42	42.6	26.1
Maharashtra	25	16.6	6.3	104.7	92.4	45	43.7	33.4
Odisha	53	19.9	8.5	119.4	82.0	42	33.6	41.5
Punjab	28	15.9	6.8	84.3	80.8	33	52.8	10.6
Rajasthan	49	25.9	6.6	109.9	82.4	51	67.8	74.6
Tamil Nadu	21	15.7	7.4	111.8	112.3	59	84.1	26.0

(continued)

Table 4.12 (continued)

States	Health (2012)			Education (2010–11)		Participation in and achievement of key social sector programmes (2013–14)		
	Infant mortality rate (per 1000 live births)	Birth rate (per 1000)	Death rate (per 1000)	Gross enrolment ratio (GER[a]) (6–10 years)	Gross enrolment ratio (GER[a]) (11–13 years)	Average person days per household under NREGA	Women's share in employment under NREGA	Achievement of *Indira Awas Yojana* (IAY) against target of house constructed (%)
Uttar Pradesh	53	27.4	7.7	126.9	79.9	35	22.2	26.7
West Bengal	32	16.1	6.3	92.7	86.3	37	35.4	52.1
All India	**42**	**21.6**	**7.0**	**115.5**	**85.2**	**46**	**52.9**	**44.1**

Note: [a]The gross enrolment ratio (GER) is the percentage of children of *any age* enrolled in the official school age group. Because many children enter school late or repeat a grade along with the children of an official age group, the GER often exceed 100%

Source: adapted from *Economic Survey 2013–14* (Table 13.7, pp. 236–37)

compared to an all India average of 21.6. In the case of death rate, it was lowest in Maharashtra and West Bengal (6.3) and highest in Odisha (8.5) followed by Madhya Pradesh (8.1) and Assam (7.9) against a national average of 7.0.

Education

Against the All India average (115.5) of the gross enrolment ratio (GER) in the age group 6–10 years during 2010–11, GER was highest in Madhya Pradesh (135.2) followed by Bihar (127.7), while Punjab (84.3) had the lowest followed by Kerala (91.4) and West Bengal (92.7). Against the all India average (85.2) of the gross enrolment ratio (GER) in the age group 11–13 years during 2010–11, GER was highest in Himachal Pradesh (113.8) followed by Tamil Nadu (112.3) and lowest in Bihar (64.6) followed by Assam (67.9). The relatively lower 11–13 years GER compared to 6–10 years GER indicates that the transition of students from primary to upper primary classes is relatively lower than the entry to primary classes. It is also to be noted that pupil–teacher ratios at all India levels of education—primary, middle and high schools—are very high in states like Uttar Pradesh and Bihar affecting the quality of education.

Key Social Sector Programmes

Against the national average of 46 person days per household under the Mahatma Gandhi NREGA during 2013–14, the highest was in Tamil Nadu (59 person days) followed by Kerala (57 person days) and lowest in Assam (24 person days) followed by Punjab (33 person days). While the all India average share of women employed under Mahatma Gandhi NREGA was 52.9% during 2013–14, the highest was in Kerala (93.4%) followed by Tamil Nadu (84.1%), and the lowest was in Uttar Pradesh (22.2%) followed by Assam (24.8%).

The overall nationwide target achievement for the Indira Awas Yojana (IAY) in 2013–14 was 44% during 2013–14, Kerala achieved the highest (97.7%) followed by Andhra Pradesh (83.3%) and Karnataka (82.6%), while the lowest target achievement was by Punjab (10.6%) followed by Himachal Pradesh (17.1%). Although there are state-wise indicators for some social sector programmes as above, it is not always possible to evaluate the performance of states based just on numbers.

The interstate comparisons of performance based on different available indicators provide some clear policy directions. While some states have done very well for some socio-economic indicators, they are poor performers in terms of other such indicators.[36] For example, although Bihar had performed best in terms of growth rate of average *gross state domestic product* (GSDP) during 2005–06 to 2012–13 (9.9%), and yet, according to poverty headcount ratio (HCR) in 2011–12, it had the highest poverty incidence among the major Indian states as has been noted above. Due to very deep rooted poverty in Bihar, there is a dire need to devise a focused strategy for poverty eradication. There have been signs of improvements on several

[36] *Economic Survey 2013–14*, p. 239.

fronts towards coordinated efforts not only from the State and Central governments, but also from many other actors, including local and non-governmental organisations (NGOs) as well as international agencies.[37] Various Central and State governments, particularly in the new millennium, have, in general, been very much conscious of the fact that human development dimension needs to be taken into account while formulating and implementing social sector programmes, and arriving at criteria for devolution of funds from Centre to states.

4.4 Inclusive Growth under Co-operative Federalism during 2014–17

Since the 1990s, there has been a resurgence of interest in analysing and measuring inequality because of an increasingly visible worldwide exclusion of a vast majority of people[38] from the fruits of economic growth in terms of household income opportunity, economic security and quality of life. During the post-liberalisation period, the Indian Governments have all been very concerned of India's continued regional inequality in particular alongside with its increasing GDP growth rates.

4.4.1 The 14th FC Recommendations on Centre–State Fiscal Relations

The Fourteenth Finance Commission (FFC) was constituted by the President of India on 2 January 2013 to make recommendations on specified aspects of Centre–State fiscal relations during 2015–16 to 2020–21. It submitted its report on 15 December 2014. After it was passed in the Parliament on 24 February 2015, the NDA Government with Narendra Modi as its Prime Minister accepted the major recommendations for devolution of taxes and other transfers from the Centre to the states and between states for the period 2015–16 to 2020–21. In his letter to the States' Chief Ministers, the Prime Minister noted:

> …. following the acceptance of the 14th FC recommendations, we are moving away from rigid centralized planning, forcing a 'One size fits all' approach on states…

---

[37]*Institute for Human Development* (2010, p. 1).

[38]Following a 2004 report 'A Fair Globalization: Creating Opportunities for All', Stiglitz (2007, p. 8) noted that '59% of the world's people were living in countries with growing inequality, with only 5% in countries with declining inequality".

Table 4.13 State-wise share in divisible pool of Union taxes

States	Share (%)
Andhra Pradesh	4.305
Arunachal Pradesh	1.370
Assam	3.311
Bihar	9.665
Chhattisgarh	3.080
Goa	0.378
Gujarat	3.084
Haryana	1.084
Himachal Pradesh	0.713
Jammu & Kashmir	1.854
Jharkhand	3.139
Karnataka	4.713
Kerala	2.500
Madhya Pradesh	7.548
Maharashtra	5.521
Manipur	0.617
Meghalaya	0.642
Mizoram	0.460
Nagaland	0.498
Odisha	4.642
Punjab	1.577
Rajasthan	5.495
Sikkim	0.367
Tamil Nadu	4.023
Telangana	2.437
Tripura	0.642
Uttar Pradesh	17.959
Uttarakhand	1.052
West Bengal	7.324
All States	**100**

Source: http://ficci.in/SPdocument/20563/Highlights_14thFinance_Commission_Report.pdf

The key features/changes of the major recommendations accepted by the government are the following:

- Recommended shares of the States (see Table 4.13) in the net[39] proceeds of Union tax revenues increased to 42% from earlier 32%, which being the largest

[39]The term 'net' in the net proceeds refers to the difference between the extra FFC transfers and the reduced Central ('Plan') Assistance to the states (CAS).

Table 4.14 Grant-in-aid for Revenue Deficit States (2015–20)

States	Rs. crores
Andhra Pradesh	22,113
Assam	33,79
Himachal Pradesh	40,625
Jammu and Kashmir	59,666
Kerala	9,519
Manipur	10,227
Meghalaya	1,770
Mizoram	12,183
Nagaland	18,475
Tripura	5,103
West Bengal	11,760
Total	**1,94,821**

Source: http://ficci.in/SPdocument/20563/Highlights_14thFinance_Commission_Report.pdf

ever jump in percentage of vertical tax devolution, compared to the earlier changes within a range between 1 and 2% increases.[40]

- Criteria and weights for calculating tax devolution will be population (17.5%), demographic change (10%), income distance (50%), area (15%) and forest cover (7.5%).[41]
- After identifying over 30 centrally sponsored schemes (CSS) that could be delinked from Centre's support, only eight CSS had finally been recommended for delinking after considering the national priorities and legal obligations.
- Existing sharing pattern under various CSS needed to be changed—States should be sharing higher fiscal responsibility for CSS implementation.
- In calculating grants to States, entire revenue expenditure will be taken into account without making distinction between 'Plan' and 'Non-plan'.
- Distribution of grants to States for local bodies will be based on 2011 population data (90% weight) and area (10% weight).
- Eleven states, called special category states (SCS) distinguished from the rest called general category states (GCS), have been identified for receiving post devolution revenue deficit grant (see Table 4.14).

It is also to be noted that in the FFC's proposed new horizontal formula for the distribution of the divisible pool among the states, although forest cover has been a

[40]For example, the Twelfth (2005–10) and Thirteenth (2010–15) Finance Commissions had recommended a state share of 30.5% (increase of 1%) and 32% (increase of 1.5%), respectively, in the Central net divisible tax revenue.

[41]*Population* is as per 1971 census; *demographic changes* are changes in population since 1971; *income distance* is computed by calculating difference between three year average gross state domestic product (GSDP) for each state with respect to the state with highest per capita GSDP; *area* has a floor limit of 2% for smaller states in deciding horizontal devolution; and *forest cover* takes into account the opportunity cost in terms of area not available for other economic activities.

new variable added compared to the Thirteenth FC, an earlier variable relating to fiscal discipline has been excluded. With greater fiscal space, i.e. with the flexibility in implementing delinked CSS schemes as per local needs, states can meaningfully contribute to the overall growth and development in their regions, thereby adding to the aggregate growth of the nation. This should ideally ensure efficient utilisation of government resources, unless of course these greater discretionary funds are wasted for being used towards populist and non-productive purposes.

According to the assessment made by the current NDA government, led by the Prime Minister Narendra Modi:

> Implementing these recommendations will move the country toward greater fiscal federalism, conferring more fiscal autonomy on the states. For example, based on assumptions about nominal GDP growth and tax buoyancy and the policy measures that are contemplated for 2015–16, it is estimated that the additional revenue for the states could be as much as Rs 2 lakh crores relative to 2014–15. Of this, a substantial portion represents the difference that is purely due to the change in the states' share in the divisible pool.[42]

Government's preliminary estimates,[43] as shown in Table 4.14, also suggest that all States stand to gain from FFC transfers in absolute terms. But, when assessed incorporating the distributional effects of variation in population, Net State Domestic Product (NSDP) at current market price, or States' own tax revenue (OTR) receipts, the biggest gainers tend to be the special category states (SCS), mostly those in the north-east India. The major gainers in per capita terms turn out to be Arunachal Pradesh, Mizoram and Sikkim for the SCS states; Goa, Kerala, Chhattisgarh and Madhya Pradesh for the general category states (GCS).

Generally speaking, a collateral benefit of moving from the Central 'Plan' Assistance to the States (CAS) to FFC transfers seems to improve the overall progressivity because, on average, States with lower per capita Net State Domestic Product (NSDP) are expected to receive more revenue than those with a higher per capita NSDP. This is because CAS transfers, being predominantly discretionary, tended to be less progressive than Finance Commission transfers. The current NDA government is very optimistic about the potential far-reaching impact of the FFC recommendations along with the creation of NITI Aayog on India's inclusive development.

4.4.2 Cooperative Federalism and Inclusive Policies since the Mid-2014[44]

Although the term 'Federation' has not been used in the Indian Constitution, yet it provides a structure of governance that is essentially federal in nature. Article-1 in

---

[42]*Economic Survey 2014–15* (Vol. 1, p. 42).

[43]*Ibid.* (Table 1.4).

[44]*Economic Survey 2016–17*, pp. 165–66.

the Constitution describes India as a 'Union of States', which implies that Indian Federation is not the result of an agreement by the states. Indian Constitution has often been described as 'federal in form but unitary in spirit'. Within this basic framework of Indian Federation, the Constitution has given overriding powers to the Central government, which appoints Governors to oversee the States. The Centre can even take over the executive of the States on the issues of national security or breakdown of constitutional machinery of the State. States must, on the other hand, exercise their executive power in compliance with the laws made by the Central government and must not impede on the executive power of the Union; also, no state has the right to secede from the federation. Federalism with India's cultural and ethnic pluralism is said to have given the country's political system great flexibility, and therefore the capacity to withstand stress through accommodation. However, continuation of the same requires not simply federalism, but *cooperative federalism*. The current NDA Government that comes to power on 26 May 2014 with an electoral campaign of ushering in a new era for Indian federalism–*cooperative federalism* highlighting the fact that it requires the delegation of authority at right level (centre, state and local) for making and implementing policy, particularly the inclusive ones.

The Government claims that it has a vision of an inclusive society 'in which equal opportunities are provided for the growth and development of all sections of the population including the marginalised, vulnerable and weaker sections to lead productive, safe and dignified lives'. Accordingly, programmes have been updated/initiated by the Government towards attaining the objective of an inclusive society. For the economic and social empowerment of people belonging to the minority communities, the existing schemes such as *Nai Roshni* (New light) scheme (2012–13) for leadership development of minority women that has been updated in 2015 and *Padho Pardesh* (Studies in Foreign Countries) scheme (2013–14) of interest subsidy on educational loans for overseas studies for the students belonging to the minority communities are being implemented. For skill development and economic empowerment of minorities, schemes like *Seekho Aur Kamao* (Learn and Earn) that has been implemented since 2013–14, *Upgrading Skill and Training in Traditional Arts/Crafts for Development* (USTTAD) that had been announced in 2014 but launched in 2015 and *Nai Manzil* (New Goal) scheme to provide education and skill training to the youth from minority communities are all currently in operation. *Seekho Aur Kamao* and USTAD schemes are often linked to the current NDA Government's 'Make in India' campaign because these schemes have potential for making artisans and artists connected with buyers.

According to Census 2011, the number of persons with disabilities in India constituted 2.2% of the population. The Department of Empowerment of Persons with Disabilities (DEPwD) has launched *Sugamya Bharat Abhiyan* (Accessible India Campaign) as a nationwide campaign for achieving universal accessibility for persons with disabilities (PwDs) with a focus on three verticals: (i) built environment, (ii) public transportation and (iii) information and communication technologies. The 'Inclusiveness and Accessibility Index' launched by the Government as part of the *Sugamya Bharat Abhiyan* is argued to help the industries and corporates to participate in the Accessible India Campaign (AIC) by voluntarily evaluating their readiness for making the workplace accessible for PwDs. The Government claims that the Index is a first-of-its-kind initiative in the country and 'will be an ideal instrument for the integration, assimilation and inclusion of PwDs into the mainstream'. It is expected that the Index will enable the corporate and non-corporate organisations to introspect over their inclusive policies and organisational culture in aid of PwDs, employment of such workforce and adaptations to meet the needs of PwDs. Further, the 'Rights of Persons with Disabilities Bill—2016' passed by the Parliament on 16 December 2016 aims at securing and enhancing the rights and entitlements of PwDs. The bill has proposed to increase the reservation in vacancies in government establishments from 3% to 4% for those with benchmark disability and high support needs.

As can be seen from both Table 4.6 (above) and Table 4.15 (below), there had been a declining trend in the overall social sector expenditure (as a percentage of GDP) during 2011–15. But this declining trend has substantially been reversed in 2015–16 (Table 4.16). This perhaps indicates the current NDA Government, like the earlier two governments (UPA-I and UPA-II), has, at least for the time being, made its commitment towards social sector development in general and inclusive policy measures in particular. It is, however, yet to be seen the effectiveness of cooperative federalism especially in terms of policy-making of various social sector schemes cooperatively with level(s) of government (centre, state and local) as appropriate and also delegating responsibility for managing them to the right level.

The idea of *competitive federalism* has been later on added to the initial amalgam of policy objectives enunciated by the Modi Government in order to make the states compete with each other to attract investments as well as provide better public goods and services. There are, however, structural constraints as Arora (2015) argues:

> What has become increasingly evident is that the States are unevenly equipped to engage in fair competition, since regional disparities in the provision of basic needs and social sector services are overwhelming. Moreover, there are vast differences in governance capabilities, and while special category States *a la* the Planning Commission, may have withered away with it, the need for asymmetric federalism remains. Equity may not be central to the mandate of the Finance Commission, but no government which espouses cooperative federalism can afford to ignore it. Enhanced devolutions across the board do not address this problem, which requires a new asymmetric federalism framework that remains to be defined.

4.4.3 Redistributive Resource Transfers (RRT) and Their Impact on States

In order to find out some reason for India's prolonged spatial/regional inequality, the *Economic Survey 2016–17* argues (p. 285) that the Indian growth take-off since 1980 has been associated with *Peninsular India* constituting the states like Gujarat,

Table 4.15 Preliminary estimates of gain from additional FFC transfers from the centre to the states

States	General and special category states	Benefits from FFC (Rs. crore)	Benefits per capita (Rs.)	Benefits as per cent of own tax revenue (OTR)	Benefits as per cent of Net State Domestic Product (NSDP)
Andhra Pradesh (united)	GCS	14,620	1,728	27.4	2.2
Arunachal Pradesh	SCS	5,585	40,359	1,758.1	51.0
Assam	SCS	7,295	2,338	95.5	5.8
Bihar	GCS	13,279	1,276	105.3	4.9
Chhattisgarh	GCS	7,227	2,829	67.5	5.2
Goa	GCS	1,107	7,591	44.1	3.0
Gujarat	GCS	4,551	753	10.3	0.8
Haryana	GCS	1,592	628	7.8	0.5
Himachal Pradesh	SCS	8,533	12,430	207.7	14.6
Jammu and Kashmir	SCS	13,970	11,140	294.4	22.4
Jharkhand	GCS	6,196	1,878	89.1	4.8
Karnataka	GCS	8,401	1,375	18.1	1.8
Kerala	GCS	9,508	2,846	37.0	3.1
Madhya Pradesh	GCS	15,072	2,075	55.9	4.5
Maharashtra	GCS	10,682	951	12.2	0.9
Manipur	SCS	2,130	8,286	578.7	19.5
Meghalaya	SCS	1,381	4,655	198.0	8.6
Mizoram	SCS	2,519	22,962	1,410.1	33.3
Nagaland	SCS	2,694	13,616	886.5	18.7
Odisha	GCS	6,752	1,609	50.2	3.2
Punjab	GCS	3,457	1,246	18.3	1.4
Rajasthan	GCS	6,479	945	25.5	1.6
Sikkim	SCS	1,010	16,543	343.7	10.7
Tamil Nadu	GCS	5,973	828	10.0	0.9
Tripura	SCS	1,560	4,247	181.8	6.9
Uttar Pradesh	GCS	24,608	1,232	46.8	3.5
Uttarakhand	SCS	1,303	1,292	23.2	1.4
West Bengal	GCS	16,714	1,831	67.0	3.0
Total		204,198	1,715		

Source: adapted from *Economic Survey 2014–15* (Table 1.4, pp. 41–43)

Table 4.16 Trends of social sector expenditure by Central and State Governments combined (2013–16)

Items	2013–14	2014–15	2015–16 (Revised estimate)
(As a percentage of GDP measured at current prices)			
Total expenditure	26.6	25.1	28.2
Expenditure on social services *of which*	6.6	5.7	6.9
Education	3.1	2.6	2.9
Health	1.2	1.1	1.3
Others	2.3	2.0	2.7

Source: *Economic Survey 2016–2017* (p. 160)

Maharashtra, Tamil Nadu, Karnataka, Kerala and Andhra Pradesh 'with better geography—being close to the ocean'..... These states of *Peninsular India* 'have indeed grown faster and advanced more rapidly economically' in comparison with other states—the so called Other Indias which include hinterland India (the India of rivers), India of forests, India of natural resources and India of 'special category' status.[45] The *Survey* also examines the impact of redistributive resource transfers to the states through fund disbursal by the Centre via different channels: (i) a share of central taxes; (ii) plan and non-plan grants; and (iii) plan and non-plan loans and advances.[46] These funds constitute 'gross devolution to states' entailing a strong redistributive element for averting regional inequalities by correcting fiscal imbalances. The concept of 'redistributive resource transfers' (RRT) is utilised in this examination. RRT to a state is defined as gross devolution to the state adjusted for respective state's share in aggregate GDP. Thus, RRT is neither the same as gross devolution, nor 'a definitive metric of redistribution'; it is instead just '*one specific* measure of transfers'.[47]

Figure 4.1 shows, along with 2015 per capita gross devolution, the ranking of states in the descending order of RRT received in per capita terms in 2015. The top ten recipient states are Sikkim, Arunachal Pradesh, Mizoram, Nagaland, Manipur, Meghalaya, Tripura, Jammu and Kashmir,

Himachal Pradesh and Assam (all 'special category' states). Gross devolution per capita is at Rs. 32,000 on average for the top ten recipients of which Rs. 26,000 (81%) is estimated as RRT in 2015. The orange and green dotted lines in Fig. 4.1 are the all India rural and urban annualised per capita poverty lines for 2015, respectively. As can be seen from Fig. 4.1, '(a)nnual per capita RRT flows for all the north-eastern states (except Assam) and Jammu and Kashmir have exceeded the

[45]*Economic Survey 2016–17* (p. 285).

[46]While (i) is stipulated by Finance Commissions, (ii) and (iii) used to be decided by the erstwhile Planning Commissions.

[47]*Economic Survey 2016–17* (p. 288).

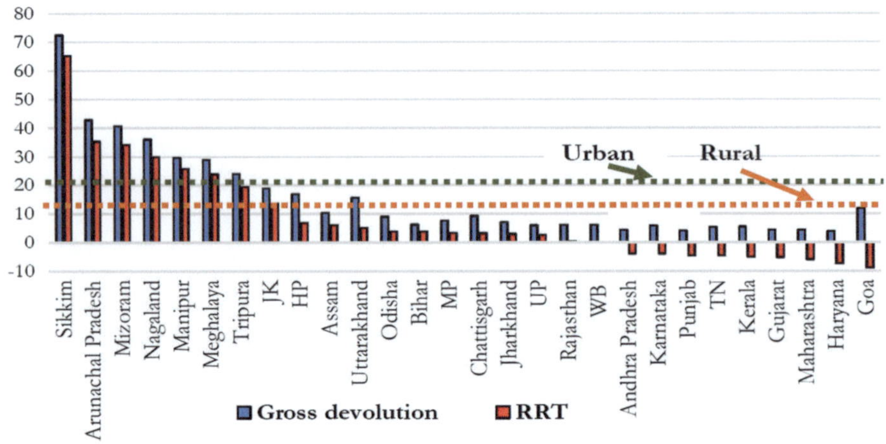

Fig. 4.1 Gross devolution and RRT per capita (Rs. Thousand 2015). (Source: adapted from *Economic Survey 2016–17*, Fig. 1, p. 288.)

annual per capita consumption expenditure that defines the all India poverty lines, especially the rural'[48]. According to the *Survey*:

> (P)oorer states receive the highest transfers, exactly as one would expect [in a federal system]. However, despite such flows over the past few decades most of the high RRT recipient states (excluding Himachal Pradesh and Uttarakhand) are at lower levels of per capita GSDP.[49]

The *Survey* results[50] are striking:

> The higher the RRT, the slower is per-capita GSDP growth, the smaller is state's share of manufacturing in GSDP,[51] and the lower is state's own tax revenue.

Although the so called RRT curse 'may not be fully valid especially for the north-east Indian states with poor connectivity in particular and poor infrastructure (physical, financial and digital) in general, the Centre could find ways of ensuring that the resources it redistributes are used more productively. The *Survey* suggests[52] the following three steps:

(i) redirecting a certain portion of RRT to household as a part of a *Universal Basic Income* (UBI) scheme;

(ii) conditioning transfers on states' better fiscal performance; and

(iii) making states' better governance and sound institutional practices.

---

[48]*Ibid.* (p. 289).

[49]*Ibid.* (pp. 289–90).

[50]*Ibid.* (p. 290).

[51]The average share of manufacturing in GSDP over the years during 2011/12–2014/15.

[52]*Economic Survey 2016–17* (p. 296).

Chapter 5
Development under Digital Divide in India

5.1 Introduction

The emergence and development of new technologies is a complex and dynamic socio-economic process. It is imperative that the development of high-technology industries,[1] like information and communication technology (ICT), especially in developing countries, be studied in a holistic manner. Any methodological approach for studying the social shaping of technology needs to take into account the social forces that influence economic and policy matters, while simultaneously acknowledging the impact of economic factors and policy initiatives on the evolution of society.

The analytical framework to be adopted in this chapter will use a combination of actor-network theory (ANT) and national innovation system (NIS) approach to capture the essence of the socio-economic dynamics of the evolution of the ICT industry in India. This composite framework seems to be well suited to the analysis of the ICT sector in India. The basis of ANT is the idea that society and technology are composed of networks linking various actors and actants (Ryder 2003). In fact, ANT does not posit a stable social structure; rather a constant interaction between different elements is posited. This interaction is the channel through which technological innovation translates into social transformation. For instance, the advent of the Internet has spawned changes in social networking possibilities and opened new vistas for personal communications.

The policy-oriented approach of NIS focuses on national level analysis for examining the impact of technology on society. NIS is defined by Metcalfe (1995) as a set of institutions, which jointly and individually, contribute to the development of new technologies and provide the framework within which governments form and influence the innovation process. He states that the division of labour and peculiarities of information, which result in a predominance of coordination by

[1]Contemporary high-technology industries usually include industries like information and communication technology, biotechnology, nanotechnology and robotics.

D. Dutta, *Development under Dualism and Digital Divide in Twenty-First Century India*, Dynamics of Asian Development, https://doi.org/10.1007/978-981-10-6344-2_5

non-market means, shape the nature of each country's NIS. The institutions like private firms, universities, public research centres, which constitute the NIS, make complementary contributions, but may differ in terms of their motivation for and commitment to the dissemination of knowledge (Cimoli 1998).

In adopting a composite ANT-NIS framework for this chapter, the dynamic cross-flow of influences that shape social, economic and policy outcomes will be captured (Dutta 2009). The framework adopted conceives of certain local characteristics attributable to the actors and actants belonging to both private and public sectors as ultimately influencing the national innovation system (NIS) through the sociopolitical process. The NIS matrix, in turn, influences the public sector and private sector outcomes in terms of investment location, technology choice, human capital intensity, etc. The public and private sectors also impinge upon the local characteristics with regard to investment, availability of educational and research infrastructure, incentives for human capital accumulation, rewards for entrepreneurship and governance structures. The local characteristics shape private sector development via, for instance, entrepreneurial activity. They also influence the success of public sector endeavours by responding appropriately to the available educational and employment opportunities. The private sector plays a role in public sector activities through the formal and informal policy advocacy process. The public sector influences the private sector through procurement decisions, policy directions and provision of governance and public services. Thus, in this framework, each element in the network influences the other. The socio-economic outcome, in terms of technology choice, innovation activity, entrepreneurial initiatives, human capital investment, policy-making, economic growth and income distribution, is the result of a complex interactive process.

This framework provides a broad matrix that can be used to analyse the socio-economic aspects of the ICT[2] industry's growth in India. The Indian social, political and economic system as it emerged following the end of colonial domination was somewhat diverse. The broad national endeavour was to create a unified sociopolitical entity without sacrificing the underlying diversity of the nation. It resulted, among other things, in the persistence of diversities and the adoption of a federal political system. In this regard, it is notable that certain southern Indian states had a lead in terms of technological capabilities and institutions.[3] A strong

[2]The term 'information and communication technology' (ICT) is broadly used to refer the family of related technologies that process, store and transmit information by electronic means (OECD 2004, p. 63). While information technology (IT) refers to an interconnected intelligent network of various components such as sensors and detectors, computers and knowledge-based systems, control and display systems, communication technology (CT) network includes telephone, wireless transmission and reception, satellite and mobile telecommunications, fibre optic communication system, computer-modem/router, Internet, Wi-Fi/Ethernet, World Wide Web. Two technologies together form a national information and communication infrastructure, which in turn is linked to the global information and communication infrastructures.

[3]For instance, the states of Karnataka and Andhra Pradesh, which were largely composed of the erstwhile princely states of Mysore and Hyderabad, respectively, had a strong public works infrastructure, complementary engineering talent and educational institutions.

desire for rapid technological progress also formed the basis of the Indian NIS. The public sector, which dominated the economy, made major investments in the southern states in terms of research centres and production facilities. Subsequently, private sector investments in the ICT sector also showed a distinct preference for the southern region. This, in turn, encouraged the growth of the private engineering colleges and resulted in further human capital accumulation. This appears to have had a huge spillover effect and a major impact on economic growth.

The *success* of India's ICT service industry will be measured in terms of its positive effect on the underlying socio-economic *dynamics* leading to inclusive growth and development. As has been discussed in Chap. 4, the phrase 'inclusive growth and development' has been broadly used here to imply the gradual integration of India's unorganised (i.e. traditional or informal) segment into its organised (modern or formal) one through employment generation and, thereby, poverty eradication. The vastness of India's unorganised segment containing virtually all the poor and vulnerable people can be understood from the following statistics:

Although the share of the organised segment in net domestic product/gross value added (at factor cost in current prices) has increased from 30% during 1980–1981 to 44.7% during 2012–2013 (Table 3.9), its share in employment has declined from 9.18% of total workers in 1983 to only 6.27% in 2012–2013 (Table 3.10). As a result, the unorganised segment continues to contain over 93% of India's labour force (in terms of mostly disguised as well as unemployed labours), in spite of the decline in its share in net domestic product from 70.0% in 1980–1981 to 55.3% in 2012–2013.

In the light of the above statistics, there had been an urgent need felt by the Indian policy-makers in the past three decades for connectivity of India's vast rural informal segment with the counterpart of formal segment initially through telecommunication technology, and then through Internet and other wireless technologies. Although informational connectivity through mobile telephones has been now in place, very little had been done in the provision of mobile learning (M-learning) until the turn of the twentieth century. In India, where language, context and culture vary from region to region, potential ICT users belong to very large and highly diverse groups of which many are illiterate. Using an earlier experimental study in India, Chandran (2010, p. 35) confirmed:

> During the mobile learning sessions, the students, who divided on language, religion, class and community, were dominated by play impulse rather than study anxiety or cultural inhibitions. …In other words, technology was able to transcend the relative deprivation in the multicultural groups.

Both informational connectivity and mobile learning have direct implications for the emergence of a new breed of small business entrepreneurs: agricultural, industrial and commercial in addition to various service-related enterprises. Their gradual integration to the modern or formal segment depends on further support from both state and central Governments. After a comprehensive coverage of the origin and growth of the Indian ICT industry, we would like to focus particularly on growth of India's ICT-enabled service sector and various government incentive policies as well as initiatives for bridging the digital divide between the technological haves and have-nots that exist in the Indian society.

5.2 Origin and Growth of the Indian ICT Sector

The Indian information and communication technology (ICT) industry essentially began in 1968 with the establishment of Tata Consultancy Services Limited (TCS) as a subsidiary of India's Tata Group. TCS was probably established to provide ICT services for using computers within the conglomerate and in Indian industries. It had an alliance with Burroughs Corporation of the USA, which helped it gain business in the USA. TCS agreed to the prevalent export commitments imposed by the Indian government in return for the import of hardware, which gave the company an early export orientation. Meanwhile, important events had taken place in the global computer industry. In 1969, IBM decided to sell software separately, thereby effectively de-linking the production of software and hardware. In 1972, Intel invented the microprocessor leading to the development of mini- and microcomputers. The subsequent continuous fall in hardware prices and corresponding acceleration in computing capabilities led to an explosive growth in computer usage (Parthasarathy 2004). This led to a corresponding increase in the demand for software services. By then a plethora of older computer systems in existence required extensive maintenance.

In 1978, the Prime Minister Morarji Desai's Janata Government—India's first non-Congress central government—imposed restrictions on foreign ownership of multinational company (MNC) subsidiaries, which led to the withdrawal of the American MNC, International Business Machines Corporation (commonly known as IBM), from the Indian market. This proved to be fortuitous since some former IBM employees in India set up software[4] consultancies of their own. It also allowed smaller hardware companies to grow and exposed Indian software professionals to various platforms. Further, it led to the rise of TCS as a major Indian ICT player. This early start, however, remained an insignificant trickle in terms of ICT growth due to prevalent government policies. Although these policies resulted in little domestic demand for, and restrictions on hardware imports, they contributed to the

[4]Computer software or simply 'software' is a generic term created with programming languages for machine-readable instructions either for a computer's processor to perform non-task-specific system operations (*i.e.* running the computer system) hence called 'system software', or for any user of the computer to accomplish specific tasks (other than running the computer system) hence called 'application software'. System software and application software are jointly categorised as software services having a service characteristic of intangibility, unlike packaged softwares which are tangible software products. Software services and products are also lately being labelled under the heading of computer and information services as in Mani (2014).

TCS's intention for export orientation and onsite work,[5] to meet hardware import commitments or to avoid using hardware available in India. It is also hypothesised that the intangible nature of software kept it outside the rigorous socialist industrial micromanagement framework (Khanna and Palepu 2004).

Overall, the experience gained by Indian software engineers working on a variety of platforms in the post-IBM domestic scenario proved useful. At the same time, the skewed education policies of the Indian socialist era saw technology institutes churning out a large number of engineers whose talents had little relevance in the constricted Indian domestic industry. Naturally, many of them migrated to the USA and rose to significant positions in technology MNCs. This most likely resulted in these corporations recognising the talent of Indian professionals and investing in India. These MNC entries include Texas Instruments in 1985, Microsoft in 1987, Hewlett Packard in 1989, Motorola in 1991 and Oracle in 1994 (Patibandla and Petersen 2002).

The development of the ICT industry in India has received considerable state support since the 1980s. Besides private sector initiatives, the main impetus for the rapid expansion of ICT in India arose from the initiatives of the technology mission for telecommunications initiated in the 1980s. This initiative headed by a technocrat, Sam Pitroda, during the period when Rajiv Gandhi was prime minister, pushed forward the technological frontiers of Indian information and communication technologies (Dutta and De 2009, pp. 205–06). Afterwards, the central and the state governments in India actively encouraged the ICT industry through a variety of policy measures. The Indian Constitution provides for devolution of administrative responsibility for various government functions by separating the roles of the central and the state governments. Issues like foreign trade and large-scale industrial policy are handled by the central government. State governments are responsible for land allocation, local taxes and provision of basic infrastructure. Coordination between the centre and the states is, however, required in some cases such as setting up of industrial parks. For supporting the ICT industry, major targeted incentives were the setting up of software technology parks, tax breaks for both central and state-level taxes, provision of high-quality infrastructure, administrative and marketing support, allocation of land at preferential rates and initiatives to develop technology clusters. These measures are described below in detail.

By the late 1980s, it was apparent that India's socialistic policies had not helped India much in terms of economic growth and poverty reduction. Therefore, a slow

[5]*Onsite* software development means providing software professionals at the client's business location. In onsite work, the software service company sends software professionals overseas to the client's establishment to execute the project. Much of the development, design and management inputs come from the foreign client. Side by side with the *onsite* software development, there started *offshore* software development as well. *Offshore* software development means the outsourcing of a substantial part of software development to be carried out at the business location of the software services provider. In offshore work, the project is largely executed at the facilities of the service provider using the managerial and project management skills of the software service providing firm (Arora et al. 2001).

process of economic liberalisation started. During the post-liberalisation era, Government policies had acted as a catalyst to facilitate the growth of IT exports especially by establishing the Software Technology Parks of India (STPI) in 1991 as an autonomous organisation under Ministry of Communication and Information Technology. The major supports under the STP Scheme are to provide (i) Single Window Clearance to Software Exporting Units; (ii) Fiscal benefits, (iii) Infrastructure Supporting Data Communication and Incubation, and (iv) Interface between Government and Industry.

In the early 1990s, the IT-enabled services[6] (ITeS) industry began to evolve as well, when foreign companies such as American Express, British Airways, General Electric (GE) and Swissair set up their offshore operations in India.[7] By then, certain Indian ICT companies, like Infosys Technologies Limited, Satyam Computer Services Limited, Wipro Technologies and Reliance Infocomm not only had been set up, but also adopted varied approaches towards improving the quality of their products and services.[8] The central measure for achieving quality by the various major Indian ICT firms had been the adoption of *Six Sigma Methodology*[9] and the multivariate management approaches like *Total Quality Management* TQM),[10] *Supply Chain Management* (SCM)[11] and *Customer Relationship Management* (CRM).[12]

---

[6]During the earlier years, different service lines of IT-enabled services (ITeS) offshored to India included customer care, finance, human resources, billing and payment services, administration and content development (*Economic Survey 2004–2005*, p. 148). To-day, IT-enabled services (ITeS) have expanded and include business process outsourcing (BPO) covering banking/financial/insurance sector assignments, as well as knowledge process outsourcing (KPO)/ legal process outsourcing (LPO), call centre-related assignments, medical lab, diagnostic and dental services, medical transcription services, e-publishing data conversion or digitization, type-setting, copy editing, content and design, graphics CAD/CAM multimedia, animation work, etc. (ESC 2014).

[7]*Economic Survey 2004–2005*, p. 148.

[8]A detailed analysis is available in Dutta and Sekhar (2005).

[9]*Six Sigma Methodology* is an approach to achieve near perfection quality for eliminating defects (driving towards six standard deviations between the mean and the nearest specification limit) in any process—from manufacturing to transactional and from product to service.

[10]TQM precedes the *Six Sigma Methodology*. Originating in the 1950s, TQM revolves around the objective of *doing things right the first time*. Gaining immense popularity since the 1980s, this management approach focuses primarily on market satisfaction. By viewing the organisation as a collection of processes, TQM has begun gaining increasing recognition as a generic management tool. The key principles of TQM include management commitment, customer focus, constant improvement, and employee empowerment.

[11]Portraying itself as a set of individualised processes during the post-World War II period, the concept of SCM has shown a systematic growth and development since then. Having additional names like B2B or business-to-business, the SCM today has grown manifold with the growth of the ICT sector, where the two most important elements of an effective supply chain are communication and transmission of data. Examples of supply chain advancement in the field of ICT include *Electronic Data Interchange* (EDI), *Extension Markup Language* (XML).

[12]Being a core customer-focused strategy, CRM concentrates on maintaining the customer base by tracking all the possible minute information about the customer and developing software systems

This sizable economic phenomenon of the Indian ICT industry has naturally left its mark on the socio-economic fabric of India. It is evident from the Indian growth experience that ICT services-driven growth shows certain patterns (Arora and Athreye 2002; Arora and Gambardella 2004; World Bank 2004; Basant and Chandra 2007; Dutta and De 2009; D'Costa 2011; Mani 2012, 2014). The growth of ICT service industries has been accompanied by increased employment, urban consumption growth and demand for technical education, at the national and the regional levels. Regions endowed with better educational facilities have generally grown faster, which has given rise to spatial and developmental consequences in terms of distributive and political economic issues related to the wider society.

While exports were the initial impetus for the ICT service industry in India, domestic demand has now been growing steadily. The high-technology services-driven growth witnessed in India, which is spearheaded by the vibrant ICT service sector, appears to be less intensive in physical capital than the manufacturing industry-oriented growth efforts of China and other East Asian economies. This allows for relatively lower physical investment and therefore higher current consumption (McKinsey and Company 2007). It appears that this is due to the higher human and organisational capital intensity of ICT-driven growth in India (De and Dutta 2007).

Several earlier authors have explored the link between the institutional environment, policy initiatives and human resource development in India, and its effect on the growth of the Indian ICT service industry. Arora and Athreye (2002) assess the contribution of software to India's economic development paying particular attention to human capital formation. Caniëls and Romijn (2003) study the prominent information technology cluster in the southern Indian city of Bangalore. They examine the beneficial effects of regional industrial clusters from the viewpoint of passive and active collective efficiencies. Parthasarathy (2004) also examines the development of the ICT cluster in Bangalore from the viewpoint of the social embeddedness of economic activity. His paper envisages state policy as slowly losing autonomy and embedding itself in private capital in order to encourage economic growth. Basant and Chandra (2007) explore the role of educational and research institutions in high-technology city clusters in India. Their research develops a framework for analysing the role of academic institutions in city clusters.

(Footnote 12 continued)

that comes in handy for the various specific business purposes like marketing, support, sales. In short, CRM presents a customer-centric approach than a product-centric approach to sustain in the market. The adoption of CRM stems from the increasing recognition on the long-term relationship with customers as one of the chief assets of any organisation irrespective of their size. Thus, the focus is more on *customer retention* than on new *customer acquisition*. Information technology plays a pivotal role in gathering statistical information on the various needs of customers. There are many methodologies designed to achieve the objective of customer retention. The most popular one being *Retentiongram Model* that enables informed choices to be made with due emphasis on the different strategies for different customer segments.

Currently, there have been many efforts underway in many developing countries including India for connecting the rural sector to not only the entire national economy, but also the global economy so that the rural population can have the benefits from being connected to the wider markets by selling their products at better prices and profits. As Mathur (2011, pp. 129–130) points out, the impact of ICT in terms of both static and dynamic efficiency gains:

> Static gains are one-time, and come from more efficient use of scarce resources, allowing higher consumption in the present. It is useful to distinguish two kinds of static efficiency gains. One kind pertains to increase in operating efficiency, while the other comes from reduced transaction costs. In both cases, the channel for gains is through more effective and lower cost. The second type of potential benefit comes from reductions in economic inequality, to the extent that such reductions are an agreed-upon social goal, and therefore a social benefit. However, a focus on IT for rural development is, at least on the surface, supportive of reduced inequality along with increased efficiency and growth. The rural development through information technology includes improvements in the capabilities of the population such as education, health and nutrition, independently of any direct or indirect economic impact. The ability to participate in democratic decision-making also falls into this category. Broad-based improvements in capabilities can also have positive impacts on long-run economic wellbeing, but this is not a necessary condition for desiring such improvements.

5.2.1 Growth of India's ICT-Enabled Service Sector

Software development and information technology-enabled services (ITeS) including business process outsourcing (BPO), business process management (BPM), software engineering R&D services and product development have emerged as one of the most dynamic and vibrant sectors in India's economy. ITeS sector had begun to evolve in the early 1990s when foreign companies such as American Express, British Airways, GE and Swissair set up their offshore operations in India. Today along with a number of Indian companies, a large number of foreign affiliates also operate ITeS services in India. The different service lines of ITeS offshored to India include customer care, finance, human resources, billing and payment services, administration and content development.[13] ITeS is the single largest contributor to services exports. As per AT Kearney's Global Services Location Index 2014, India ranked first and remains the pre-eminent destination for offshore services, with excellence in IT, BPO and voice services. The sector continues to be one of the largest employers in the country, directly employing nearly 3.5 million people as per the *National Association of Software and Service Companies* (NASSCOM). As per the Central Statistics Office (CSO), computer and related services with a share of 3.3% in India's GDP grew by 14.4% in 2013–2014. As per NASSCOM's estimate, the revenue of the IT-BPM industry at US$119

[13] *Economic Survey 2004–2005*, p. 148.

billion grew by 12% in 2014–2015, while the export market at US$ 98 billion grew by 12.3% over the previous year. The BPM sector is being driven by greater automation, expanding omnichannel presence and application of analytics across the entire value chain. The year also witnessed hyper-growth in the technology start-up and software product landscape, with India ranking as the fourth largest start-up hub in the world with over 3100 start-ups in the country. The domestic IT-BPM market is estimated at US$ 20.9 billion in 2014–15, with a growth of 10%. Software products and services revenue for 2015–2016 are projected to grow at 12–14% to reach US$ 133–136 billion as per NASSCOM. Export revenues are projected to grow by 12–14% to reach US$ 110–112 billion and domestic revenues by 10–15% to reach US$ 23–24 billion during 2015–2016.[14]

5.2.2 Software-Specific Incentive Policies during 1970–1995

The central government instituted a series of holistic policies to encourage software industry development since 1970s. These policies incorporated the prevailing economic agenda and therefore evolved from an import substitution mode to an export-oriented model. Van Dijk (2003) and Athreye (2005) describe these policies in some detail. The major measures as described by them are listed below:

(i) The Software Export Scheme of 1972 permitted imports for hardware development, subject to recovery of the price of hardware through foreign exchange earnings.

(ii) In 1976, hardware import duties were lowered from 100 to 40%. Software export applications were given faster clearance, and software firms had the option of taking export incentives and avail of the advantages of Export Processing Zones.

(iii) The Software Export Policy of 1981 allowed import of hardware for export purposes. While import duties on hardware were raised to boost the use of domestic hardware, software exporters could import computers on ‘loan’.

(iv) The New Computer Policy of 1984 allowed more foreign exchange and satellite communication facilities for software firms. Small firms were allowed to use the national computer network facilities for export purposes.

(v) The Software Policy of 1986 recognised software sector growth as an independent policy direction from hardware growth. Hardware import rules were liberalised, and software exporters were given relief from hardware import duties. At the same time, export obligations were increased with strict fines for failure to meet these obligations.

[14]*Economic Survey 2014–2015*, pp. 116–17.

(vi) The Software Technology Park (STP) scheme of 1988 led to the establishment of software technology parks which were endowed with high-quality infrastructure like satellite links, uninterrupted electricity supply, office space and computer equipment. Support services included marketing and training. Firms operating from STPs were given tax exemption for 5 years out of the initial 8 years of operation.

(vii) The New Economic Policy of 1991 resulted in the reduction of satellite communication charges, removal of STP export obligations and lowering of hardware import duties.

(viii) There were reductions in software import duties also. Duties on application software were reduced to 20% in 1994. By 1995, duties on both applications and systems software were reduced to 10%. In comparison with the high import duties of 60% in 1986, this was a major incentive.

(ix) General income tax deductions were also given to software exports from areas other than STPs. This scheme is now phased out.

Several state governments had also provided incentives such as subsidised land, focussed infrastructure, assured electricity supply and exemption from local taxes. In addition, some states have provided 'soft' facilities like innovation promotion and incubation centres, information technology policy guidelines, marketing support and inter-firm cooperation facilities. States that render significant support measures have become major centres for software industry activities. These include Andhra Pradesh, Gujarat, Karnataka, Maharashtra and New Delhi. In fact, the state capital of Karnataka, Bangalore, has become almost synonymous with the Indian software success story (Van Dijk 2003). The software industry had not only recorded a CAGR (compound annual growth rate) exceeding 50% in production during the 5 years (1995–1996 to 1999–2000) of the twentieth century, but also had a turnover of US $6 billion and exports of US $ 4 billion during 1999–2000.[15]

5.2.3 *ICT-Specific Incentive Policies during 1996–2011*

The ICT industry received far greater political and policy prominence during the period of the National Democratic Alliance (NDA) regime (March 1998–May 2004).[16] Acknowledging that the ICT industry had been facing several constraints such as low level of research and development (R&D) investment, lack of a sizable

---

[15] *Economic Survey: 2000–2001*, p. 142.

[16] This NDA regime was composed of a coalition of national and regional parties. During this period in the early part of the new millennium, the national government and several state governments expressly supported the ICT industry and projected ICT-based development efforts as a means of improving the well-being of the people. Within this regime, several politicians including Pramod Mahajan—the national IT minister, Chandrababu Naidu—the chief minister of the state of Andhra Pradesh, and S. M. Krishna—the chief minister of the state of Karnataka, gave active public support to the ICT industry (Dutta and De 2009, p. 206).

domestic software market, poor enforcement of copyright protection laws, the NDA regime led by Prime Minister Atal Bihari Vajpayee designed a series of major policy initiatives to enhance competitiveness in the software industry and strengthen the ICT sector in general. One of these policy initiatives was the formation of a *National Task Force on Information Technology and Software Development* in May 1998. The Task Force had a mandate to formulate the draft of a long-term National IT Policy. The main objective of the Task Force was to recommend immediate steps the Government needed to take, to remove bottlenecks and provide a boost to India's IT industry in general, and the software industry in particular. The Task Force submitted three key reports[17] to the government during a period of ten months (July 1998–April 1999). Its first report was focused on software industry development: the *Information Technology Action Plan: Part I* was comprised of 108 recommendations.

The major recommendations[18] of the Task Force in this report included the opening of Internet Gateway access; encouragement for private sector Software Technology Parks (STPs); zero customs and excise duty on IT software; income tax exemptions for software and services exports; encouragement to set up venture capital funds; 1–3% of the Budget of every Ministry/Department for IT applications; networking of all Universities and research institutions; allowing US Dollar linked stock options to employees of Indian software companies; new schemes for students, including attractive package for buying computers; and as range of other measures. The Government had accepted almost all the recommendations and had directed all concerned departments to implement them. In addition, the Government set up a new Ministry of Information Technology (MIT) in October 1999, as the nodal agency for facilitating all initiatives in the Central Government, the State Governments, academia, the private sector and among successful Indian IT professionals abroad.[19]

- The Task Force's third report had focused on the long-term (strategic) national IT policy. The main thrust of its major policy recommendations had been the urgent necessity for raising both productivity and quality of the Indian software industry.
- In order to promote quality movement in India's software industry, various initiatives have been taken by the Government, NASSCOM and other organisations. Some of these initiatives are in the form of incentives and grants, while others include promotion and Memorandum of Understandings (MoU).

---

[17]The three reports are *Information Technology Action Plan-Part I* (July 4, 1998), *Information Technology Action Plan-Part II* (October 26, 1998), and *Information Technology Action Plan-Part III* (April 16, 1999). While the first two reports are on software and hardware industries respectively, the third one is on long-term national IT policy.

[18]*Economic Survey: 1998–99*, p. 109.

[19]*Economic Survey: 1999–2000*, p. 125.

It is noteworthy that India's software industry has achieved distinction for providing quality services.[20] By December 1999, 170 Indian software companies acquired international quality certification. The NDA Government approved setting up of an IT venture capital fund of Rs. 100 crore[21] for software companies and then took a series of measures to develop a road map for India in e-commerce.[22] These included ICT infrastructure; legal and regulatory framework; technology for electronic commerce (e-commerce) including test-beds; issues related to international domain names; and related areas. Afterwards, the Government also enacted the Information Technology (IT) Act, 2000, not only to provide a legal framework for e-commerce and prevention of computer crimes, but also to accelerate induction of IT in critical sectors of the Indian economy. The Act aimed to recognise electronic contracts, electronic filing/documentation, digital signatures, etc. Rules under the Act had been notified, and the Act came into force on 17 October 2000. The Controller of Certifying Authority had been appointed. Moreover, announcement of IT policies by many state governments had further strengthened India's position in the software-driven IT sector in the world. Exports of the Indian software and services sector increased from Rs. 17,150 crore (US$3.95 billion) in 1999–2000 to Rs. 58,240 crore (US$12.8 billion) in 2003–2004.

The string of state-level electoral defeats of pro-reform technology-oriented chief ministers in Andhra Pradesh, Karnataka and Madhya Pradesh and the national level failure of the NDA to return to power in 2004 might be interpreted as a popular backlash against these new technology based policy initiatives, based on the belief that IT enterprises, software exports, business process outsourcing (BPO) activities and IT-based governance were a panacea for India's long standing development challenges. The initial fears of such a backlash against the new technology sector did, however, materialise neither at the state levels, nor at the central level. In May 2004, the accession of the Congress-led United Progressive Alliance (UPA-I) government at the Centre with Dr. Manmohan Singh as its Prime Minister continued support for the IT industry. A number of steps had been taken to meet the challenge of zero duty regime in 2005 under the Information Technology Agreement (ITA-1). Tariffs on raw materials, parts, other inputs and capital goods had been rationalised during 2004–05 to make domestic manufacturing of electronics and IT products viable and competitive.[23] Further policy initiatives had been

---

[20]Quoted from *Economic Survey: 2000–2001*, p. 143.

[21]Rs. 100 crore is approximately equal to US$21.5 million (at the then exchange rate).

[22]*Economic Survey: 1999–2000*, p. 125 and *Economic Survey: 2000–2001*, p. 143.

[23]The related policy initiatives taken during 2004–2005 for the Electronics and IT sector are as follows: (i) Customs duty on parts of computer, static converters for automatic data processing machines and parts thereof have been fully exempted. (ii) Computers have been exempted from excise duty. (iii) Import of second-hand capital goods has been permitted without any age restriction. (iv) The export obligation under the Export Promotion Capital Goods (EPCG) scheme can also be fulfilled by the supply of Information Technology Agreement (ITA-1) items to the Domestic Tariff Area (DTA) provided the realization is in free foreign exchange (*Economic Survey 2004–2005*, Box 7.2, p. 149).

taken during 2005–06 to improve the competitive edge of the IT sector. These policy initiatives included the following:

> (i) Customs duty on all the 217 tariff lines covered under the Information Technology Agreement (ITA-1) of WTO had been abolished; (ii) All goods required in the manufacture of ITA-1 items had also been exempted from customs duty subject to Actual user condition; (iii) An additional duty of 4 per cent had been imposed on items bound by ITA-1 (except IT software) and their inputs, raw materials, parts, capital goods covered under various customs notifications; (iv) Expenditure incurred on in-house R&D facility for scientific research by a company engaged in the business of electronic equipments, computers, telecom, etc. had been allowed a weighted deduction of 150 per cent of the expenditure incurred. Time limit for availing this benefit had been extended up to March 31, 2007; (v) In order to improve information security with growing applications of IT, an Information Security Management System had been set up. A security cooperation agreement had been signed with Microsoft to exchange computer security related information and training of technical personnel; and (vi) An expert committee had been set up to review the IT Act (*Economic Survey 2005–2006*, Box 7.3, p. 148).

In December 2006, the Information Technology Amendment Bill had been introduced in the Parliament, which proposed to put in place technology applications, security practices and procedures relating to such applications, as well as addressing the issue of technological neutrality in IT laws as recommended by the United Nations Commission on International Trade Law (UNCITRAL) on Electronic Signature. Subsequently, the Information Technology Amendment Act was enforced in 2008 and the rules of important sections had been notified in October 2009 addressing the needs of national cyber security:

> The Act has, inter alia, added provisions to deal with new forms of cybercrimes like publishing sexually explicit material in electronic form, video voyeurism and breach of confidentiality. The Indian Computer Emergency Response Team (CERT-In) has been designated as the nodal agency for coordinating matters related to cyber security and emergency response. CERT-In has published a crisis management plan for countering cyber attacks and cyber terrorism. It has also created a panel of IT security auditors. The Certifying Authorities (CAs) licensed by the CCA have issued more than 14,00,000 Digital Signature Certificates. These are being used in applications such as Real-Time Gross Settlement System & Electronic Fund Transfer, email, e-procurement, share trading and issue of import/export licences and filing of company returns.[24]

During the earlier period of the UPA government's second term from 2009 to 25 May 2014,[25] it was found that several issues relating to the IT/ITeS sector needed attention:

> These include shifting from low-end services to high-end services like programming in the light of competition in BPO from other countries and policies in some developed countries like UK to employ locals; addressing data protection issues as half of offshore work does not come to India; concluding totalisation agreements with target countries to resolve the

[24]*Economic Survey 2009–10*, pp. 228–29.

[25]The NDA government with Narendra Modi as the Prime Minister came to power on 26 May 2014.

social security benefits issue as is being done now; and increasing the coverage and depth of IT and ITeS services in the domestic sector.[26]

In the 2010–2011 Budget, the government allocated expenditure for improving IT infrastructure and delivery mechanism, reduction in surcharge from 10 to 7.5% for IT companies and Government's e-Governance Plan.[27]

5.3 Success Story of India's Telecom and Related Communication Services

India's technology mission for telecommunications that was initiated in the 1980s had pushed forward the technological frontiers, which resulted in an international success story of the Indian telecom network being ranked as the second largest in the world, after China in 2011. In spite of a so-called 2G spectrum scam,[28] involving India's telecom sector in 2008, the total number of telephones increased from 206.83 million on 31 March 2007 to 926.53 million as on 31 December 2011. The growth in wireless connections had been phenomenal, reaching 893.84 million connections at the end of December 2011, taking their share to over 96% of total telephones in the country. Teledensity, which is an important indicator of telecom penetration, increased from 18.31% in March 2007 to 76.86% in December 2011. Urban teledensity as of December 2011 reached a high level of 167.85%, while that of rural teledensity was low at 37.48%. This showed significant urban-rural divide with the potential for further growth in rural areas. Teledensity variation also existed among different circles as well. While some circles such as Delhi (235.6%), Mumbai (188.95%), Chennai (170.18%), Kolkata (168.45%) and Himachal Pradesh (118.63%) showed high teledensity, in some circles such as Bihar (47.17%) and Assam (45.85%) it was very low in December 2011.[29]

The growth of wireless connections had been phenomenal, reaching 893.86 million connections at the end of December 2011. As a result, the share of wireless telephones had increased from 80.3% in March 2007 to 96.4% in December 2011.

---

[26] *Economic Survey 2010–11*, p. 252.

[27] The e-Governance initiatives in India go back to mid-1990s for wider sectoral applications with emphasis on citizen-centric services. Subsequently, many States/UTs started various e-Governance projects. Because these e-Governance projects could make only lesser than the desired impact, Government of India later on launched National e-Governance Plan (NeGP) in 2006 (www.digitalindia.gov.in/content/about-programme).

[28] The Indian telecommunications sector had gone through a so-called 2G spectrum scam and political scandal in which politicians and government officials under the UPA regime under-charged mobile telephone companies for frequency allocation licenses, which they then used to create 2G spectrum subscriptions for cell phones. These licenses were issued in 2008 under A. Raja, Minister of Communications & IT from 2007 to 2009, which the Supreme Court of India subsequently cancelled on 2 February 2012 declaring them 'unconstitutional and arbitrary'.

[29] *Economic Survey 2011–12* (pp. 240 and 267).

However, the growth of wire line connections has been decreasing every year. Improved affordability of wireless phones has made the universal access objective more feasible. The liberalisation efforts of the government in the telecom sector became evident in the growing share of the private sector in total telephone connections. As against a meagre 5% in 1999, the share of private operators increased to 86% in December 2011. A competitive stimulus provided by a liberal policy regime increased telecom penetration together with a substantial reduction in tariffs.[30]

Since the announcement of the Broadband Policy in 2004, several measures had subsequently been taken to promote broadband penetration in the country. As a result, there are 13.30 million broadband subscribers as on 31 December 2011 and 19.69 million internet subscribers at the end of March 2011. However, broadband has lagged behind the growth of telephones in India. Special efforts are being made to increase the penetration of broadband, especially in rural and remote areas. The upcoming decade is likely to usher in an information era through mobile value added services (MVAS) and broadband for all. The successfully concluded auction of the broadband wireless access (BWA)/3G spectrum and National Optical Fiber Network (NOFN) was expected to enhance wireless broadband penetration and help connect the remotest locations across India.[31]

5.3.1 India's New Telecom Policy 2012[32]

In June 2012, the Government approved the National Telecom Policy (NTP 2012) with a few changes and additions to the original draft of the New Telecom Policy, introduced by the Department of Telecommunications (DoT) in October 2011. This policy replaced the existing telecom policy formulated in 1999 and defined the general direction of the new telecom policy with the following major guidelines. Accordingly, it would:

- provide appropriate incentives for rolling out reliable and affordable broadband access to rural and remote areas: DoT had earlier proposed to lay special emphasis on providing reliable and affordable broadband access to rural and remote areas by a combination of optical fibre, wireless, VSAT and other technologies, which were to be funded from the Universal Service Obligation Fund (USOF), while the access to Optical Fibre Network (OFN) was proposed to be open, non-discriminatory and technology neutral;

---

[30] *Ibid.* (pp. 266–67).

[31] *Ibid.* (p. 240).

[32] http://www.medianama.com/2012/06/223-indias-new-telecom-policy-2012-whats-changed-additions-omissions/.

- launch secure transactional services including online authentication of identity and financial services by leveraging mobile devices and SIM cards with enhanced features;
- promote R&D, design, development and manufacturing in the domestic telecom equipment manufacturing, provide appropriate fiscal incentives to telecom equipment manufacturing through a Modified Special Incentive Package Scheme (M-SIPS) and to Indian product manufacturers for domestic deployment and exports;
- intend to facilitate resale at the service level in both wholesale and retail, by approving and introducing MVNOs (Mobile virtual network operators) while ensuring due compliance with security and other license-related obligations;
- intend to establish and strengthen the Institute of Advanced Radio Spectrum Engineering and Management Studies (IARSEMS) in order to undertake policy research in radio spectrum engineering, management/radio monitoring and related aspects as a government agency;
- also intend to strengthen and develop National Telecom Institute for Policy Research, Innovation and Training (NTIPRIT) to enable research in India centric technologies and policies in telecom domain, capacity building and set up a comprehensive repository in NTIPRIT for distributing telecom-related information, standards, benchmarks, resources and program curriculum.
- also establish a National Mobile Property Registry to address security, theft and other issues likes reprogramming of mobile handsets and create an appropriate regulatory framework to provide a reliable means of public communication by Telecom Service Providers during disasters while strengthening the regulator to ensure telcos comply with the prescribed performance standards and Quality of Service (QoS) parameters;
- seek to appropriately consider restructuring of the Public Sector Undertakings, under the Department of Telecommunications, with respect to management, manpower and equity and recognise strategic importance of Telecom PSUs in nurturing/enhancing the Government's intervention capabilities in matters of national security or international importance, including execution of bilateral projects funded by the Government of India;
- recognise and enhance the opportunities available through/within Telecom PSUs for deployment of indigenously developed Telecom products, with Indian IPR, to provide vital support for domestic manufacturing of Indian Telecom products in the long run;
- formulate appropriate policies in the area of enterprise and data services to fuel further growth of India's ICTE sector and attract investments; and
- take requisite measures to strengthen various DoT units when necessary, to achieve the objectives of this policy as well as operationalise the policy by bringing out detailed guidelines, when appropriate, while also intending to take suitable facilitatory measures to encourage existing service providers to migrate to the new regime in a level playing field.

5.4 Digital Divide in India and Government's Initiatives for Its Bridging

The dramatic but uneven development consequences of the growth of the ICT industry in India has been noted by several studies as summarised in Dutta and De (2014, Sect. 4). Although it is apparent that the rise of the ICT industry has provided unique opportunities and challenges to the Indian socio-economic fabric, it has also resulted in large disparities in incomes and living standards. On the one hand, the rise of ICT firms and related high-technology services has resulted in huge opportunities for employment, economic growth and human capital development. On the other hand, certain regions and sections of society have been unable to reap the economic benefits of the ICT sector boom. States endowed with better educational facilities have attracted greater ICT investment resulting in human capital accumulation[33] and increased urban consumption in ICT industry intensive states such as Karnataka and Andhra Pradesh of India's southern region. While India's South and the West maintained their lead in terms of private technical education and IT output growth, the North and the East were beginning to catch up. The North, however, showed some growth in these areas, but the East was yet to come on par in the early 2000s. The overall *digital divide*[34] in India as a whole during 2001–2014 can be assessed from Table 5.1. Although mobile cellular subscription has drastically increased from less than 1% in 2001 to 74.48% in 2014, the number of Internet users has increased very slowly from less than 1 to 18% during the same period.

5.4.1 Initiatives to Bridge Digital Divide under the UPA-I & II Governments (2004–14)

After the United Progressive Alliance (UPA-I) government came to power at the Centre with Dr. Manmohan Singh as its Prime Minister in May 2004, apart from continuing support for the IT industry, it also started using IT as a tool for raising the living standards of the masses, which became the vision of the government's IT policy. Towards this end, the Department of Information Technology (DIT) took up an ambitious programme of personal computer (PC) Internet penetration to the rural and undeserved urban areas. The Department also announced a programme to establish State Wide Area Network (SWAN) up to the block level to provide

[33]The number of engineering colleges per million population and the number of engineering students per million population can be considered as proxies for the human capital production apparatus and human capital output, respectively.

[34]'Digital divide' refers to a substantial asymmetry between two or more population in the distribution and effective use of information and communication resources, which may be within a country or across different countries.

Table 5.1 Extent of digital divide in India: 2001–2014

	2001	2002	2003	2004	2005	2006	2007	2008	2009	2010	2011	2012	2013	2014
Mobile cellular subscriptions (per 100 people)	0.62	1.21	3.10	4.70	8.00	14.52	20.16	29.53	44.12	62.39	73.20	69.92	70.78	74.48
Fixed telephone subscriptions (per 100 people)	3.64	3.85	3.84	4.16	4.45	3.57	3.39	3.23	3.11	2.91	2.69	2.50	2.32	2.10
Fixed broadband subscriptions (per 100 people)	0.01	0.01	0.01	0.02	0.12	0.20	0.27	NA	0.65	0.91	1.09	1.21	1.19	1.24
Secure internet servers (per 1 million people)	0.11	NA	0.25	0.41	0.58	0.71	0.95	1.22	1.48	2.11	2.84	3.49	3.82	5.54
Internet users (per 100 people)	0.66	1.54	1.69	1.98	2.39	2.81	3.95	4.38	5.12	7.50	10.07	12.58	15.10	18.00

Source: *World Development Indicators*, World Bank (accessed on 11 December 2015)

connectivity for e-Governance. DIT also set up Community Information Centres (CICs) in hilly, far-flung areas of the North-East and Jammu and Kashmir to facilitate the spread of benefit of information and communication technology. It was also proposed to set up CICs in other hilly, far-flung areas of the country like Uttaranchal, Andaman and Nicobar & Lakshadweep.[35]

In order to ensure that the benefits of IT and ITeS reach the common people, the Government initiated a move to make available tools and fonts in various Indian languages freely to the general public during 2006–2007. The National e-Governance Plan (NeGP) was approved by the Government of India on 18 May 2006 with the following vision[36]:

> "Make all Government services accessible to the common man in his locality, through common service delivery outlets and ensure efficiency, transparency and reliability of such services at affordable costs to realize the basic needs of the common man".

The NeGP comprises of Mission Mode Projects (MMPs) and core e-infrastructure. The NeGP identifies 27 Mission Mode Projects (MMPs) and eight components of its e-infrastructure.[37] The eight components of the Plan are broadly divided into two categories: three core infrastructural components, and five others. The first category covers mainly core infrastructural components: State Wide Area Network (SWAN), State Data Center (SDC) and Common Service Centres (CSCs), while the other category covers five broad areas like standards, capacity building, awareness and communications, assessment, and research and development, which go a long way to ensure successful implementation, institutionalisation and sustainability of NeGP.

As Fig. 5.1 depicts, the 27 MMPs include eight integrated projects; eight central projects and 11 state projects.

The eight integrated projects located at the core of the figure include:

(1) *e-BIZ*—seeks to address several issues related to approvals and permissions for businesses, reducing the points of contact between the business entities and the Government agencies, standardising required information, establishing a single-window services, and reducing the burden of compliance.
(2) *National Service Delivery Gateway*—acts a messaging middleware providing intelligent routing services from a Service Seeker to a Service Provider.
(3) *Common Service Centres*—propose to set up to 87,419 centres for providing common services in 17 States.
(4) *e-Procurement*—establishes a one stop-shop providing all services related to government procurement.
(5) *e-Office*—provides a middleware for streamlining, aligning, optimising and automating all internal processes across government boundaries.

---

[35] *Economic Survey 2004–2005*, p. 148.

[36] Chauhan (2009, p. 7).

[37] *Ibid.* pp. 7–12.

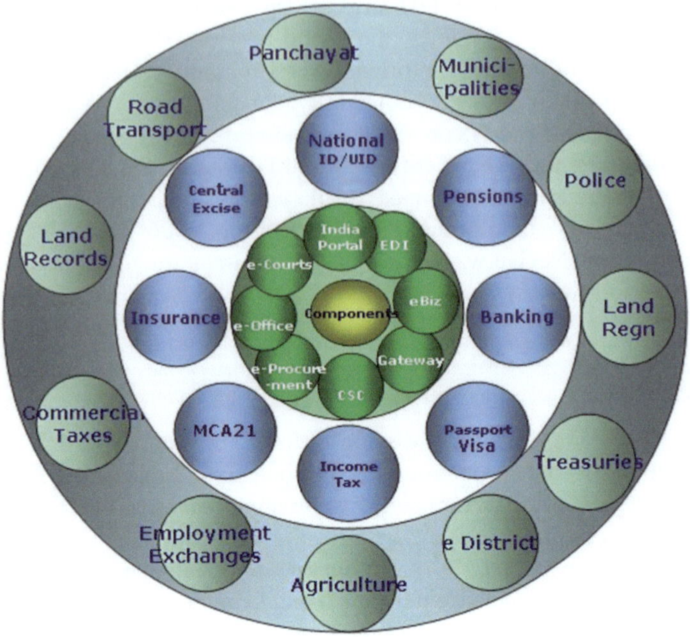

Fig. 5.1 Mission mode projects

(6) *e-Courts*—offer online availability of judgments and cause list, e-filing of cases and notifications through e-mails.
(7) *India Portal*—provides one-stop access to government services.
(8) *Electronic Data Interchange (EDI) for Trade*—introduces electronic filing and clearance of import and export documents, e-payment of duties or charges by Ports, Airports, Customs, etc., and electronic exchange of documents between community partners and Customs, Ports and other government agencies.

The eight central projects comprise:

(1) *Income Tax*—includes 19 defined services to be provided online like e-filing of tax returns through intermediaries, online submission of forms, online payment of taxes through selected banks, issue of refunds through Electronic Clearance System.
(2) *MCA21*—offers availability of all Ministry of Company Affairs (MCA) services including filing of documents, registration of companies and public access to corporate information through a secure portal.
(3) *Insurance*—provides insurance-related services through the four public sector general insurance companies.
(4) *Central Excise*—enables filing of service tax and Excise Returns, e-Payments of custom duties, automated clearance of courier consignments, etc.

(5) *National ID/UID*—creates a central database and generates unique identifiers for residents across the country primarily for effective reach of social sector benefits.
(6) *Pensions*—track and handles pension settlements.
(7) *Banking*—integrates core banking solutions of various banks.
(8) *Passport, Visas and Immigration*—enables applications for new passports, renew old passports, track application status and handle immigration formalities for all international incoming flights.

The 11 State projects involve:

(1) *Agriculture*—provides services like market prices, soil information, crop diseases and management, good practices for horticulture, sericulture.
(2) *Employment Exchange*—enables to match the requirements of employers and potential employees, provides guidance to the unemployed and facilitates online registration of vacancies by employers.
(3) *Commercial Taxes*—improve efficiency of VAT administration by enabling electronic filing of returns and clearance of refunds, online payment of taxes, etc.
(4) *Land Records*—identify and automates 14 services like integration of textual and spatial land records data, integration of registration and mutation processes, automatic updating of land records providing conclusive title to land owners.
(5) *Road Transport*—includes services like vehicle registration and driving licenses.
(6) *Gram Panchayat*—issues trade licenses, certificates, house related services, receipt of fund progress reports, individual beneficiaries of various schemes, etc.
(7) *Municipalities*—provide G2C services like issuing birth and death certificates, payment of utility bills, issuing licenses.
(8) *Police*—implements Common Integrated Police Application (CIPA) and hardware in Police Stations.
(9) *Property Registration*—replaces manual systems of verification and scrutiny of documents, capturing and preserving copies of documents, and conducting searches and of maintaining back office records.
(10) *Treasuries*—involve payment of salaries to government employees, payment of expenses, etc.
(11) *e-District*—automates backend processes to enable the delivery of G2C services through Common Services Centers.

In addition to the eleven State projects defined, each State can add up to five state-specific projects.

3 Main Core Components:

Three main core components that were identified by the NeGP are presented below:

State Wide Area Network (SWAN)
The Government has approved the SWAN Scheme for establishing State Wide Area Networks (SWANs) across the country in 35 States and Union Territories, at a total outlay of Rs. 3,334 Crore over a period of 5 years. The objective of SWAN Scheme is to establish converged network consisting of data, voice and video circuits with minimum 2 Mbps capacity, linking the State with the Union Territories Headquarters, right up to the Block and Tehsil headquarters, through the district and the Sub-division headquarters. The aim is to create a secure government closed user group (CUG) network, for the purpose of delivering Government-to-Citizen (G2C) and Government-to-Government (G2G) services.

State Data Centre (SDC)
State Data Centre (SDC) has been identified as one of the important element of the Core infrastructure components for supporting NeGP. SDC provides key functionalities such as central repository of the state, secure data storage, online delivery of services, Citizen Information/Services portal, State Intranet portal, disaster recovery, remote management and service integration, among others. The entire scheme involves an outlay of Rs. 17,000 million. It is expected that the State Data Centre shall be set up and operated by 2009 across different states in the country.

Common Service Centres (CSCs)
CSC involves a scheme for providing support for establishing 100,000 broadband Internet-enabled Common Service Centers (CSCs) in rural areas of the country. The Scheme has been approved at a total cost of Rs. 5742 Crores over 4 years, of which the Government of India is estimated to contribute with Rs. 856 Crore and the State Governments with Rs. 793 Crores. Other resources would be mobilised from the private sector.

5 Broad Components:
Each of the five other broad components is explained as follows:

Standards
Various Working Groups and Task Forces have been constituted considering various areas of interventions to formulate guidelines and standards. These areas include technical standards and e-governance architecture, network and information security, e-governance information security standard, localisation and language technology standards, metadata and standards for application domains, conformity assessment framework which is extremely relevant for any e-governance project, policies on identity and access management, and e-forms.

Capacity Building
A comprehensive Capacity Building Scheme has been approved covering all States and Union Territories. The major component of the Capacity Building Scheme is the formation of professional core teams for providing technical support to the policy-makers, executive bodies and implementing authorities. The responsibilities of the core teams include providing training and orientation of key stakeholders associated with policy-making and implementation of state e-Governance

Programme, and providing a platform to promote knowledge sharing. In addition, it creates Capacity Building Management Cell at the national level, to oversee the smooth implementation of capacity building scheme and to take midterm corrective actions, as appropriate. The Scheme will also facilitate recruitment of professionals, preparation of training content, scheduling of training programs, study and adoption of international best practices.

Awareness and Communications

The success of the Plan hinges not only on accessibility and availability to information and various services but also awareness regarding the Programme, effective branding of NeGP and finally a communication strategy that addresses the above two. This component focuses on creating and implementing the strategy to achieve the following objectives: (i) building distinctive brand of NeGP which will be utilised across Departmental communications; (ii) creating awareness among citizens about the initiative and its objectives; (iii) motivating stakeholders, with an emphasis on the point that NeGP is not about computerisation or technology but making interaction with government easier and (iv) creating a demand driven atmosphere which would ensure that the service delivery and its quality are met. The aim is also to create a set of communication guidelines that can be used by other Ministries and/or Departments to design their own communications plan.

Assessment

A significant part of scarce resources are being invested in e-Government projects. Even with its perceived potentials, e-Government projects are fraught with risks and the success rate across the world is not very encouraging. Given this scenario and the fact that e-Government projects are inherently complex, it therefore becomes imperative that a robust assessment strategy and framework is devised for evaluating performance of e-Government projects. This would not only provide valuable understanding on individual projects but also provide for a backward integration into the process of project appraisal and capacity building.

Research and Development

Inputs from research activities are needed in the areas of e-Governance Technical Standards including interoperability standards, e-Government Enterprise Architecture Frameworks, Information Security, Data and Metadata Standards, and Quality and documentation that includes e-Governance Quality Manual, e-Governance Project Life-Cycle, Project Management, Program Management Conformance Assessment Frameworks and Service-Level Agreement guidelines, among others. In addition, research results are needed for preparing deliverables that are being aimed at producing publications related to e-government standards, published at government websites for reference and as discussion papers for working group members. In addition, they are also required for reviewing technical papers, proposals, documents, guidelines, and for providing technical inputs on various open standards and technologies, architectures and middleware to the e-Governance directorate. The approach includes collaborations with industry and academics in the area of e-Governance research and innovations. In particular, the

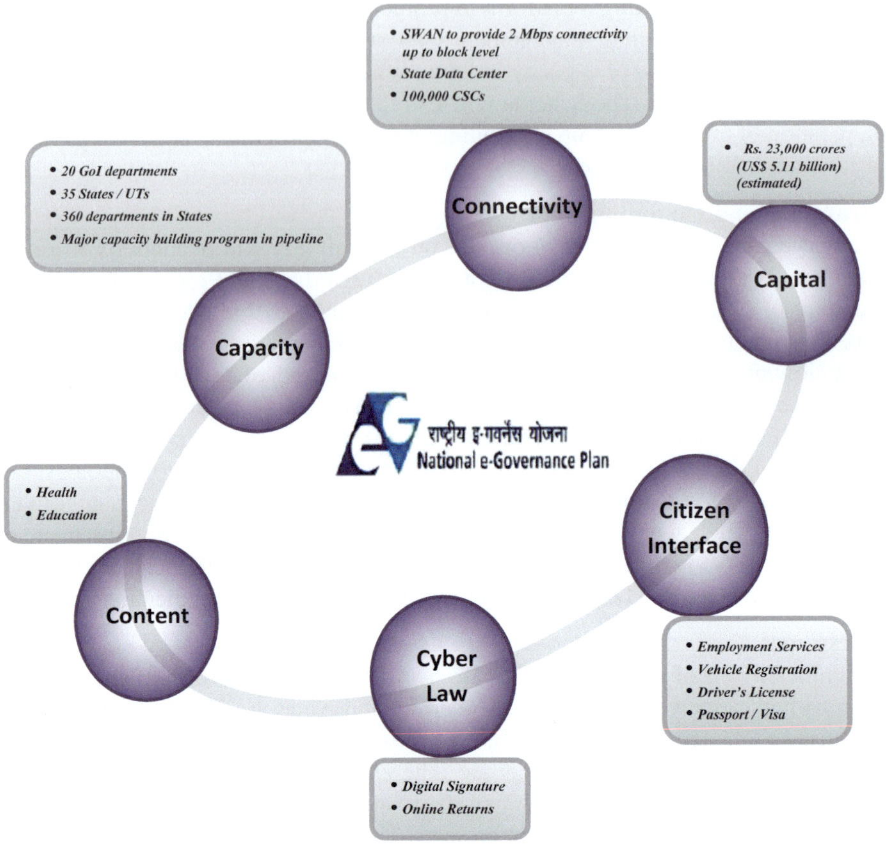

Fig. 5.2 Integrated approach for implementing NeGP

Microsoft Innovation Lab has been set up for developing innovative e-Governance solutions and research in the area.

NeGP Implementation Strategies

The implementation strategy for NeGP is based on an integrated approach and on seven guiding principles. The integrated approach is based on the integration of the following perspectives and is shown in Fig. 5.2:

Connectivity—deploying a State Wide Area Network, State Data Centers and 100,000 Common Service Centers (CSCs);
Capacity—building human and institutional capacity in 20 Government of India Departments, 35 States and Urban Territories, 360 Departments at States;
Content—providing services in vertical domains like Health and Education;
Cyber law—providing the regulatory framework for digital signatures, etc.
Citizen Interface—providing enhanced G2C services like vehicle registration, driver's license, and visas.

Capital—assuring financial resources.

During 2006–2007, a planned outlay of Rs. 5,742 crore had been approved of which the share of the Central Government and the State Governments would be Rs. 856 crore and Rs. 793 crore, respectively. The balance was expected to be invested by the private sector.[38] During 2007–2008, the Government also approved a scheme for facilitating the establishment of 1 lakh broadband Internet-enabled Common Service Centres (CSCs) in the rural areas, in such a public–private partnership mode.[39]

The *Economic Survey 2009–2010* reported (p. 228) that there were 27 Mission Mode Projects (MMPs) under the National e-Governance Plan (NeGP) consisting of nine Central MMPs, 11 State MMPs and seven integrated MMPs (including eight programme support components) which, *inter alia*, achieved the following by December 2009:

> Out of the 100,000 broadband Internet-enabled Common Service Centres (CSCs) planned to be rolled out in rural areas on PPP basis, 58,954 have been rolled out. Eleven States/Union Territories have completed implementation of the State Wide Area Networks (SWANs) scheme which is envisaged to provide secured network from State headquarters up to block level with a minimum bandwidth capacity of 2 Mbps. Proposals of State Data Centres (SDC) for 31 States/Union Territories have been approved with a total outlay of Rs 1,378.50 crore. Twenty States/Union Territories have completed the institutional framework for State-level strategic decision making including setting up of State e-Governance Mission Teams (SeMT) and deployed SeMT personnel.

Recognising the potential of broadband services in the growth of GDP and in creation of an enabling environment for promoting a knowledge-based society, government had, as has already been noted above, announced a broadband policy in 2004. Afterwards, several measures had been taken to promote broadband usage in the country. As a result, there were 13.30 million broadband subscribers as on 31 December 2011 and 20.99 million Internet subscribers at the end of March 2011. However, broadband has lagged behind the growth of telephones in India. Special efforts had also been made to increase its penetration, especially in rural and remote areas. The Universal Service Obligation Fund (USOF) was established with the fundamental objective of providing people in rural and remote areas access to 'basic' telephony services at affordable prices. Subsequently, its scope was widened to provide subsidy support for enabling access to all types of telephony services including mobile services and broadband connectivity and for creation of infrastructure like optical fibre cables (OFC) in rural and remote areas.[40]

As was reported in *Economic Survey 2011–2012* (p. 267), various schemes under implementation for taking communication facilities to rural and remote areas with the support of the USO fund were as follows:

---

[38]*Economic Survey 2006–2007*, Box 7.4, p. 147.

[39]*Economic Survey 2007–2008*, Box 8.3, p. 194.

[40]*Economic Survey 2011–2012*, p. 267.

1. All 5,79,889 villages, i.e. about 97.69% of the Census 2001 inhabited revenue villages, had been covered with village public telephone (VPT) facility as of 31 December 2011.
2. Setting up and managing of 7,353 infrastructure towers in 500 districts spread over 27 states for provision of mobile services in specified rural and remote areas was targeted; 7,296 of them (99%) had been set up by December 2011.
3. In order to provide broadband connectivity to rural areas, the USOF signed an agreement with Bharat Sanchar Nigam Limited (BSNL) on 20 January 2009 to provide 8,88,832 wire line broadband connections to individual users and government institutions and set up 28,672 kiosks over a period of 5 years. As on 31 December 2011, 3,38,617 broadband connections and 6426 kiosks had been provided under this scheme in rural and remote areas.
4. Another scheme had been launched under the USOF to provide sufficient back-haul capacity to integrate voice and data traffic from the access network in rural areas to their core network by strengthening the OFC network. This scheme considered OFC network augmentation between the block headquarters and district headquarters to begin with. The USOF, through this scheme, was put in charge for providing subsidy support for augmentation, creation and management of intra-district OFC network on the condition that it would be shared with other telecom operators at the rates prescribed in the agreement. The state of Assam had been taken up first for this implementation.
5. Recognising the vital role that information communication technology (ICT) can play in the empowerment of rural women, a scheme called *Sanchar Shakti* had been launched in March 2011 for pilot projects aimed at facilitating access of self-help groups (SHGs) to ICT-enabled services. Financial support from the USO Fund was expected to be provided towards value added services (VAS) subscriptions for SHGs in accordance with the provisions of underlying subsidy agreements. The initial memorandums of understanding (MoUs) had been signed for proof of concept (PoC) for nine mobile VAS projects in the states of Tamil Nadu, Kerala, Maharashtra, Uttar Pradesh, Uttarakhand, Andhra Pradesh, Rajasthan and the Union Territory of Puducherry.

Other Major Initiatives under the UPA-II Government

National Optical Fibre Network

Government had approved a project of National Optical Fibre Network (NOFN) in October 2011 for providing broadband connectivity to approximately 2.5 lakh gram panchayats at a cost of Rs. 20,000 crore.

The network will provide connectivity to various public institutions like gram panchayats, primary health centres (PHCs) and schools in rural areas. It will also result in investment from the private sector both for providing different services and for manufacturing of broadband-related telecom equipment. The project will be funded by the USOF. The third-generation (3G) and broadband wireless access (BWA) auctions that took place last year are expected to act as catalysts for enabling Internet access to even the remotest parts of India and further boost the use of mobile broadband and mobile data as well as applications. The upcoming decade will usher in an information era through mobile value added services (MVAS) and 'broadband for all'.[41]

National Knowledge Network

Earlier, Government had also approved another project on establishment of National Knowledge Network (NKN)[42] in March 2010 with an outlay of Rs. 5990 crore over a period of 10 years, and with National Informatics Centre being its implementing agency. The objective of the NKN project with its multi-gigabit capability was to facilitate an ultra-high speed backbone for e-Governance and also to establish a strong and robust Indian network all universities, research institutions, libraries, laboratories, health care and agricultural institutions across the country and the globe. The Ministry of Communications & Information Technology records NKN's following achievements[43] by 31st May 2014:

- 1261 links to Institutions have been commissioned and made operational. This includes 341 links to institutions under NMEICT, which have been migrated to NKN.
- 66 Virtual Classrooms have been set up.
- NKN connectivity has also been extended to 286 NIC district centres.
- 89 Nos of Core Links have been commissioned and operational.
- NKN connectivity has been extended to State Wide Area Network (SWAN) in 26 States/Union Territories and State Data Centre (SDC) in 23 States/UTs.

As noted in *Economic Survey 2011–2012* (pp. 242–43), significant progress had been made in laying down core e-infrastructure and in most of the Mission Mode Projects (MMPs). More than 97,000 common service centres (CSCs) had been established across the country as Web-enabled service access points for making public services available to citizens on an anytime, anywhere basis. Initiatives under the NeGP also included online services related to income tax, Ministry of Corporate Affairs (MCA) 21, passports and central excise. The government also initiated new e-Governance projects for education, health, public distribution system and postal services. This would ensure common people can access quality education, cost efficient and quality health care and postal services at affordable costs. The number of public services available to citizens in electronic mode would be expanded through the Electronic Delivery of Services (EDS) Bill, approved by the union cabinet on 20 December 2011. In order to leverage the rapid growth in penetration of mobile technology and connectivity and also to ensure accessibility to all services to the common people, public services under all e-Governance projects would

---

[41] *Economic Survey 2011–2012*, pp. 267–68.

[42] The Government's decision to set up National Knowledge Network was first announced in the 2008–2009 Budget Speech under the Chairmanship of Principal Scientific Adviser to the Government of India for its coordination and monitoring.

[43] http://deity.gov.in/content/national-knowledge-network.

be delivered through mobile devices like mobile phones and *Aakash* tablets.[44] Further, basic banking services, i.e. cash withdrawal, cash deposit, balance inquiry, and transfer of money from one account to another, would be extended to every panchayat through the CSCs and money transfer facility to every village by December 2013, leveraging ICT and mobile technology. This would help make financial inclusion a reality with the help of ICT.

Direct Cash/Benefit Transfer

In October 2012, the UPA-II Government constituted a high-power National Committee on Direct Cash Transfers in a bid to reduce corruption at the cutting edge. The purpose of Direct Benefits Transfer (DBT) was to ensure that 'benefits go to individuals' bank accounts electronically, minimising tiers involved in fund flow thereby reducing delay in payment, ensuring accurate targeting of the beneficiary and curbing pilferage and duplication'. The Committee had been mandated to 'provide an overarching vision and direction, as well as to determine broad policy objectives and strategies, to enable direct cash transfers … to individuals eligible for benefits flowing out of the government's many welfare programmes'. Three Mission Mode Committees (MMCs)—on technology, financial inclusion and implementation—had been designed to implement the direct cash transfer system. While focus of the Technology Committee was on the technology, payment architecture and IT issues, that of the Financial Inclusion Committee was on ensuring universal access to banking and other financial services at affordable costs to disadvantaged and low-income sections of the society. The Implementation Committee's task was to work out the details of the Electronic Transfer of Benefits for all their departments under different Ministries involved. Afterwards, in the meeting of the National Committee on Direct Cash Transfer led by the Prime Minister, Manmmohan Singh, a decision was taken that Direct Benefit Transfer (DBT) would be rolled out from 1 January 2013 in 43 identified districts. The following Table 5.2 gives a list of 25 schemes implemented for DBT as on 10 April 2013.

The UPA-I & II Governments had thus taken various initiatives to promote the growth of the IT-ITeS industry and had been a key catalyst for increased IT adoption—through sectors reforms that encourage IT acceptance, National e-Governance Plan (NeGP) and the Unique Identification Development Authority of India (UIDAI) programme that created large-scale IT infrastructure and promoted corporate participation. During the UPA-II Government, the Draft National Policy on Information Technology 2011 emphasised adoption of technology-enabled approaches to overcome developmental challenges in education, health, skill development, financial inclusion, employment generation and governance so

[44]*Aakash* is an Android-based tablet computer promoted by the Indian Ministry of Human Resource Development as part of an initiative to link 25,000 colleges and 400 universities in an e-learning program. It is produced by the British-Canadian company Data Wind. The *Aakash* tablet was officially launched by India's then Minister of Human Resource Development, Kapil Sibal in New Delhi on 5 October 2011.

Table 5.2 List of 25 schemes implemented for Direct Benefit Transfer (DBT)—as on 10.04.2013

Sl. No.	Ministry/Department	No. of schemes		CS/CSS	Name of the scheme	Share of centre	Funds flow
1	M/o Social Justice & Empowerment	6	1	CSS	Post-Matric Scholarship for SC Students	100%	MSJE to State Govt to District to Bcncficiarics
			2	CSS	Pre-Matric Scholarship for SC Students	100%	MSJE to State Govt to District to Bcncficiarics
			3	CSS	Pre-Matric Scholarship for Children of those encaged in unclean occupations	100%	MSJE to State Govt to District to Bcncficiarics
			4	CS	Uparadation of merit of SC Students,	100%	MSJE to State Govt to District to Bcncficiarics
			5	CSS	Post-Matric Scholarship for OBCs	100%	MSJE to State Govt to District to Bcncficiarics
			6	CS	Top Class Education Scheme		
2	M/o Human Resources Development, D/o Higher Education	3	1	CS	Scholarship to Universities/College Students	100%	MHRD-Bcncficiary through Canara Bank Account
			2	CS	Fellowship Schemes of UGC		MHRD-UGC Bcncficiary through Canara Bank Account
			3	CS	Fellowship Schemes of AICTE		MHRD-AICTE-Institution-Bcncficiary
3	M/o Human Resources Development, D/o School Education & Literacy	2	1	CS	National Means cum Merit Scholarship	100%	SBI to Bcncficiary Accounts
			2	CS	National Scheme for Incentive for the girl child for secondary education	100%	Canara Bank to Bcncficiary Accounts
4	M/o Tribal Affairs	3	1	CSS	Post-Matric Scholarship Scheme for ST Students	100%	MOTA to State Govt, to District to Bcncficiarics
			2	CS	Top Class Education System	100%	MOTA to Institutes to Bcncficiarics
			3	CS	Rajiv Gandhi National Fellowship	100%	MOTA to UGC. to Bcncficiarics
5	M/o Minority Affairs	3	1	CSS	Matric Scholarship Scheme,	100%	Through State Govt to District to Bank to Bcncficiary
			2	CS	Maulana Azad National Fellowship	100%	Through UGC to bcncficiary
			3	CSS	Merit cum Means Scholarship Scheme	100%,	Through State Govt to Institutions to Bcncficiary

(continued)

Table 5.2 (continued)

Sl. No.	Ministry/Department	No. of schemes		CS/CSS	Name of the scheme	Share of centre	Funds flow
6	M/o Women and Child Development	2	1	CSS	Indira Gandhi Matritva Sahyog Yojana (IGMSY)		
			2	CS	Dhanalakshmi Scheme,		
7	M/o Health & Family Welfare	1	1	CSS	Janani Suraksha Yojana		
8	M/o Labour and Employment	5	1	CS	Scholarship to the Children of beedi workers	Cess on sale of bccdi to financc Beedi Welfare	Money flows to bcncficiarics from Bccdi Welfare Fund
			2	CS	Housing subsidy to beedi workers		
			3	CSS	Stipend to children in the special schools under the Child Labour Project	100%	Funds Released to District Societies
			4	CS	Mipena to trainees unaer tne iscneme 01 Welfare of SC/ST job seekers through Coaching, Guidance and Vocational	100%	Field Institutes of DGET
			5	CSS	Payment of stipend to trainees under the Scheme of Skill Development in 34 Districts affected by Left-Wing Extremism (LWE)	100%	State Treasury, Directorate of Employment and Training, institutes
	Total No. of Schemes	25					

Source: http://dbtmis.planningcommission.nic.in/dbtentry/homepage.aspx

as to enhance efficiency across the board in the economy. It sought to bring ICT within the reach of the whole of India while at the same time harnessing the immense human resource potential in the country to enable it to emerge as the global hub and destination for IT-ITeS Services by 2020.

5.4.2 Initiatives to Bridge Digital Divide under the NDA Government (2014–2017)

After the Bharatiya Janata Party (BJP) led National Democratic Alliance's (NDA) Modi government came to power on 26 May 2014, the mid-year union budget 2014–2015 was its first policy document. The government rose to power on the promise of good governance and development for all—particularly by uplifting rural India through the provision of urban amenities and technology upgrades.

Acknowledging that previous e-Governance initiatives undertaken by various State Governments and Central Ministries have played a significant role in shaping the progressive e-Governance strategy, the Modi Government wanted to speed up e-Governance implementation across the various arms of Government at National, State and Local levels. Because the UPA-I Government's approval of the National e-Governance Plan (NeGP) did not constitute financial approval(s) for all the Mission Mode Projects (MMPs) and components under it, the Modi Government wanted to rectify this limitation.[45]

Recognising the need for greater penetration of IT services[46] domestically, in Budget 2014–2015, 'Digital India' strategy has been envisioned as an ambitious umbrella programme to prepare India for knowledge-based transformation. This would ensure broadband connectivity at village level, improved access to services through IT-enabled platforms, greater transparency in government processes and increased indigenous production of IT hardware and software. One of the important components of this programme is people's empowerment through availability of entitlements on the cloud, coupled with Aadhaar Authentification Platform. A National Rural Internet and Technology Mission for services in villages and schools and E-Kranti for government service delivery are other initiatives. Recognising the importance of IT, the government's 'Make in India' mission has included IT and business process management (BPM) among the twenty-five focus sectors.

The Finance Minister Arun Jaitley announced in the budget a countrywide programme with a new direction called 'Digital India' in order to bridge the digital divide between digital 'haves' and 'have-nots'. He proposed a *National Rural Internet and Technology Mission* (NRITM) for services in villages in order to

[45]http://www.digitalindia.gov.in/print/node/23.

[46]A wide spectrum of IT services (ITS) include system management and maintenance, mobile applications, Cloud Computing, next generation user interfaces, graphics processing unit (GPU) accelerated computing, consultancy services, system integration, chip design, E-Governance, E-Commerce. (ESC 2014).

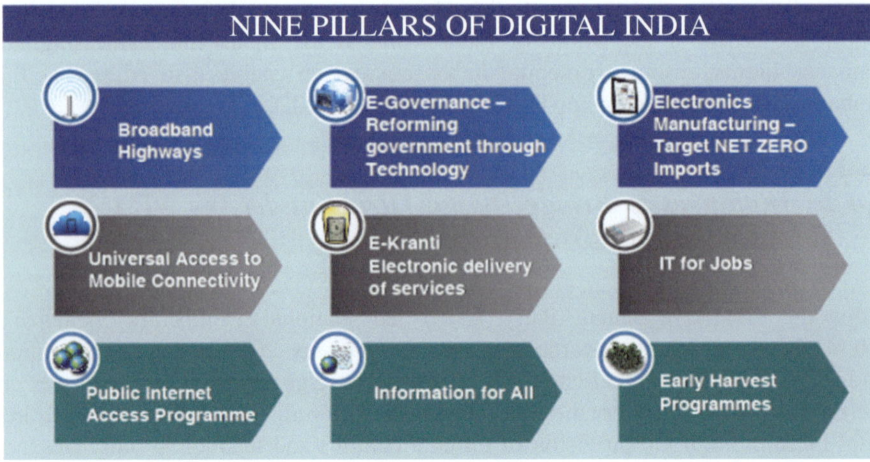

Fig. 5.3 Nine pillars of Digital India *Source* http://www.digitalindia.indiaincorporated.com/videos-graphics/#filter

bridge the rural-urban divide. Jaitley also proposed 'e-Kranti' for governance and services delivery at different levels of government. The 'Digital India' programme with nine pillars (see Fig. 5.3) is basically a good governance programme for transparency and better service delivery of various government schemes through the use of information and communication technology (ICT). The NRITM was announced mainly for services in village through broadband connectivity and other ICT-driven and ICT-enabled platforms like virtual classrooms in rural schools for skill development of rural youth.

It was argued by some critics that Jaitley's new ICT programmes and schemes as part of digital infrastructure were very similar to programmes announced by the United Progressive Alliance-led (UPA-II) government. The most notable one was the UPA-II government's programme of the National Optical Fibre Network (NOFN) which was announced in 2011 presumably to bridge the digital divide by connecting 2.5 lakh of village panchayats in 2 years. The total length of the fibre optics network is approximately 5,00,000 km altogether. When completed, it is expected to link rural and urban India with a 100 megabits per second (mbps) information superhighway, although it's completion was far behind the target. Mudgal (2014, p. 44) notes that the UPA government's floundering NOFN project's estimated cost of Rs. 20,000 crore was supposed to be met from the Universal Service Obligation Fund[47] (USOF) which has a huge cache of funds. He questions

[47]The New Telecom Policy (NTP) 1999 of Department of Telecom, Government of India, had Universal Service as one of its main objectives. It strives to provide a balance between the provision of Universal Service to all uncovered areas, including the rural areas, and the provision of high-level services capable of meeting the needs of the country's economy and encourage development of telecommunication facilities in remote, hilly and tribal areas of the country. The

why Jaitley's 'Digital India' aimed at doing pretty much the same with such a paltry allocation of Rs. 500 crore only. His general comment is, however, noteworthy:

> The issues of rural broadband connectivity, community media, virtual classrooms or hospitals, IT-enabled MIS [management information schemes] services, tracking of food grain delivery systems, and rural media penetration are intertwined and platform agnostic. It is immaterial whether connectivity comes through fibre optics, satellite telephony, [Global System for Mobiles/Code Division Multiple Access] GSM/CDMA-based mobile phone networks, or a combination of all, but what matters is the efficacy of the end use. The ultimate policy push has to come not from token budgetary allocations but from pursuing a policy of spectrum commons where resources like spectrum and cable networks are seen through the lens of their social rather than market value. …The moot question remains if the government is willing to look at spectrum, broadband and rural media penetration as issues of growth and poverty mitigation.[48]

As a follow up of the key decisions taken at the first meeting of the Apex Committee on 'Digital India' programme held in November 2014, the Union Cabinet chaired by the Prime Minister, Narendra Modi, gave its approval for the Approach and Key Components of 'e-Kranti': National e-Governance Plan (NeGP)-2.0 on 25 March 2015. 'A strength, weakness, opportunities and threats (SWOT) analysis of NeGP reveals several issues related to adopting new technologies, transforming processes and improving implementation that need to be addressed urgently'.[49] The objectives and key principles of 'e-Kranti' are as follows in Table 5.3:

In order to implement the objectives of 'e-Kranti' or National e-Governance Plan (NeGP)-2.0, the 'Digital India' programme had been designed by the Department of Electronics and Information Technology (DEITY) under the Central Government's Ministry of Communications & Information Technology until 18 July 2016, when DEITY has been upgraded to a new Ministry.[50] Meanwhile, the telecommunications sector—one of the key drivers of socio-economic development—had grown faster. There had been approximately 33.4 million new telephone connections added during April to October 2015, which was way ahead of the 29.65 million increases in number of connections in the corresponding period of 2014.[51] Several other major initiatives taken by the NDA government are the following.

(Footnote 47 continued)

resources for meeting the Universal Service Obligation (USO) were to be generated through a Universal Access Levy (UAL), at a prescribed percentage of the revenue earned by the telecom licensees to be decided in consultation with the Telecom Regulatory Authority of India (TRAI).

[48]Mudgal (2014, 45).

[49]http://pib.nic.in/newssite/PrintRelease.aspx?relid=117690 (accessed on 23 August 2016).

[50]During the recent Cabinet reshuffle in July 2016, although Ravi Shankar Prasad, the former Communications and Information Technology Minister, has been made in-charge of the Law Ministry, he retains the Department of Electronics and Information Technology (DEITY) by making it as a new Ministry. Shri Prasad has, therefore, been now in-charge of two Ministries—Law Ministry, and the new Ministry of Electronics and Information Technology (MEITY).

[51]*Economic Survey 2015–2016*, vol. 2, p. 148.

Table 5.3 Objectives and key principles of e-Kranti

Objectives	Principles
i. To redefine NeGP with transformational and outcome oriented e-Governance initiatives such as Reforming Government through Technology, Undertaking and Strengthening Government Process Re-engineering, electronic databases, complete workflow automation and IT-based Government Redressal in all Government Department ii. To enhance the portfolio of citizen-centric services iii. To ensure optimum usage of core Information and Communication Technology (ICT) iv. To promote rapid replication and integration of eGov applications v. To leverage emerging technologies for Education (e-Education), Health (e-Health), Farmers, Financial Inclusion, Justice, Planning, and National and Cyber Security vi. To make use of more agile implementation models	i. Transformation and not Translation ii. Integrated Services and not Individual Services iii. Government Process Re-engineering (GPR) to be mandatory in every MMP (Mission Mode Project) iv. ICT Infrastructure on Demand v. Cloud by Default vi. Mobile First vii. Fast Tracking Approvals viii. Mandating Standards and Protocols ix. Language Localisation x. National GIS (Geo-Spatial Information System) xi. Security and Electronic Data Preservation

http://pib.nic.in/newssite/PrintRelease.aspx?relid=117690 (accessed on 23 August 2016)

BharatNet/National Optical Fibre Network (NOFN)

The earlier UPA government's National Optical Fibre Network (NOFN) project has been renamed by the NDA government as BharatNet, touted as the 'backbone for Digital India'. The project is aimed at providing 100 Mbps broadband connectivity to approximately 2.5 lakh gram panchayats across India. Under this project, in order to further bridge the connectivity gap between gram panchayats and blocks, it is planned to provide broadband connectivity by utilising existing fibre of three Central Public Sector Enterprises (PSEs), namely Bharat Sanchar Nigam Limited (BSNL), RailTel and Power Grid, and by laying incremental fibre, wherever necessary. It is expected that the access providers/service providers like mobile operators, Internet Service Providers (ISP), cable TV operators and content providers can launch various services in rural areas. It is also noted that under the BharatNet project various applications for e-health, e-education, e-governance, etc. will be provided. Up to 30 November 2015, 1,03,643 km of pipes and 74,994 km of optical fibre cables (OFC) have been laid. Further, OFC has been laid in 32,049 gram panchayats[52] out of approximately total of 2.5 lakh.

According to J. S. Deepak, the Union Secretary for Information Technology and Communications, the progress of the BharatNet project implementation has been

[52]*Economic Survey 2015–2016*, vol. 2, p. 149.

slow due to a variety of reasons, including the 'inability of Bharat Broadband Network Limited' to procure optical network termination equipment in time as well as 'major gaps in the implementation strategy'. On 30 April 2016, the Telecom Commission approved a revised strategy for a three-phase implementation[53] of the BharatNet/NOFN project.

- The first phase envisages providing one lakh gram panchayats with broadband connectivity by laying underground OFC lines by March 2017.
- The second phase will provide connectivity to all 2.5 lakh gram panchayats using an optimal mix of underground fibre, fibre over power lines, radio and satellite media, and is expected to be completed by December 2018.
- In the third phase from 2018 to 2023, state-of-the-art, future-proof network, including fibre between districts and blocks, with ring topology to provide redundancy, would be created.

Rural Wireline Broadband Scheme for provision of Broadband Connections
The Rural Wireline Broadband Scheme provides wireline broadband connectivity to rural and remote areas. As on 31 October 2014, a total of 6,35,929 broadband connections have been provided and 14,653 kiosks have been set up under the scheme in rural and remote areas.[54]

Spectrum Auction
The NDA government's successful spectrum auction [as opposed to the 2G Spectrum scam briefly noted in footnote 237 above] had added high value to the national exchequer. The Department of Telecommunications (DoT) conducted auction of spectrum in March 2015 simultaneously in 2100 MHz,[55] 1800 MHz, 900 MHz and 800 MHz bands. Total spectrum on offer was 470.75 MHz, out of which 418.05 MHz (88.8%) was allocated to bidders. The value realised was Rs. 1,09,874.91 crore (67.8% more than the value of the allocated spectrum at reserve price).[56]

Machine to Machine Communications
Recognising the futuristic role of machine to machine communication (M2 M) to facilitate the role of new technologies in furthering public welfare and enhanced customer choices through affordable access and efficient service delivery, a 'National Telecom M2 M Roadmap' has been prepared. It puts together various standards, policy and regulatory requirements and approach for the industry on how

---

[53]http://gadgets.ndtv.com/internet/news/centre-asks-states-to-follow-andhra-pradesh-for-bharatnet-project-838548 (accessed on 25 October 2016).

[54]*Economic Survey 2015–2016*, vol. 2, p. 149.

[55]The megahertz, abbreviated MHz, is a unit of alternating current (AC) or electromagnetic (EM) wave frequency equal to one million hertz (1,000,000 Hz). One *MHz* represents one million cycles per second. The speed of microprocessors, called the clock speed, is measured in MHz.

[56]*Economic Survey 2015–2016*, vol. 2, p. 148.

to look ahead to M2 M. The roadmap was released in May 2015 and is expected to work as a reference document for all M2 M ecosystem partners and also to augment the policy goals of Digital India.[57]

Expansion of Direct Benefits Transfer (DBT)
Following the previous government's support for the *Aadhaar* program, the current government has introduced a potential large-scale, technology-enabled, real-time Direct Benefit Transfer (DBT) system, namely the JAM (Jan Dhan-Aadhaar-Mobile) number Trinity solution. The JAM Trinity refers to the consolidation of three spokes in the wheel of economic policies meant to drive the financial inclusion measures as well as make various payments secured. The three critical spokes of the JAM Trinity are *Jan Dhan*, *Aadhaar* and Mobile connectivity. JAM offers 'possibilities for effectively targeting public resources to those who need them most, and including all those who have been deprived in multiple ways'. The progress is already evident with overhauling of the subsidy regime and moving to Aadhaar-based DBT (see Fig. 5.4). JAM is also 'paving way for expenditure rationalisation and is ensuring the removal of, so far undetected, fake and duplicate entities from the beneficiary lists, resulting in substantial savings of public money for giving a renewed focus on social welfare schemes'.

The Modi Government has also been targeting to bring as many as 147 schemes under its purview from the existing 74 ones by March 2017. As Sharma (2016) reports:

> (T)he Prime Minister's Office (PMO) is closely monitoring the ambitious target even as 71 out of 84 central ministries and departments have now opened their internal DBT cells. … The Prime Minister in the recent past has spoken about Rs 28, 000 cr savings through the DBT and the government expects that the savings figure could touch Rs 1 lakh cr with the scheme's ambit being extended.

In the case of rural areas which do not have any bank, the postal network coming on the DBT platform for banking would be expected to solve the issue.

TRAI Favours Neutral Wi-Fi Infrastructure to Bridge Digital Divide[58]
According to an assessment of India's current broadband connectivity by the Telecom Regulatory Authority of India (TRAI), India does not have an impressive ranking worldwide. In some areas, the ranking is lower than that in countries like Sri Lanka and some other African nations. Huawei, the Chinese telecom major, ranked India at 44 in a recent Global Connectivity Index, calling it a 'starter' in the area of information communications technologies deployment, but adding that the situation might change in 2017.

Recently, R. S. Sharma, the TRAI Chairman, notes:

> The fundamental on which Digital India rests is a ubiquitous broadband connectivity or broadband as a utility service. Digital India is the most transformative project of the current government with a vision to change India into a knowledge economy. We are providing

[57]*Ibid.*

[58]Abbas (2016).

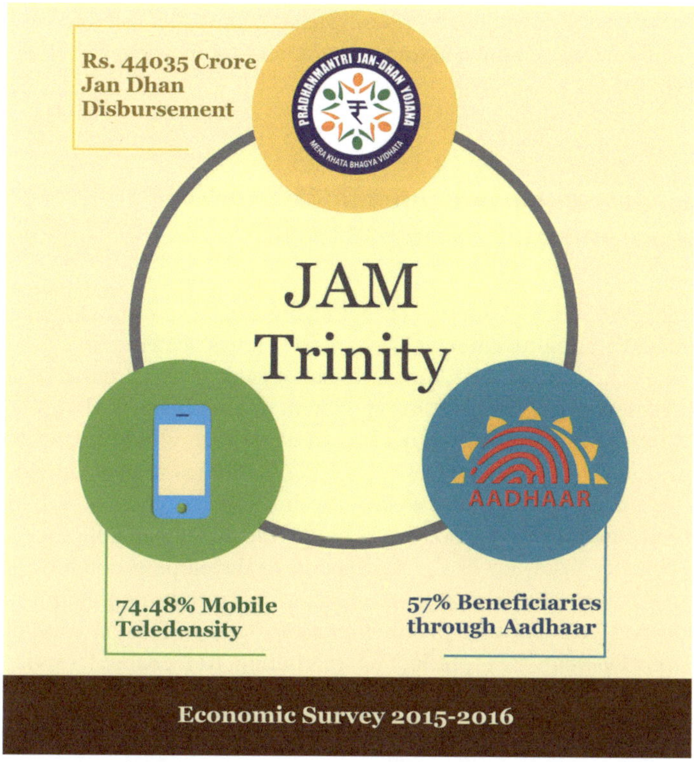

Fig. 5.4 JAM Trinity in 2014–2015 (The source of the JAM related figures in 2014–2015 on Jan Dhan disbursement and Aadhaar beneficiaries is *Economic Survey 2015–2016* (Table 1, p. 56), while the source of the figure on India's mobile teledensity in 2014 is Table 1)

> appropriate recommendations to the government to solve broadband connectivity problem. In regions like the US, UK, and France, there are millions of Wi-Fi hotspots but in India, it is just 35,000, which is a pity. We are recommending that the government use a neutral Wi-Fi architecture so that anyone, irrespective of internet service provider, will be able to latch on to any hotspot, and use the network and pay accordingly.

According to the TRAI recommendations, a neutral Wi-Fi network would avoid duplication of infrastructure. Broadband connectivity, a cornerstone of the government's Digital India initiative, will depend on leveraging cable TV infrastructure, satellite bandwidth and executing BharatNet/NOFN through the build-own-operate-ransfer (BOOT) model. Such measures taken jointly would be expected to lead to a substantial improvement in digital connectivity. TRAI had suggested to the government that the BOOT model be adopted for its BharatNet/NOFN strategy with active participation from entrepreneurs to operate, use and market the network, besides utilising cable TV infrastructure for speedier broadband penetration. 'If 100 million cable TV homes carry 10 Mbps or more bandwidth, then we can have a reliable broadband infrastructure', Sharma said, adding that satellite-based communications would facilitate digital connectivity in remote areas but policy impediments were holding this back.

5.5 The Overall Socio-Economic Dynamics of India's ICT Service Industry during 1995–2017

Over the past two decades or so, the application of new technologies especially, information and communication technology (ICT), has been credited for its positive role in economic growth and development. As a general purpose technology (GPT) like society-wide power-delivery-system of electricity, ICT has wide-spread use in a variety of products and processes in an economy; it is applicable across a broad range of uses in the society as a whole; and also has strong complementarities with existing technologies such as electricity and biotechnology as well as new ones such as nanotechnology and robotics. Although the developed countries are reaping very high benefits from the ICT, its diffusion in developing counties is still very limited. Empirical studies focusing on impact of ICT on development usually make a distinction between ICT as a *production sector* and ICT as an *enabler of socio-economic development*. ICT production (including ICT-enabled services production) for commercial use requires large capital (physical and human) investments in information infrastructures (including telecommunications), hardware and software. ICT as an *enabler of socio-economic development* involves ICT consumption (public and private).

A pre-condition of private ICT consumption in developing countries depends largely on public investment in ICT infrastructure and also on the type of ICT strategy adopted for harnessing wider development objectives. It is often argued that for developing countries benefits from ICTs are more likely to accrue from ICT consumption rather than ICT production. Globalisation accompanied by the rapid development of ICT has largely boosted international trade in services since the mid-1990s. India's ICT sector—divided mainly into computer software product development, IT services (ITS) and IT-enabled services (ITeS) as well as telecommunications—has emerged as one of the most dynamic and vibrant sectors in India's economy. This emergence is driven by a number of factors such as (i) recent growth in India's per-capita income followed by a surge in consumer and industrial demand for IT and telecommunication services, (ii) continued export demand for both ITS and ITeS due to the competitive advantage created by India's talent pool in these sectors, and (iii) supportive government policies towards the ICT sector in general.

Production of India's ICT sector (computer software and services) during the year 2013–2014 was estimated to be Rs. 622,223 crore (US$ 103 billion) registering a growth of 22% (9% in US$ terms) over the year 2012–2013. India's Gross Domestic Production (GDP) at current prices was estimated to be Rs. 11355,073 crore (US$ 1879.66 billion). ICT sector's contribution in India's GDP at current prices during the year 2013–2014 was 5.48%.[59]

Out of the total production of India's ICT sector, 81.55% was exported and only 18.45% was consumed by the domestic market. Export registered a growth of 25.31% (12.01% in US$ terms) during the year 2013–2014 over the year 2012–2013. In value terms, total software services export by Indian companies (together with the software business of their overseas subsidiaries) during 2013–2014 was estimated to be Rs. 507,500 crore (US$ 84.09 billion)[60] up from Rs. 405,000 crore (US$ 75 billion) estimated in the year 2012–2013. During the year 2013–2014, India's domestic ICT market was estimated to be Rs. 114,779 crore (US$ 19 billion) registering a growth of 21.86% (8.32% in US$ terms) over the year 2012–2013.[61]

India has established her brand equity in the global IT market. Although India recently exported ITS/ITeS to 150 countries of the world as in 2013–2014, the USA remained the top destination for this services accounting for a share of over 57.59% of total exports (in US$ term), followed by the UK (the 2nd top with a share of 17.04%), Singapore (the 3rd top with a share of 4.30%), Austria (the 4th top with a share of 2.44%), and Australia (the 5th top with a share of 2.12%).[62]

5.5.1 Recent Start-Ups and Dynamism

One part of the Indian economy that is witnessing unusual dynamism in the very recent years is the start-up sector, focused on e-commerce and financial services. The second edition of the start-up report titled: *Start-up India—Momentous Rise of the Indian Start-up Ecosystem* launched by the IT industry body NASSCOM along with Zinnov in 2015 notes:

> India ranks third, after the US and the UK, among global startup ecosystems with more than 4,200 New-age companies….. Indian technology startups landscape has seen a tremendous growth in the emergence of innovative startups and creative entrepreneurs. In terms of providing a conducive ecosystem for the startups to thrive, India has moved up to third position and has emerged the fastest growing base of startups worldwide. India is one amongst the first five largest startup communities in the world with the number of startups crossing 4,200, a growth of 40 per cent, by the end of 2015.

[59]ESC (2014).

[60]This estimated figure of Rs. 507,500 crore (US$ 84.09 billion) in 2013–2014 seem to be a simple average of the three corresponding figures published by the Reserve Bank of India (RBI) and the National Association of Software and Services Companies (NASSCOM): (i) RBI's estimation of Rs. 506,330 crore (US$ 83.7 billion) based on balance of payment statistics, (ii) RBI's estimation of Rs. 501,180 (US$ 82.8 billion) based on the annual survey, and (iii) NASSCOM's estimation of Rs. 522,890 crore (US$ 86.4 billion) [See RBI (2015)].

[61]ESC (2014).

[62]*Ibid.*

Another key highlight of the study report is that India is the youngest start-up nation in the world and 72% of the founders are less than 35 years old. It also says more than 50% of the 1,200 start-ups focus on e-com, consumer services and aggregators; and female founders/cofounders in start-up ecosystem is around 9%.

According to the Indian Government's report in *Economic Survey 2015–2016*:

> As of January 2016, there were 19,400 technology-enabled start-ups in India, of which 5,000 had started in 2015 alone. No less than 2000 of the start-ups have been backed by venture capital/angel investors since 2010, of which 1005 were created in 2015 alone. Indian start-ups raised $3.5 billion in funding in the first half of 2015, and the number of active investors in India increased from 220 in 2014 to 490 in 2015. As of December 2015, eight Indian start-ups belonged to the 'Unicorn' club (valuations greater than $1 billion).[63]

5.5.2 Re-skilling: Online Education-Technology Platforms[64]

A recent report by consulting firm McKinsey & Co, tabled at the NASSCOM India Leadership Forum in February 2017, warned that nearly half of the 3.9 million people employed in India's ICT service industry will be unable to keep pace with new technologies within 3 to 4 years. This has reignited the already present concern felt across industries (such as e-commerce, banking and manufacturing) that there is urgent need for re-skilling of the employees not only to keep current jobs, but also to transition into more secure jobs in areas (such as data analytics, machine learning and artificial intelligence).

In response to the above need for re-skilling in India, two kinds of online education-technology or ed-tech companies with vastly different approaches have been jostling for a market share in India: (i) US-based foreign biggies such as *Udacity*, *Coursera* and *edX* that view India as their largest market outside their home territories; and (ii) homegrown companies such as *AcadGild*, *UpGrad* and *Simplilearn*.

Increasingly high numbers of enrolment indicates the ed-tech boom in India. For example, *Coursera* that offers technology and business courses sourced from more than 150 global universities has two million learners in India and adding about 60,000 more every month—a pace faster than that of its global platform. Bengaluru-based Simplilearn, which had to discontinue its radio and television campaigns following a surge in enquiries, targets adding 150,000 learners during 2017–2018, up from about 100,000 in 2016–2017.

In this mass-market model of online learning, it is typical that the courses are priced competitively. As completion heats up, question may arise whether it will be a winner-takes-all market. Expert opinions converge to its answer that the foreign and local ed-tech companies solve different needs in different market segments.

[63] *Economic Survey 2015–16* (Vol. 1, Box 1.4, p. 17).

[64] This section is based on Khan (2017).

Many of the foreign ed-tech providers follow Massive Online Open Courses (MOOCs) model with the biggest strength is its credibility because the courses are created by the world's reputed educational institutions. Although learning is free, but courses leading to certificates require a payment. Homegrown ed-techs, on the other hand, have an advantage in terms of being able to offer greater teacher-student interactivity as opposed to the self-learning approach of the MOOCs model.

5.5.3 *Online Start-Ups in India's Informal Segment*[65]

Another recent development in India's private sector is the emergence of online start-ups like *Babajob*, *UrbanClap*, *Taskbob* and *Housejoy* as a slew of technology platforms to connect millions at the bottom of India's social strata pyramid—casual workers or free agents like maids, cooks, drivers, carpenters, electricians, plumbers —to the potential markets for them. 'With supply aplenty and no organised market, this part of the job market has remained largely primitive, unorganised and sub-optimally productive with virtually no mechanism to connect supply with demand or set expectations around wages and service standards'. This has now begun to change thanks to the above mentioned online technology platforms. These technological platforms are expected to help slowly integrating India's informal segment into its formal one. A range of business models are emerging. Babajob

> "These platforms have the power to scale. They can aggregate a lot of people, match supply with demand and shape pricing," says Nandan Nilekani, co-founder of Infosys and architect of the *Aadhaar* card.

Unlike China, India may not be able to create millions of manufacturing jobs. The services sector will be a critical in farm-to-non-farm transition for India's millions of farm workers.

> "These platforms can remove inefficiencies, boost productivity and create significant value (for the Indian economy)," Nilekani adds.

5.6 Post-Demonetisation Initiatives for Digital Transactions

5.6.1 *Bharat Interface for Money (BHIM)*

Since the demonetisation of two highest denomination currency notes (Rs. 500 and Rs. 1,000) on 8 November 2016, there has been a continuous push for digital

[65]This section is based on Goyal (2016).

transactions in India. Using the Unified Payments Interface (UPI)—the mobile-based national payment system that allows money transfer between bank accounts—was thought by the Government to be the most promising path to follow. It led to the development of the Bharat Interface for Money (BHIM) by the National Payments Corporation of India (NPCI).[66] BHIM is a common app that can be used by anyone who has a bank account with a linked mobile number and was launched by Prime Minister Narendra Modi on 30 December 2016. An update or BHIM 1.1 came, within a week of its launch, on 4 January 2017 after users raised concerns about its security features. As of 6 Jan 2017, 'BHIM has already attracted 5 million users and enabled close to 700,000 transactions, according to CEO of NITI Aayog, Amitabh Kant'.[67]

5.6.2 Aadhaar Pay (or BHIM-Aadhaar Interface)

The National Payments Corporation of India (NPCI) successfully finalised the Unified Payments Interface (UPI) platform by facilitating its interoperability through the power of mobile phones in achieving digitalisation of payments and financial inclusion. This makes the 'M' an integral part of the government's digital flagship 'JAM'—*Jan Dhan, Aadhaar, Mobile*—initiative.[68] On 14 April 2017, the Prime Minister of India launched BHIM-Aadhaar Pay platform—a biometric-based payment system. The merchant version of the Aadhaar Enabled Payment System (AEPS) is called *Aadhaar Pay*. The BHIM-Aadhaar Pay ap allows users to make payments using the fingerprint scanner through the authentication of a user's biometric details already stored in Aadhaar database. The app is available for download to merchants across the country. Any citizen without having any access to smart phones, Internet, debit or credit cards is able to transact digitally through the BHIM-Aadhaar Pay platform.

5.6.3 Is Aadhaar a Security Threat?

The biometric-based (fingerprints and iris scans) 12-digit unique identity numbers of India's billion-plus population constitute a database named 'Aadhaar' and issued

---

[66]National Payments Corporation of India (NPCI) is an umbrella organisation for all retail payments system in India. It was set up with the guidance and support of the Reserve Bank of India (RBI) and Indian Banks' Association (IBA). Its core objective is to 'consolidate and integrate the multiple systems with varying service levels into nation-wide uniform and standard business process for all retail payment systems. The other objective was to facilitate an affordable payment mechanism to benefit the common man across the country and help financial inclusion'.

[67]Gupta (2017).

[68]*Economic Survey 2016–17*, p. 3.

by the Unique Identification Authority of India (UIDAI).[69] Because this identity number cannot be duplicated, the government is trying to use it for many purposes including social welfare benefits transfer to the recipients' bank account, marriage certificates, passports, pension claims, and even SIM card registration for mobile phone connections. In fact, no country seems to be using biometric-based data in such a wide range of applications as India is attempting for. It is often argued that the use of Aadhaar-related biometric database does not have any constitutional or legal approval either. Only the Aadhaar Act 2016 targeted for delivery of financial and other subsidies, benefits and services has been passed by the Parliament.

The UIDAI itself has admitted in the past that the Aadhaar project involves risks/issues such as 'ownership risks (ownership of the project by stakeholders), technology risks (nowhere in the world a project of this size has been implemented) and privacy concerns (there may be groups raising privacy issues–many ID Projects in Western countries have been stalled due to the opposition of privacy groups)'.[70] Recent reports based on a study conducted by the Centre for Internet and Society (CIS) reveal that data of 130 million Aadhaar cardholders have been leaked from four government websites. In response to these reports, the government has put in place new safeguards in 2017. The Ministry of Electronics and Information Technology (MEITY) has circulated a set of 27dos and 9 don'ts on data handlings to all government departments. This includes instructions on masking Aadhaar data and bank details as well as encrypting data. The government has also mandated regular audits to check safety of personal data. A letter from the MEITY has also spelt out legal consequences of any such data breach by warning:

> Publishing identity information, i.e. Aadhaar number along with demographic information is in clear contravention of the provisions of the Aadhaar Act 2016 and constitutes an offence punishable with imprisonment up to 3 years. Further, publishing of financial information including bank details, being sensitive personal data, is also in contravention of provision under IT Act 2000 with violations liable to pay damages by way of compensation to persons affected.[71]

[69]The expenditure incurred by the government on the Aadhaar project has been US$ 1.27 billion over the period from 2009 to 2017 as reported by Singh (2017).

[70]Krishna (2015).

[71]Sharma (2017a).

Chapter 6
Conclusion

At the outset of nation building after India's independence in 1947, an attempt was made by the first Prime Minister to move India with socio-economic structural dualism inherited from the colonial administration towards a 'socialistic pattern of society' without accepting either of the two major ideologies of capitalism and socialism in their strict sense. The government needed necessary and inevitable compromises to make with the vested interest groups in a multi-class Indian society, which essentially led the Indian polity towards the State-led capitalism with State control from its 'commanding heights'. From the mid-1960s and onwards, the country gradually relaxed various kinds of control mechanisms, especially in the case of industrial licensing and import policies. During the 1980s, India was pushed towards a stage of transitional capitalism. In spite of being a mixed economy with strong public sector, the Indian State has remained to be fundamentally capitalist because of its separation of the immediate producers from the means of production, irrespective of the juridical forms of property ('private' or 'public'). While it may be true that the Indian State enjoys some degree of relative autonomy from any single major dominant class, it would, however, be naive to believe that the Indian State could effectively function in the interest of the 'society as a whole' or, more specifically, in the real interest of the vast majority of the poor people.

The bureaucracy of the civil administrative apparatus, inherited from the British regime, had grown at a phenomenal rate (about 6% of the total work force) and pocketed a substantial proportion of national cake in the form of unproductive rent. Another source of unproductive leakage from the national exchequer had been a huge amount of subsidies to the rich capitalist farmers. Generally speaking, the economically deprived class of the Indian society had been all along left at the mercy of 'trickle down' effect of whatever moderate growth had taken place. Over time, the rhetoric of pro-poor promises by the State had been intensified in terms of several laws and programmes such as land reform laws, anti-monopoly laws, labour laws, progressive tax laws and anti-poverty programmes. The resulting consequences of these measures had done very little to benefit the poor. 'It is', as Krishna (1988, p. 15) noted, 'a significant novelty of India's political revolution that the relative balance of class forces does not operate at the stage of legislation, planning

D. Dutta, *Development under Dualism and Digital Divide in Twenty-First Century India*, Dynamics of Asian Development, https://doi.org/10.1007/978-981-10-6344-2_6

and pronouncements to prevent a progressive stance, but it effectively blocks and perverts their redistributive effects at the implementation stage'. The case of the functional impotence of the revamped Panchayati Raj Institutions (PRIs) during the 1990s was another example of such institutional failures. In fact, corruption in the PRIs had become rampant in India's most states (Aiyer 2002, p. 3296).

The fact that the unorganised segment continues to contain over 93% of India's labour force, in spite of the continual decline in its share in net domestic product, tends to support the view that economic reforms are, by and large, all about the organised segment and its benefit at the cost of the unorganised segment. The PRIs are expected to rescue the people, closely linked to rural India's unorganised segment, from their never-ending sufferings at all levels of the Indian society. Since the beginning of the new millennium, the Government of India has been attempting to integrate a comprehensive district-level development programme into the national development strategy, with a view to involve backward districts into overall growth process. Over the past two decades, the central and state governments together have been trying to take necessary steps to ensure genuine participation of the panchayats at the village and intermediate levels in the district planning committees. It can also be seen that increased economic liberalisation and its deepening involvement in the ongoing processes of economic globalisation have been associated with not only growing income and regional inequality, but also economic effects that appear to have disadvantaged the unorganised (marginalised) segment of the Indian economy. Furthermore, there has been little economic trickle down of the benefits of economic growth to the rural poor and those in impoverished regions of India.

If one looks at the political economy of the Indian nation, one could easily identify the three contending dominant economic classes such as the industrial capital class, the capitalist farmers and the rentier class including State bureaucrats, politicians and professionals in its modern/organised segment. But the working-class masses in the traditional/unorganised segment do have a significant political role to play in contemporary governments (now-a-days mostly coalitions of political parties) coming to power in India's both federal and state elections. Over the past decade, the recent governments have made significant efforts for using digital information and communication technology (ICT) as a powerful tool in accelerating development process by bringing previously unattainable markets within the reach of poor, improving the delivery of government services in general and social sector benefits to the poor in particular. But still digital dividends of the rapidly spreading digital technologies in the Indian society as a whole are far from satisfactory. The *World Development Report 2016: Digital Dividends* finds that India has not yet taken full advantage of the digital revolution. Using the metrics of connectivity and complements, the Report notes that, by most accounts, the digital divide across age, gender, geography and income within India is significantly higher than in China; only India's score in digital adoption by governments to provide services to the poor masses, through its successful digital ID programmes such as Aadhaar, is higher than in China (Basu 2017).

Apart from increasing budgetary allocations for some anti-poverty programmes and employment-generation schemes, the current government has been designing policy structures for their effective implementation. Using contemporary ICT-based social-networking media, this government is more and more resorting to political mobilisation of the masses by setting common agenda expressed in simple slogans like promising 'achhe din' or 'good days' for the common people. Due to the social-networking media's instant power of two-way interaction between the leader and the led, the government in power has become more and more sensitive to the masses' basic needs gap in income, education, sanitation, housing and water supply. Realising that the rectification of this gap is the key to its political survival, the current government seems to be making genuine efforts for fulfilling the promises made during both the pre- and post-election campaigns, through a number of social welfare schemes—some existing/redesigned and some newly launched.

On the economic reforms front, the current NDA government has been lately on a somewhat back foot mode, especially after its failure in 2015 to amend the Land Acquisition Law 2013 due to opposition from within the NDA's affiliated organisations like Swadeshi Jagran Manch, Bharatiya Kisan Sangh and Bharatiya Mazdor Sangh Sangh Parivar. Because land is a state matter, currently, National Institute for Transforming India (NITI) Aayog has been active in pushing for liberal land-leasing laws in states. In fact, in June 2016, the NITI Aayog has set up a special cell to build consensus with states on the Centre's land-leasing policy.

The most alarming issue in Indian economy now is jobless growth, which greatly undermines its ability to reap the *demographic dividend*. Because of almost one million new entries in job market every month, the Indian economy today needs to generate about 120 million non-farm jobs over the next decade to gainfully employ its increasingly bigger labour force. According to the *Economic Survey 2015–16*, growth rate of labour force (2.23%) was significantly higher than that of the rate of employment (1.4%) during the decade of 2001–11 (Jaffrelot 2016). There is a very little hope for a high percentage of job creation in highly capitalistic multinational companies which have shown interest in participating in India's 'Make in India' programme. It is often argued that government's attention must also be on strengthening the small and medium enterprises (SMEs) that have, generally speaking, labour intensity four times higher than that of many large firms. This, however, requires their better access to discretionary credit and fiscal as well as non-fiscal incentives. In fact, in the wake of the current government's cancellation of over one lakh companies in a single stroke during the post-demonetisation period due to their alleged indulgence in black money dealing, the government may find a way to bring them back in operation through carrot and stick approach; it can be expected to salvage the jobs at least in the case of SMEs and without diluting the regulatory oversight of the government.

The current government recognises that the economic reform process has been far from complete even after more than twenty-five years of economic liberalisation: jobs have not kept up pace with economic growth; manufacturing sector has not emerged to be as vibrant as in many East Asian economies; and the lack of fully defined guidelines for exit paths is creating immense economic, political and fiscal costs, although the government has been undertaking a number of initiatives such as introducing a new bankruptcy law and rehabilitating stalled projects (Jaitley 2016). It is often argued that the economic reforms in India have always been 'gradualist '—every government has shied away from unshackling those areas of the economy that are considered politically 'sensitive'—suggesting that Indian politics is responsible for it (Sharma 2016).

A number of administrative reforms that have been launched by the current government over the past three years to make the administrative machinery more efficient, decisive and cohesive via reviewing and monitoring of outcomes by the prime minister's office are in right direction. The key reforms include Pro-Active Governance and Timely Implementation (PRAGATI) initiative in various infrastructural projects (roads and railways) and social sectors. PRAGATI provides 'a forum for all stakeholders of key projects to voice their views, assigns clear responsibilities with strict timelines, expedites developmental projects by bringing the Centre and states on the same platform, and brings key projects under close supervision of the highest officials' (Kant 2017). In 2016, eight Groups of Secretaries (GoSs) have been formed to 'break silos, stimulate thinking across ministries and develop a roadmap for growth with a commitment from all stakeholders'. They have been working on themes ranging from 'Accelerated Growth with Inclusion and Equity' to 'Employment Generation Strategies' and 'Energy Conservation and Efficiency'.

Lately, the current government has also been caught in conflict with the Supreme Court of India—the highest constitutional court. The Central government had proposed to replace the present collegium system by establishing National Judicial Appointments Commission (NJAC) for the appointment and transfer of judges to the higher judiciary in India. After the completion of all formalities, the NJAC Act and the related Constitutional Amendment Act came into force on 13 April 2015. On 16 October 2015, the Constitution Bench of Supreme Court, by a majority opinion, had struck down the NJAC as unconstitutional after hearing the petitions filed by several persons and bodies including Supreme Court Advocates on Record association (SCAoRA), the first and lead petitioner. While stating that the central government did not want a confrontation, but Ravi Shankar Prasad, the Minister of Law and Justice termed the verdict as 'a setback to parliamentary sovereignty'. This also led Arun Jaitley, the Finance Minister, to express his following personal view:

> A constitutional court, while interpreting the Constitution, had to base the judgment on constitutional principles. There is no constitutional principle that democracy and its institutions have to be saved from elected representatives. The Indian democracy cannot be a tyranny of the unelected and if the elected are undermined, democracy itself would be in danger.

Jaitley's reference of 'a tyranny of the unelected' is certainly to the Supreme Court of India. This reference invites two comments. *Firstly*, India being a parliamentary democratic federal republic and operating under the constitution of 1950, separation of powers between legislatures, executives and the judiciary is constitutionally mandatory, and therefore, the term 'tyranny' is impertinent. *Secondly*, the term 'unelected' is misplaced because in modern democracies, this term refers to the unelected government entities such as independent central bank, regulators and various appeal bodies known as 'non-majoritarian institutions' in political science. Unlike the Supreme Court of India which is a constitutionally driven institution, this category of unelected government entities is granted specialised public authority for making democratic systems of government more robust.

It is interesting to note that a recent report, *Democracy in India: A Citizens' Perspective*, as a part of a global survey on attitudes to democracy, conducted in India in 2013 as a replication of a similar one in 2005, shows faith in India's unelected institutions. However, the proportion of people who said 'they were satisfied with the way democracy worked in India' slightly went down, although remained very close to 50% in both 2005 and 2013; the proportion of those who said 'they were dissatisfied' more than doubled from 6 to 11% during the same period; and the rest responded saying 'either indifferent or of no opinion'. Also, support for authoritarianism has been higher among the elites of the modern segment (richer, better educated people and those with high media exposure) (Rukmini 2015).

In a society like India with inherent *structural dualism*, where the vast traditional/unorganised/informal segment still coexists side by side with the small, but economically powerful and predominantly self-centred elitist, modern/organised/formal segment. In the light of the latter segment's job absorption capacity of only about 6% of total labour force, the current trends of overall jobless growth, mass dependence on social sector subsidies, under-funded health and education sectors, relatively higher digital divide, gradual loss of faith on democracy and above all the compulsion of increasingly high unproductive military expenses do indicate that the reduction of India's *structural dualism* is a distant reality. Let us hope that the current and future governments, after capitalising on its current demographic and digital dividends, and with good governance, would be able to steer the Indian society free from the tyranny of *structural dualism* decades before it celebrates the centenary of independence in 2047.

References

Abbas, M. (2016, October 31). Tri favours neutral Wi-Fi infrastructure to bridge digital divide. *The Economic Times*.
Agrawal, A. N., & Varma, H. O. (1996). *India: Economic information year-book*. New Delhi: National Publishing House.
Ahluwalia, I. (1983). *Industrial stagnation in India since the mid-sixties*. New Delhi: Indian Council of Research in International Economical Relations.
Anon. (2002, September 8). Govt ditches disinvestment, for now. *The Economic Times*. http://www.economictimes.com/today.
Anon. (2015, July 6). Socio economic survey shows rural India poorer than expected. *The Economic Times*. http://economictimes.indiatimes.com/news/economy/indicators/socio-economic-survey-shows-rural-india-poorer-than-expected/articleshow/47952567.cms.
Anon. (2016, November 3). GST rate structure finalised, panel fixes rates at 5%, 12%, 18% & 28%. *The Economic Times*. http://economictimes.indiatimes.com/news/economy/policy/gst-rate-structure-finalised-panel-fixes-rates-at-5-12-18-28/articleshow/55225712.cms?prtpag.
Anon. (2017, July 1). GST rates: Here's your complete guide. *The Economic Times*. http://economictimes.indiatimes.com/news/economy/policy/gst-rates-heres-your-complete-guide/printarticle/59395255.cms.
Arora, A., & Athreye, S. (2002). The software industry and India's economic development. *Information Economics and Policy, 14,* 253–273.
Arora, A., & Gambardella, A. (2004). The globalization of the software industry: Perspectives and opportunities for developed and developing countries. *NBER Working Paper Series*, Working Paper #10538.
Arora, A., Arunachalam, V. S., Asundi, J., & Fernandes, R. (2001). The Indian software services industry. *Research Policy, 30,* 1267–1287.
Arora, B. (2015, May 22). The distant goal of cooperative federalism. *The Hindu*.
Athreye, S. S. (2005). The Indian software industry. In A. Arora & A. Gambardella (Eds.), *From underdogs to tigers: The rise and growth of the software industry in Brazil, China, India, Ireland, and Israel* (pp. 7–39). Oxford: Oxford University Press.
Aiyar, M. S. (2002). Panchayati Raj: The way forward. *Economic and Political Weekly, 37*(31), 3293–3297.
Bamat, T. (1977). Relative state autonomy and capitalism in Brazil and Peru. *Insurgent Sociologist*, Spring Issue.
Bardhan, P. (1980), "Interlocking Factor Markets and Agrarian Development: A Review of Issues," *Oxford Economic Papers*, 32 (1).
Bardhan, P. (1983). Notes on the theory of the state—The perspective form a development country. *Paper presented at a Colloquium on "Marxism and the State,"* Dept. of Philosophy, University College, London.

D. Dutta, *Development under Dualism and Digital Divide in Twenty-First Century India*, Dynamics of Asian Development, https://doi.org/10.1007/978-981-10-6344-2

Basant, R., & Chandra, P. (2007). Role of educational and R&D institutions in city clusters: An exploratory study of Bangalore and Pune Regions in India. *World Development, 35*(6), 1037–1055.

Basu, K. (2016, February 12). India's digital transformation. *The Hindu*.

Berger, S., & Piore, M. J. (1980). *Dualism and discontinuity in industrial societies*. NY: Cambridge University Press.

Bhargava, P. K. (1984). Transfers from the Center to the States in India. *Asian Survey, 24*(6), 665–687.

Boudon, R. (1971). The uses of structuralism, London: Heinemann. [French edition (1968)].

Brass, P. R. (1982). Pluralism, regionalism and decentralising tendencies in contemporary Indian Politics. In A. J. Wilson & D. Dalton (Eds.), *The States of South Asia– Problems of national integration* (Essays in honour of W. J. Morris), London: C. Hurst.

Brecher, M. (1959). *Nehru—A political biography*. London: Oxford University Press.

Breedlove, W., & Armer, M. (1996). Economic disarticulation and social development in less-developed nations: A cross-national study of intervening structures. *Sociological Focus, 29*(4), 359–378.

Caniels, M. C. J., & Romijn, H. A. (2003). Dynamic clusters in developing countries: Collective efficiency and beyond. *Oxford Development Studies, 31,* 3.

Chadha, G. K., & Sahu, P. P. (2002). Post-reform setbacks in rural employment: Issues that need further scrutiny. *Economic and Political Weekly, 37*(21), 1998–2026.

Chakravarty, M. (2012, December 9). India's employment elasticity almost zero. *Live Mint*.

Chand, G. (1966). *"Nehru and Planning", in Nehru legacy—A symposium*. New Delhi: National Book Club.

Chandran, S. (2010). Sustainable distance education through mobile learning: A case study in multicultural context. *OIDA International Journal of Sustainable Development, 02*(04), 35–40.

Chaudhuri, S. (2002). Economic reforms and industrial structure in India. *Economic and Political Weekly, 37*(2), 155–162.

Chauhan, R. (2009). *National E-Governance Plan in India*, UNU-IIST Report No. 414, United Nations University for Software Technology, Macao.

Cimoli, M. (1998). National system of innovation: A note on technological asymmetries and catching-up perspectives. *Interim Report, IT-98-030/June*, International Institute for Applied Systems Analysis, Laxenburg, Austria.

Cypher, J. M., & Dietz, J. L. (2009). *The process of economic development* (3rd ed.). Routledge: London and New York.

Clague, C. (Ed.). (1997). *Institutions and economic development: Growth and governance in less-developed and post-socialist countries*. Baltimore & London: The Johns Hopkins University Press.

Cypher, J. (2001). Developing disarticulation within the mexican economy. *Latin American Perspectives, 28*(3), 11–37.

Das, P., & Saibal, K. (2016). Public expenditure, demography and growth: Theory and evidence from India. IZA Discussion Paper No. 9721.

D'Costa, A. P. (2011). Geography, uneven development and distributive justice: The political economy of IT growth in India. *Cambridge Journal of Regions, Economy and Society, 4*(2), 237–251.

D'Costa, A. P. (2014). Compressed capitalism and the challenges for inclusive development in India. In D. Dutta (Ed.), *Inclusive growth and development in 21st century—A structural and institutional analysis of China and India*, Vol. 9 in Series on Economic Development and Growth. Singapore: World Scientific Publishing Co.

De, S., & Dutta, D. (2007, September), Impact of intangible capital on productivity and growth: Lessons from the Indian information technology software industry. *Economic Record, 83* (Special Issue), S73–S86.

de Janvry, A. (1981). *The Agrarian question and reformism in Latin America*. Baltimore and London: The Johns Hopkins University Press.

de Janvry, A., & Sadoulet, E. (1983). Social articulation as a condition for equitable growth. *Journal of Development Economics, 13*(3), 275–303.
Deaton, A., & Dréze, J. (2002). Poverty and inequality in India: A re-examination. *Economic and Political Weekly, 37*(36), 3729–3748.
Dorn, J. (2016). The genesis and evolution of China's economic liberalization. *Cato Working Paper No. 38*, Washington DC: Cato Institute.
Drèze, J., & Sen, A. (2014). An uncertain glory: India and its contradictions. London: Penguin [First published by Allen Lane in 2013].
Drazen, A. (1982). Unemployment in LDCS: Worker heterogeneity, screening, and quantity constraints. *World Development*, Special Issue.
DuRand, C. (1984). Toward a theory of the state in socialism—The case study of China. *Monthly Review*, *6*(2).
Dutta, D. (1989). Poverty, planning and politics: The past decade of India. *Scandinavian Journal of Development Alternatives, 8*(1), 117–132.
Dutta, D. (1990). Nehru: The architect of Indian State and planning. *Scandinavian Journal of Development Alternatives, 9*(2 & 3), 85–99.
Dutta, D. (1998). Fifty years of economic development in India: Rhetoric and reality. In P. K. Basu, N. D. Karunaratne & C. A. Tisdell (Eds.), *Fifty years of Indian development: India in retrospect, future directions and investment outlook*, Economics Conference Monograph No. 5, The University of Queensland.
Dutta, D. (2004). Effects of globalisation on employment and poverty in dualistic economies: The case of India. In C. Tisdell & R. K. Sen (Eds.), *Economic globalisation–Social conflicts, labour and environmental issues*. Cheltenham, UK & Massachusetts, USA: Edward Elgar.
Dutta, D. (2009). Social shaping of India's computer software technology sector: A methodological framework of analysis in terms of actors and networks. In M. Sanyal et al. (Eds.), *Post-reform development in Asia.* Hyderabad, India: Orient BlackSwan.
Dutta, D. (2011). Recent economic development in the Indian economy. *Ecodate*, *25*(3).
Dutta, D. (2014). Convergence of structuralism and institutionalism in development economics and studies—Revisited. In D. Dutta (Ed.), *Inclusive growth and development in 21st century—A structural and institutional analysis of China and India*, Vol. 9 in Series on Economic Development and Growth (pp. 3–33). Singapore: World Scientific Publishing Co.
Dutta, D., & De, S. (2009). Political economy of IT in India: Challenges and policy responses. *International Journal of Interdisciplinary Social Sciences, 4*(9), 201–212.
Dutta, D., & De, S. (2014). Socio-economic dynamics of the ICT industry's regional growth in India. In D. Dutta (Ed.), *Inclusive growth and development in 21st century—A structural and institutional analysis of China and India*, Vol. 9 in Series on Economic Development and Growth (pp. 191–217). Singapore: World Scientific Publishing Co.
Dutta, D., & Sekhar, A. (2005). Major Indian ICT firms and their approaches towards achieving quality. In R. Jha (Ed.), *Economic growth, economic performance and welfare in South Asia* (pp. 225–248). Hampshire & N.Y.: Palgrave Macmillan.
Economic Survey. Delhi: Ministry of Finance, Government of India (various issues).
Economy At A Glance. Statistics of India, TATA Services Ltd (various years).
Felix, F. (1977). The technological factor in socioeconomic dualism-toward an economy-of-scale paradigm for development theory. In M. Nash (Ed.), *Essays on economic development and cultural change in Honor of Bert F.* Hoselitz, Chicago and London: University of Chicago Press.
Ghuman, B. S. (1997). Liberalisation and regional patterns of industrialisation: The Indian experience. Paper presented to the International Conference, *South Asian Development in 1997 and beyond: Its relevance for Australia*, 12–14 September, University of Sydney.
Gopal, S. (Ed.). (1983). *Jawaharlal Nehru—An anthology*. New Delhi: Oxford University Press.
Goyal, M. (2016, November 20). How online startups are shaping the informal jobs sector in India. *The Economic Times*.

Grossmann, H. (1977). Archive: Marx, classical political economy and the problem of dynamics—Part II. *Capital and Class*, *3* (Autumn).

Gupta, K. (2017, January 6). New version of BHIM app launched. *Live Mint.*

Gupta, S. P. (1995). Economic reform and its impact on poor. *Economic and Political Weekly, 30* (22), 1295–1313.

Hamilton, D. (1975). Mexico: The limits of state autonomy. *Latin American Perspectives, 2*(5), 81–108.

Hey, J. D. (1981). *Economics in Disequilibrium.* NY: N.Y. University Press.

Higgins, B. (1977). Economic development and cultural change: Seamless web or patchwork quilt?. In M. Nash (Ed.), Essays on Economic Development and Cultural Change in Honour of B.F. Hoselitz. Chicago and London: University of Chicago Press.

Hoogvelt, A. (1997). *Globalization and the postcolonial world: The new political economy of development.* Baltimore, Maryland: The Johns Hopkins University Press.

Horvat, B. (1981). Establishing self-governing socialism in LDCs. *World Development*, *9*(9–10). Also in C. K. Wilber & K. P. Jameson (Ed.) (1982), *Socialist models of development.* Oxford: Pergamon Press.

Huang, J. (1995). Structural disarticulation and third world human development. *International Journal of Contemporary Sociology, 36*(3–4), 164–183.

IIPO. (1982, April–June). *Indian Institute of Public Opinion: Quarterly Economic Report*, *26* (104).

Institute for Human Development. (2010). A report on 'Poverty in Bihar: Pattern, dimensions and eradication strategies. International Seminar on 18–20 April, Patna. http://www.ihdindia.org/pdfs/poverty_seminar_report.pdf.

Jaffrelot, C. (2016, April 29). India's jobless growth is undermining its ability to reap the demographic dividend. *The Indian Express.*

Jaitley, A. (2016, July 21). 25 years of reforms: Liberalisation is significant, but we still have an exit problem, says Arun Jaitley. *The Economic Times.*

Kaldor, N. (1972). The irrelevance of equilibrium economics. *Economic Journal*, *82*(328).

Kant, A. (2017, June 28). Administrative reforms: Rebolting the steel frame. *The Economic Times.*

Karanjia, R. K. (1960). *The Mind of Mr Nehru.* London: George Allen & Unwin.

Kaur, B., Misra, S., & Suresh, A. K. (2013). Cyclicality of social sector expenditures: Evidence from Indian States. *Reserve Bank of India Occasional Papers*, *34*(1 & 2).

Khan, T. (2017, June 30). Re-skilling: Education-technology platforms vying to cash in on opportunities in India. *The Economic Times.*

Khanna, T., & Palepu, K. (2004). The evolution of concentrated ownership in India broad patterns and a history of the Indian software industry. National Bureau of Economic Research, Working Paper No. 10613, Cambridge, Massachusetts.

Kornai, J. (1972). *Rush vs. Harmonic Growth—Mediation on the theory and on the policies of economic growth.* Amsterdam: North-Holland.

Kostzer, D. (2004). Globalization and disarticulation: The road to exclusion in Latin America. Working Paper No. 36, Ministry of Labor, Employment and Social Protection, Buenos Aires, Argentina.

Krishna, G. (2015, October 5). Aadhaar may have a lethal impact on the existence of India. *The Economic Times.*

Krupp, S. R. (1965). Equilibrium theory in economics and in functional analysis as types of explanation. In D. Martindale (Ed.), *Functionalism in the Social Science: The strength and limits of functionalism in Anthropology, Economics, Political Science, and Sociology*, Monograph No. 5. The American Academy of Political and Social Science, Philadelphia.

Kurien, C. T. (1996). *Economic reforms and the people.* Delhi: Madhyam Books.

Laski, H. J. (1968). *Authority in the Modern State*. Hamden, Conn.: Archon Books. [First Published in 1946].

Machlup, F. (1963). *Essays on economic semantics*. NY: Prentice-Hall Inc. [Original F. Machlup (1958). Structure and structural change: Weaselwords and Jargon. *Zeitschrift Für Nationalökonomie*, *18*(3)].

Mani, S. (2012). The mobile communications services industry in India: Has it led to India becoming a manufacturer hub for telecommunication equipment? *Pacific Affairs, 85*(3), 511–530.

Mahanti, T. (2000, January 24). Service sector fuelled a higher GDP growth in the nineties. *The Economic Times*.

Mani, S. (2014). Emergence of India as the world leader in computer and information services? *Economic & Political Weekly, 49*(49), 51–61.

Marglin, S. A. (1981b). The radical challenge to mainstream economics. Discussion Paper No. 829. Harvard Institute of Economic Research, Harvard University.

Mathur, A. (2011). Building a vision for the Indian rural sector through the information technology. *Journal of Advances in Management, IT & Social Sciences*, *1*(2).

McKinsey & Company. (2007). The 'Bird of Gold': The rise of India's consumer market. McKinsey & Company. www.mckinsey.com/mgi/publications.

Metcalfe, S. (1995). The economic foundations of technology policy: Equilibrium and evolutionary perspectives. In P. Stoneman (Ed.), *Handbook of the economics of innovation and technical change* (pp. 410–512). Oxford, UK: Blackwell.

Moore, B. (1966). *Social origins of dictatorship and democracy*. Boston: Beacon Press.

Moser, C. O. N. (1978, Sep./Oct.). Informal sector or petty commodity production: Dualism or dependence? *World Development*, *6*.

Mudgal, V. (2014). Union budget and the 'Digital Divide': Old wine in new bottle. *Economic & Political Weekly*, *49*(31).

Nagaraj, R. (2016). Unorganised sector output in the new GDP series: Why has it shrunk? *Economic and Political Weekly, 51*(14), 24–27.

Nagatani, K. (1981). *Macroeconomic dynamics*. N.Y.: Cambridge University Press.

Nair, K. (1979). *In defence of the irrational peasants—Indian agriculture after green revolution*. Illinois, Chicago: University of Chicago Press.

Nash, M. (1977). Modernisation: Cultural meanings—The widening gap between intellectuals and the process. In M. Nash (Ed.), *Essays on economic development and cultural change in Honour of B.F. Hoselitz*. Chicago and London: University of Chicago Press.

National Accounts Statistics. Central Statistical Organisation, Government of India, New Delhi, (various issues).

National Task Force on Information Technology and Software Development. May 1998, Government of India.

Nayyar, D. (1997). Globalization: The game, the players and the rules. In S. D. Gupta (Ed.), *The political economy of globalization*. Norwell, Massachusetts: Kluwer Academic Publishers.

NCEUS. (2008). *Contribution of the unorganised sector to GDP Report of the Sub Committee on NCEUS task force*. Working Paper No. 2, National Commission for Enterprises in the Unorganised Sector, Government of India.

NCEUS. (2009). *The challenge of employment in India—An informal economy perspective*, Vol. 1, Main Report. National Commission for Enterprises in the Unorganised Sector, Government of India.

Nehru, J. L. (1960). *India today and tomorrow*. New Delhi: Indian Council for Cultural Relations.

O'Donnell, G. (1978). State and alliances in Argentina: 1956–76. *Journal of Development Studies*, *15*(1).

OECD. (2004). *Information technology outlook*. Paris: Organisation for Economic Co-operation and Development.

Olson, M. (1982). *The rise and decline of nations: Economic growth, stagflation, and social rigidities*. New Haven, Conn: Yale University Press.

Pais, J. (2002). Casualisation of urban labour force: Analysis of recent trends in manufacturing. *Economic and Political Weekly, 37*(7), 631–652.

Papola, T. S., & Sahu, P. P. (2012). *Growth and structure of employment in India: Long-term and post-reform performance and the emerging challenge*. New Delhi: Institute for Studies in Industrial Development.

Parthasarathy, B. (2004). India's silicon valley or silicon valley's India? Socially embedding the computer software industry in Bangalore. *International Journal of Urban and Regional Research, 28*(3), 664–685.

Patibandla, M., & Petersen, B. (2002). Role of transnational corporations in the evolution of a high-tech industry: The case of India's software industry. *World Development, 30*(9), 1561–1577.

PEO. (1985). Evaluation study of Integrated Rural Development Programme (IRDP), PEO study no. 134, Programme Evaluation Organisation, Planning Commission, Government of India. http://planningcommission.nic.in/reports/peoreport/cmpdmpeo/volume1/134.pdf.

Petras, J. F. (1976). State capitalism and the Third World. *Journal of Contemporary Asia, 6*(4).

Piaget, J. (1970). *Structuralism*. N.Y.: Basic Books Inc. [Original French edition published in 1968].

Portes, A., & Walton, J. (1981). *Labour, class and the international system*. N.Y. and London: Academic Press.

Rao, V. M. (1998). Economic reforms and the poor: Emerging scenario. *Economic and Political Weekly, 33*(29 & 30), 1949–1954.

RBI. (1982). *Capital formation and saving in India: 1950–51 to 1979–80*. Bombay: Reserve Bank of India.

RBI. (1985). *Report of the Committee to Review the Working of the Monetary System*. Bombay: Reserve Bank of India.

RBI. (1999). *Annual report 1998–99*, Appendix Table II.1. Reserve Bank of India, Bombay.

RBI. (1999). *Report on currency and finance*. Bombay: Reserve Bank of India.

Report of the National Commission on Labour, Ministry of Labour, Employment and Rehabilitation (1969). Government of India.

Rukmini, S. (2015, August 7). Some have faith in unelected institutions, but India values dissent. *The Hindu* (updated on 29 March, 2016).

Ryder, M. (2003). What is actor-network theory? http://carbon.cudenver.edu/~mryder/itc_data/ant_dff.html1.

Saikia, D., & Goswami, N. (2017). Spatial industrial diversification in India: An analysis of unorganised manufacturing enterprises. *Assam Economic Review, 10*.

Sharma, A. (2016, July 20). Centre tries to bring 147 schemes under Direct Benefits Transfer. *The Economic Times*.

Sharma, M. (2016, July 25). In 25 years, India has never really embraced reform. *The Economic Times*.

Sharma, N. (2017a, June 2). Centre brings in new safeguards following cases of Aadhaar data leaks on government websites. *The Economic Times*.

Sharma, N. (2017b, June 15). 3 Years of Modi Government: A look at whether big-ticket schemes have brought 'achhe din' for common man. *The Economic Times*.

Sikarwar, D. (2017, April 17). GST: Government looking to keep single rate for each product to avoid complexity. *The Economic Times*.

Simon, H. A. (1962). The architecture of complexity. *Proceedings of the American Philosophical Society, 106*(6), 467–482.

Singh, S. (2017, April 13). Benefits of Aadhaar are real but so are fears of biometric theft. *The Economic Times*.

Skocpol, T. (1979). *States and social revolution—A comparative analysis of France*. Russia and China, NY: Cambridge University Press.

Stiglitz, J. (2007). *Making globalization work*. London: Penguin Books Ltd.

Street, J. H., & James, D. D. (1982). Institutionalism, structuralism, and dependency in Latin America. *Journal of Economic Issues, 16*(3), 673–689.

Stokes, R., & Anderson, A. (1990). Disarticulation and human welfare in less developed countries. *American Sociological Review, 53*(February), 63–74.
Sundrum, R. M. (1987). *Growth and income distribution in India: Policy and performance*. New Delhi & Newbury Park, Calif: Sage Publications.
Tanzi, V. (1982). Fiscal disequilibrium in developing countries. *World Development, Special Issue, 10*(12), 1069–1082.
Taylor, L. (1983). *Structuralist macroeconomics*. New York: Basic Books Inc.
Therborn, G. (1980). *The ideology of power and the power of ideology*. London: Verso Editions.
UNESCO. *Social Transformation*. Retrieved May 6, 2015, from www.unesco.org/new/en/social-and-human-sciences/themes/international-migration/glossary/social-transformation/.
Van Dijk, M. P. (2003). Government policies with respect to an information technology cluster in Bangalore, India. *European Journal of Development Research, 15*(2), 93–108.
Varshney, A. (1984, September 1). Political economy of slow industrial growth in India. *Economic and Political Weekly*.
Venu, M. K. (2000, January 4). Productivity wins the day as growth in GDP hits 7.5 percent with employment dip. *The Economic Times*. http://www.economictimes.com/today.
Wadhva, C. D. (Ed.). (1977). *Some problems of India's economic policy* (2nd ed.). New Delhi: Tata McGra Hill Publishing Company Limited.
Waters, M. (1995). *Globalization*. London & New York: Routledge.
WDR. (2016). *World development report 2016: Digital dividends*. World Bank Group: Washington DC.
Weisskopf, T. E. (1983). Alternative models of economic development. *Économies et Sociétés, 17* (2).
WG-SFR. (2012). *Report on the Working Group on State's Financial Resources for the Twelfth Five Year Plan (2012–2017)*. Planning Commission, Government of India.
Wolpe, H. (1980). *The articulation of modes of production-essays from economy and society*. London, Boston and Henley: Routledge and Kegan Paul.
World Bank. (2004). Sustaining India's services revolution: Access to foreign markets, domestic reform and international negotiations. The World Bank.
World Bank Country Study. (1996). *India: Five years of stabilization and reform and the challenges ahead*. Washington, DC: The World Bank.
Wright, E. O. (1982). The status of the political in the concept of class structure. *Politics and Society, 11*(3).
Zaidi, B. (2017, June 5). How self-employed professional, entrepreneurs, SMEs can get ready for GST. *The Economic Times*.

MIX
Papier aus verantwortungsvollen Quellen
Paper from responsible sources
FSC® C105338

If you have any concerns about our products,
you can contact us on
ProductSafety@springernature.com

In case Publisher is established outside the EU,
the EU authorized representative is:
Springer Nature Customer Service Center GmbH
Europaplatz 3, 69115 Heidelberg, Germany

Printed by Libri Plureos GmbH
in Hamburg, Germany